AF837885

UNIVERSITY OF WESTMINSTER

Failure to return or renew your books on time will result in suspension of borrowing rights at all University of Westminster libraries.

Due for return on:

Information Systems and Library Services **Regent Library**
4 - 12 Little Titchfield Street, London W1W 7UW
Telephone 020 7911 5000 ext 2537
www.westminster.ac.uk/library

25 0313586 1

Prospects and Challenges for EU-China Relations in the 21st Century

The Partnership and Cooperation Agreement

P.I.E. Peter Lang

Bruxelles · Bern · Berlin · Frankfurt am Main · New York · Oxford · Wien

Jing Men & Giuseppe Balducci (eds.)

Prospects and Challenges for EU-China Relations in the 21st Century

The Partnership and Cooperation Agreement

"College of Europe Studies"
No. 12

343.240951 PRO

The editors of this book would like to give their thanks
to the InBev-Baillet-Latour Fund and to the College of Europe,
without whom this book would not have been made possible.

No part of this book may be reproduced in any form, by print, photocopy, microfilm or any other means, without prior written permission from the publisher. All rights reserved.

© P.I.E. PETER LANG S.A.
Éditions scientifiques internationales
Brussels, 2010
1 avenue Maurice, B-1050 Brussels, Belgium
www.peterlang.com; info@peterlang.com

ISSN 1780-9665
ISBN 978-90-5201-641-2
D/2010/5678/39

Printed in Germany

Library of Congress Cataloging-in-Publication Data
Prospects and challenges for EU-China relations in the 21st century : the partnership and cooperation agreement / Jing Men and Giuseppe Balducci, editors.
p. cm. — (College of Europe studies ; No. 12) Includes bibliographical references.
ISBN 978-90-5201-641-2 1. European Union—China.
2. European Union countries—Relations—China. 3. China—Relations—European Union countries. I. Men, Jing. II. Balducci, Giuseppe.
JZ1570.A57C667 2010 341.242'20951—dc22 2010026791

Bibliographic information published by "Die Deutsche Nationalbibliothek"
"Die Deutsche Nationalbibliothek" lists this publication in the "Deutsche Nationalbibliografie"; detailed bibliographic data is available on the Internet at <http://dnb.ddb.de>.

Acknowledgements

Since September 2008, funded by the InBev-Baillet Latour Fund, the InBev-Baillet Latour Chair of European Union-China relations has been established at the College of Europe. With the support of the Rector of the college, Prof. Dr. Paul Demaret, of the dean of IRD, Prof. Dr. Dieter Mahncke, and of our colleagues Prof. Dr. Sieglinde Gstoehl, Sabine Dekeyser, and Anne-Claire Marangoni, we organised successfully the first international conference on EU-China relations at the College of Europe in April 2009: "Prospects and Challenges for EU-China Relations in the 21st century: The Partnership and Cooperation Agreement." The editors would like to thank the InBev-Baillet Latour Fund for its financial support to the workshop and the above mentioned professors and colleagues for their great support and help.

This book is composed of papers selected from those submitted and discussed at the workshop. As Mr. Giuseppe Balducci does not work for the College of Europe anymore since September 2009, most of the editing task has been overtaken by Benjamin Barton. Thus, the editors would like to give their heartfelt thanks to him for his great contribution to the editing of the book.

Contents

Abbreviations

AA	Association Agreement
ACP	Africa Caribbean Pacific
ADB	Asian Development Bank
ADS	Approved Destination States
APEC	Asia Pacific Economic Cooperation
ASEAN	Association of Southeast Asian Nations
ATC	Agreement on Textiles and Clothing
BAP	Bali Action Plan
BIT	Bilateral Investment Treaty
BRIC	Brazil Russia India China
CCP	Common Commercial Policy
CEEC	Central and Eastern European Countries
CEO	Chief Executive Officer
COHOM	Working Party on Human Rights
CoP15	Conference of Parties
CSO	Civil Society Organisation
CSR	Corporate Social Responsibility
DSU	Dispute Settlement Understanding
EC	European Community
ECCP	European Climate Change Programme
ECFR	European Council on Foreign Relations
ECJ	European Court of Justice
ECOSOC	Economic and Social Council
ECT	Energy Charter Treaty
ECU	European Currency Unit
EEC	European Economic Community
EIA	European Integration Agreements
EIB	European Investment Bank
EIIA	European Integration Investment Agreements
EP	European Parliament
ESDP	European Security and Defence Policy
ESS	European Security Strategy

ETS	European Emission Trading Scheme
EU	European Union
EUCTP	EU-China Trade Project
FDI	Foreign Direct Investment
FOCAC	Forum on China Africa Cooperation
FTA	Free-Trade Agreement
G4	Group of Four
G7	Group of Seven
G8	Group of Eight
G20	Group of Twenty
G77	Group of Seventy-Seven
GATS	General Agreement on Trade and Services
GATT	General Agreement on Trade and Tariffs
GDP	Gross Domestic Product
GE	General Electric
GHG	Green House Gases
GLS	Global Labour Strategy
GNP	Gross National Product
GSP	General System of Preferences
HED	High-Level Economic and Trade Dialogue
ICC	International Criminal Court
ICESCR	International Covenant on Economic, Social and Cultural Rights
IEA	International Energy Agency
ILO	International Labour Organisation
IMF	International Monetary Fund
IPCC	Intergovernmental Panel on Climate Change
IPR	Intellectual Property Rights
KP	Kyoto Protocol
LDC	Least Developed Countries
MEF	Major Economies Forum
MES	Market Economy Status
MFA	Multi-Fibre Agreement
MFA	Ministry of Foreign Affairs
MFN	Most Favoured Nation
MIGA	Multilateral Investment Guarantee Agency
MNC	Multi-National Corporation

MoU	Memorandum of Understanding
MRV	Measuring, Reporting and Verifying
NATO	North Atlantic Treaty Organisation
NBS	National Bureau of Statistics
NEF	New Economics Foundation
NGO	Non-Governmental Organisation
NIPS	National Intellectual Property Strategy
NLP	New Leading Powers
NT	National Treatment
NTB	Non-Trade Barrier
OECD	Organisation for Economic Cooperation and Development
PCA	Partnership and Cooperation Agreement
PLA	People's Liberation Army
PRC	People's Republic of China
PSC	Political and Security Committee
PTA	Preferential Trade Agreement
R&D	Research and Development
RMB	Renminbi
RTD	Research and Technology Development
S&T	Science and Technology
SAIC	State Administration of Industry and Commerce
SARS	Severe Acute Respiratory Syndrome
SCM	Supply Chain Management
SIPO	State Intellectual Property Office
SME	Small and Medium Enterprise
SPS	Sanitary and Phyto-Sanitary
S&T	Science and Technology
TBR	Trade Barrier Regulations
TBT	Technical Barrier to Trade
TCA	Trade and Cooperation Agreement
TEC	Treaty of the European Community
TECA	Trade and Economic Cooperation Agreement
TFEU	Treaty on the Functioning of the European Union
TRIMS	Trade Related Investment Measures
TRIPS	Trade Related Aspects of Intellectual Property
TRM	Transitional Review Mechanism

TSSC	Textile Specific Safeguard Clause
UK	United Kingdom
UN	United Nations
UNDP	United Nations Development Programme
UNFCCC	United Nations Framework Convention on Climate Change
US	United States
USSR	Union of Soviet Socialist Republics
WB	World Bank
WBCSD	World Business Council for Sustainable Development
WIPO	World International Property Organisation
WMD	Weapon of Mass Destruction
WTO	World Trade Organisation

Foreword

Pierre DEFRAIGNE

It is an honour for me to present this collection of papers, based on the International Workshop dedicated to the European Union (EU)-China Partnership and Cooperation Agreement (PCA), organised by the College of Europe on 3 April 2009. The College has indeed put China among its main fields of research and teaching, thanks also to the InBev-Baillet Latour Fund and to the holder of the InBev-Baillet Latour Chair, Professor Jing Men.

This workshop marked the second event within the framework of the College's extracurricular activities on EU-China Relations[1] and focused on the EU-China relationship with regard to the Strategic Partnership Agreement (SPA), and conducted in the context of the world economic crisis and its recovery process. In my view the most serious hurdle to building such a genuine Sino-European partnership is the very fact that the EU, for all its impressive accomplishments, is still not regarded as a true strategic player from the Chinese perspective. Put simply, for a genuine partnership to take shape both Europe and China need to take the EU seriously.

The current impasse has occurred for two reasons. On the one hand, the EU is not yet a unified international actor, nor is it a fully-fledged civilian power. At the latest G20 summit, President Obama was standing alone with a population of 350 millions and the world's largest Gross Domestic Product (GDP). President Hu Jintao was China's sole representative with 1.3 billion people and the world's third largest GDP (in PPP) – while the EU, with half a billion inhabitants and a GDP equivalent to the United States' (US) GDP, was represented by no less than 6 Heads of State and Government. In effect, there are simply too many individual European leaders and not enough EU leadership. On the other hand, Europe is still in limbo with regard to its hard power capabilities, which can be broken down into three segments: the EU-3 (the "Big Three"); the NATO rank and file; and the total EU-27 member

1 Before the organisation of the international workshop on the EU-China PCA, Chinese Ambassador Song Zhe was invited to give a speech at the College of Europe in March 2009.

states working in the framework of the emerging foreign policy and security pillar, which undertakes peace-keeping and peace-enforcing missions in several theatres of operation.

Some circumstances might, however, change the Chinese perspective of the EU – for-better or for worse. First of all, the economic crisis is turning into a major opportunity for cooperation to overcome the first global recession for the last 60 years (1.5% global output in 2009) and the contraction of international trade (-11.9%).[2] Positive signs can be found in the international reaction to the crisis, starting with the successful G20 meeting in London,[3] which secured the basis for a new system of governance, which should replace the Bretton-Woods order that emerged out of the Second World War.

Moreover, one could argue that the rise of China, since 1979, has been made possible by several dysfunctional elements of global economic governance. Several circumstances, such as the collapse of the Bretton-Woods system on August 15th 1971 – with the subsequent decoupling of the dollar and the gold standard and the shift to a floating exchange rate system – or the rapid liberalisation of capital flows in the space of a single decade, created the necessary conditions allowing for international capital to move to China. Coupled with these conditions were the monumental decisions taken by the Communist Party to adopt market capitalism under a new guise – a socialist market economy – epitomised by China's accession to the WTO after 14 years of negotiations, two decades after its conversion to a socialist market economy.

Another contributing factor was, of course, the building-up of massive structural external imbalances between America and Asia, due to the US' over-zealous consumption patters, which are directly connected to the severe aggravation of income and wealth distribution in the US. The US accumulated excessive levels of public debt that poor American households, whose over-consumption has translated into a structural trade deficit for the US and an exponential trade surplus for China. What we have witnessed since September 15 with the collapse of Lehman Brothers – a "9/15" perhaps which might overshadow 9/11 in history books – is actually the beginning of the unscrambling of a global economic disorder which was neither fair nor sustainable, and eventually proved fundamentally unstable. This instability mainly derived from structural imbalances coupled with the drifting of global market

---

2 International Monetary Fund, 'World Economic Outlook 2009,' Washington, DC: International Monetary Fund, p. 184.

3 The G20 London Summit was held in London on 2 April 2009. More information about the outcomes of the Summit can be retrieved at http://www.londonsummit.gov.uk/en/.

capitalism that eventually led to a situation of unregulated "hyper-financialisation."

The abrupt turn taken by world economic globalisation after the Wall Street tsunami, means that since last September, regulatory policy-making has taken over from market-led policy-making – regulation is superseding deregulation. This might come as a relief for those who never put their faith in neo-classical economic theory or, *a fortiori*, in neo-liberal doctrines. The latter are from now on left orphaned by the most right-wing politicians in the West.

Yesterday, they praised the superiority of market solutions to almost any problem, but overnight they converted to neo or hyper-Keynesianism, coupled with a heavy-hand approach from governments in the banking sector and several key industrial sectors. The danger of this U-turn is all too blatant: swinging from global under-regulated markets to national interventions is exposing the global economy to the risk of protectionism and market fragmentation. A system based on global governance and on multilateral rules and cooperation is part of a sounder answer. Yet the structural changes that are required to deal with the abrupt fall in global demand are such that only governments can mobilise the resources required to complete them within a reasonable span of time. America and China are the countries which need to adjust the most: the USA will have to get rid of its propensity to fall into heavy debt, while China – whose export sector has been severely hit by the world recession – needs to progressively change its growth model in three areas: China needs to switch from export-driven to domestic demand-driven growth; it requires more egalitarian growth patters; and also, more sustainable growth. Fortunately, China's prudent financial policy has spared the Chinese economy from the financial dire straits into which the EU was pulled. This spared China having to simultaneously clean-up banks' "cupboards" whilst also having to reallocate massive resources across sectors and regions.

The Chinese political system is thus being seriously tested in carrying out this Herculean task. If it proves successful, then its output/legitimacy will be strengthened and its international authority will be bolstered, not only in Asia and in the South, but also in the West, and particularly in Europe. This is despite the fact that Europeans, rightly or wrongly, have always put the legitimacy of the process, over the legitimacy of the outcome. With the design of its massive stimulus package, even as early as last autumn, the PRC's authorities clearly realised the need for these new orientations to the Chinese economy including, the gradual establishment of a social safety net, which will pave the way for an increase in household consumption; huge infrastructural programmes (that includes the impressive railroad plan) that will contribute to strengthening the economic and political unity of China, as well as to the regional rebalancing of China from East to West and South to North – setting the foundations for the expansion of China's potentially gigantic domestic consumption; important investments, which are contributing to the greening of China (e.g. in water treatment plants).

The challenge is enormous and has been made yet more difficult by the prospect of social unrest entailed by the severe strains imposed upon the workers, by bankruptcies and job losses in the export sector. But the Chinese leadership has proved its ability to cope under extremely difficult circumstances, if only because China's development – with its very tough geographical and physical constraints – has always been a tremendous challenge. In parallel to the optimism felt for the EU's future, one is also optimistic that China will be once again up to the job, no manner how difficult it may be. Therefore, it seems clear that this dramatic change of tack with respect to China's development model, is transforming China's relationship to the world – and to the EU – in both economic and political terms. China's relative economic weight will increase further, as a result of the increase in the relative growth rate differentials between China and the West, while the global balance of power will be tilting further eastwards.

Furthermore, China's success might become a global benchmark while the credibility of the Anglo-Saxon model might have been severely harmed by Wall Street's meltdown. China will cease being a mainly powerful export house and become more and more an attractive market and a hub for further technology transfer and services, and other forms of advanced FDI. Regional integration in East Asia should deepen, subject to political developments nonetheless. China's future energy and commodity needs will sharply increase its investments in the Southern Hemisphere, but first and foremost, China will have to deepen and widen its technological capacity, which is key to enjoying a more autonomous development, as well as to better its terms of trade with the rest of the world. China is becoming a fully-fledged economic power and is acting as a responsible player. China is a reliable WTO member and has played an important and very constructive role in the success of the London G20 Summit. It still has to make more of a commitment to the international climate negotiations, but the first seedlings of China's green economy augur as a positive omen for the future.

I am sure you will enjoy reading this collection of papers. Initiatives of this kind are extremely useful and important for the consolidation of the EU-China relationship, especially after the financial and economic crisis. Indeed, academics have a key responsibility in this relationship: tearing down the Chinese Wall of European ignorance concerning the reality of the actual situation and unearthing China's potential – therefore highlighting the quality of the partnership that we have to develop together. All of this needs to occur without forgetting the fact that the EU has also some difficult internal tasks to complete.

INTRODUCTION

EU-China Relations in the 21st Century

Jing MEN & Giuseppe BALDUCCI

Over the last thirty years, EU-China relations have deepened and expanded significantly. This is indicated by the stunning growth of their economic interactions, which have made China into the EU's second most important commercial partner and the latter China's first trading partner as well as its largest source of advanced technology. Paralleling these economic changes, the EU and China have also developed their political relations through annual summits, Troika meetings and sectoral dialogues, which aim at addressing global issues as well as topics relevant to bilateral relations. In recent years, both the EU and China were interested in upgrading their relations from a Comprehensive to a Strategic Partnership. Against this background, the EU and China have at the beginning of 2007 launched negotiations on a Partnership and Cooperation Agreement (PCA), which will replace the Agreement on Trade and Economic Cooperation that dates back to 1985. The PCA is to provide a legal framework in which the two sides could further develop their cooperation.

Notwithstanding these remarkable achievements, the further development of EU-China relations is hampered by some problems. Particularly after 2005, the doubts about the strategic partnership between the two sides, the EU's rising trade deficit with China, and the suspension of the EU-China summit meeting at the end of 2008, reminded both the Europeans and the Chinese of the wisdom and efforts needed from both sides to further promote bilateral cooperation. The negotiations of the PCA are proceeding rather slowly due to the lack of breakthrough between the two sides on issues such as human rights, the Taiwan issue, market economy status and the lifting of the arms embargo.

Differences between the EU and China

The EU and China have different political systems based on different ideological origins. Such differences are compounded by the fact that the EU and China are at different stages of economic development. The EU focuses on political freedom and attaches great importance to the political and civil rights of its citizens. In contrast, China concentrates on solving economic problems so that all the Chinese can have sufficient nutrition and basic material needs. China was lagging far behind the industrialised countries when the PRC was founded in 1949. The economic reform carried out since the end of the 1970s has brought dynamism to the Chinese economy. Some Chinese benefited from government policy and became rich. Nevertheless, the uneven development in China has led to a huge gap between the big cities such as Beijing, Shanghai and most of the vast land of the Chinese interior. As a result, China feels the need to emphasize more on the economic rights of its citizens. This fails to correspond to the EU's expectations. The EU expects to exert influence on China and to turn it into a liberal democratic regime, based on the rule of law. Since the 1990s, the EU has been keeping a close eye on the development of political rights of Chinese citizens. In order to promote an open society, the EU has financed many programs and projects in China including training programs for Chinese lawyers.

Both the EU and China agreed to establish a strategic partnership in 2004. However, the description of the relationship is so ambiguous that it is not clear whether they have already a strategic partnership or they are in the process of building one. The fact that the arms embargo is still maintained after twenty years of further development of bilateral relations indicates that EU-China relations are not as well developed as the phrases used by the leaders, on both sides, sometimes suggest. The first round of strategic dialogue was held between the EU and China in 2005, one year after the two sides agreed to establish a strategic partnership. David Scott has expressed the view that strategic dialogue and strategic partnership are somehow incoherent to each other. Strategic dialogue is used to overcome strategic divergences and differences, whereas strategic partnership indicates strategic convergence. The regularly held strategic dialogue between the EU and China seems to indicate that consensus and agreement still need to be established.[1] As a matter of fact, many problems exist between the EU and China that it may be premature to define the partnership as "strategic."[2]

---

1 See David Scott, 'The EU-China "Strategic Dialogue": Pathways in the International System,' in David Kerr & Fei Liu (eds.), *The International Politics of EU-China Relations*, Oxford, Oxford University Press, 2007, pp. 13-37.

2 See Liselotte Odgaard & Sven Biscop, 'The EU and China: Partners in Effective Multilateralism?,' in D. Kerr & F. Liu (eds.), *The International Politics of EU-China Relations*, pp. 54-77; Jean-Pierre Cabestan, 'The Role of France in Sino-European Relations: Central or Marginal?,' in D. Kerr & F. Liu (eds.), *The International Politics of EU-China Relations*, pp. 129-150; and Alison Bailes & Anna Wetter, 'EU-China

Furthermore, together with the impressive growth of two-way trade between the EU and China, the EU's trade deficit has also been rising rapidly. While China's exports to the EU grew from US$19.83 bn in 1996 to US$245.19 bn in 2007, China's imports from the EU only increased from US$19.89 bn in 1996 to US$110.96 bn in 2007. The EU faces much more pressure from the rising deficit in its trade with China. In its most recent China policy paper, the EU regards China as "the single most important challenge for EU trade policy."[3] In 2008, the EU's deficit rose to 169 bn euros.[4]

EU-China relations encountered another challenge when China decided to postpone the 2008 summit meeting, due to French President Sarkozy's scheduled meeting with the Dalai Lama in Poland. Disappointment with China's decision was obvious in the EU. According to John Fox, who works for the European Council on Foreign Relations in London, "China doesn't place much value in Europe any more."[5] Many Europeans believe that the Chinese "are really taking a stand, but what this is going to do is provoke European leaders to discuss China in a more critical way."[6] Whereas in China, one day after the Chinese got to know that the EU-China summit meeting was postponed, the *Huaqiu shibao* (*Global Times*) produced a survey online among about 9,000 netizens, 91.77% of them expressed the view that the reception of the Dalai Lama by the Europeans will change their impression on the EU negatively. 96% of the netizens who participated in the survey supported the decision of the Chinese government to postpone the summit meeting.[7]

China, in its relations with the EU, has always called for equal partnership and mutual respect. In the view of the Chinese, cooperation with the EU should be mutually beneficial. Economically, as China has

---

Security Relations: The "Softer" Side,' in D. Kerr & F. Liu (eds.), *The International Politics of EU-China Relations*, pp. 153-183.

3 Commission of the European Communities, 'A Policy Paper on EU-China Trade and Investment: Competition and Partnership Brussels,' COM(2006) 632 final, Brussels, 24 October 2006, retrieved on 23 January 2009, http://trade.ec.europa.eu/doclib/docs/2006/october/tradoc_130791.pdf, p. 3.

4 Press Release of the EU, 'EU-China Trade in Facts and Figures,' 4 September 2009, retrieved on 23 September 2009, http://europa.eu/rapid/pressReleasesAction.do?reference=MEMO/09/375&format=HTML&aged=0&language=EN.

5 C. Buckley, 'Dumped Summit Exposes China-Europe disenchantment,' *Reuters*, 1 December 2008, retrieved on 15 January 2009, http://ecfr.eu/content/entry/ecfr_john_fox_china_eu_summit_cancellation_reuters.

6 'France heads into Chinese storm over Tibet,' *AFP*, 5 December 2008, retrieved on 15 January 2009, http://ecfr.eu/content/entry/ecfr_john_fox_france_china_tibet_afp/.

7 'Ouzhou naonu Sarkozy jian Dalai dianran Zhongguoren nuhuo' (Sarkozy's meeting with Dalai fuelled China's ire), *Huaqiu shibao (Global Times)*, 5 December 2008, retrieved on 15 January 2009, http://world.huanqiu.com/roll/2008-12/303457.html.

become the third largest economy in the world, a close cooperation between the EU and China is necessary to help find solutions to the international financial crisis. Politically, two of the member states of the EU are permanent members of the UN Security Council. The EU and China need to work together to maintain world peace and stability. The visit of Chinese Premier Wen to Europe in early 2009, after the cancellation of EU-China summit hosted by the French Presidency of the EU in December 2008, was described by the Chinese government as "a trip of confidence." With this trip, China intended to remind the EU that the two remain important partners in spite of so many differences.[8]

Between the EU and China, apart from the above mentioned gaps in expectations, there are other issues for which consensus also needs to be reached. For example, European access to the Chinese market, the treatment of market economy status required by the Chinese, the huge European goods trade deficit with the Chinese, the piracy and intellectual property offences to European products in China, and etc. Currently, a major negotiation topic between the two sides is how to cope with global warming and how much responsibility each should take in reducing greenhouse gas emissions. Facing pressure from the EU and the US, Chinese Premier Wen said at the High-level Conference on Climate Change Technology Development and Technology Transfer in Beijing that "developed countries (should) shoulder the duty and responsibility to tackle climate change and should alter their unsustainable lifestyle."[9] The emissions per person in China are less than one-third of the average level of the developed countries.[10] As a developing country, China's top priority is economic growth. This position is not well received in the international community. Many Europeans attributed the failure of Copenhagen Conference in December 2009 to China's insistence on its priority of development and its uncompromised attitude – that China should be treated as a developing country.

Whether China is a developing country or not is an issue in dispute. There is no doubt that China is rising rapidly since its reform policy was adopted at the end of the 1970s. China is now the third largest economy in the world, the largest trading partner of many countries in the world

8 D. Wei, 'Waijiaobu cheng Wen Jiabao Zongli fangwen Ouzhou siguo shi yici "xinxinzhilü"' (Foreign Ministry says that Premier Wen's visit to Europe is 'a trip of confidence'), *People's Daily*, 23 January 2009, retrieved on 30 January 2009, http://politics.people.com.cn/GB/1024/8715320.html.

9 'Climate Technology Meeting Highlights Developed-Developing Country Divide,' 14 November 2008, retrieved on 15 June 2009, http://ictsd.net/i/news/biores/33669.

10 'Premier Wen Jiabao Addressed at the Third East Asia Summit,' *China Daily*, 22 November 2007, retrieved on 15 June 2009, http://www.ccchina.gov.cn/en/NewsInfo.asp?NewsId=9886.

including Japan, India, Brazil, Australia, and South Korea. It is the second largest trading partner of both the European Union and the United States. In the meantime, China has the largest foreign currency reserve and acts as the largest owner of American government debt. However, if China's GDP is analysed at the per capita level, it is ranked after 100 among all the countries in the world. China's GDP per capita in 2006 was around US$2,100, whereas the GDP per capita of the fifteen members of the European Monetary Union had already reached more than US$34,000 in the same year.[11] China has developed unevenly in its regions. The coastal areas in the east and southeast of China have benefited most from the reform policy whereas China's vast inland is lagging much behind. Among the Chinese, the increasing income gap is worrisome. A report by the Chinese Academy of Social Sciences demonstrates that the disparity between the haves and have-nots has widened dramatically over the past 20 years. "The richest 10 percent of Chinese families now own more than 40 percent of all private assets, while the poorest 10 percent share less than two percent of the total wealth."[12] The sharp contrast of these data indicates China's uniqueness. "It has one foot in the developing world and another in the developed one."[13]

Mutual Expectations and Challenges

Both the EU and China would like to maintain stability and peace in the world. They expect that via joint efforts, development is sustained and conflicts are avoided. As a rising power, the EU promotes multilateralism in international relations. Such a policy conforms to the EU's interest. European integration is based on a group of well recognised rules and norms as well as effective multilateralism. The significant achievement of enlargement from the original six members to the current twenty-seven members is a result of rule-building and institutionalised multilateral cooperation between the members. In a world in search of multipolarity, the rule-based multilateral approach can allow the EU to give full play to its successful experience accumulated in the process of European integration and in the meantime, to enhance the EU's influence in international affairs. In the EU's design of world governance, multilateralism is

---

11 'Global income per capita,' retrieved on 20 October 2008, http://www.finfacts.com/biz10/globalworldincomepercapita.htm.

12 'China Suffers Widening Income Gap,' *China Daily*, 17 January 2007, retrieved on 18 June 2009, http://www.chinadaily.com.cn/china/2007-01/07/content_776436.htm.

13 Domingos Jardo Muekalia, 'Africa and China's Strategic Partnerships,' *African Security Review*, Vol. 13, No. 1, 2004, p. 5.

an indispensable element.[14] However, effective multilateralism will not be realised without support from China. The multipolarity promoted by China is not the same as the multilateralism advocated by the Europeans. As China attaches great importance to the traditional concept of sovereignty, it is difficult for the two to achieve consensus on the strategic vision for international economics and politics.

As a normative/civilian/soft power, the EU intends to help China transform into a country based on the rule of law, with respect to human rights and democracy. The EU is eager to integrate China into the international community so that not only cooperation between the two sides will be improved but also the EU's role in the world will be strengthened. In order to realise this goal, the EU invested for its first China National Indicative Programme (2002-2006) €250 mn and committed in the current one (2007-2010) for €225 mn. However, China's progress in this aspect seems to be unsatisfactory. By far, although China has signed both of the UN Covenants on Economic, Social and Cultural Rights and on Political and Civil Rights, the Chinese National People's Congress has not ratified the second covenant twelve years after its signature. Due to lack of progress, the Europeans have become increasingly frustrated in the human rights dialogue with their Chinese counterparts.

China also has expectations from the EU. China-US relations used to be the top priority in China's external relations. After the EU and China came closer in their cooperation, the Chinese government attempted to juxtapose China-EU relations with China-US relations, hoping that the EU could help balance against the US hegemonic power. Both as rising powers, the EU and China seemed to be perfect partners in China's strategic design of the future world order. However, to China's disappointment, the US remains the EU's closest partner. The newly developed China-EU relations could in no way replace the importance of the US to the EU.[15] The discussion of lifting the arms embargo in 2005 demonstrated to the Chinese that in China-EU relations, it is impossible to get rid of the shadow of the US. To cultivate relations with the EU will not help balance against the US.

---

14 See European Security Strategy: 'A Secure Europe in a Better World,' 12 December 2003, retrieved on 15 June 2009, http://www.consilium.europa.eu/uedocs/cmsUpload/78367.pdf.

15 See Jing Men, 'The EU-China Strategic Partnership: Achievements and Challenges,' *European Policy Paper Series*, No. 12 (November 2007), European Studies Centre (University of Pittsburgh), http://ucis.pitt.edu/euce/pub/policypapers/2007-EU-China_Partnership.pdf.

The differences between the EU member states in the making of the European Common Foreign and Security Policy is another problem that failed to live up to Beijing's expectations. Before 2005, the Chinese leadership believed that the EU institutions had considerable influence among its member states. If the green light had been given to the lifting of the arms embargo at the European level, the member states would not have presented much problem.[16] With hindsight, such understanding obviously misjudged the decision-making mechanism of the CFSP. The discussion of the lifting of the arms embargo in the EU exposed the divergences among the member states and the limited role of the European institutions in promoting a common CFSP position, which obliged the Chinese to adjust its EU policy and to invest more energy in the individual capitals of the member states instead of simply relying on Brussels.

Needless to say, it is in the interest of both the EU and China that bilateral relations are developing stably and smoothly. In the meantime, it is more than natural that differences exist between the two since they have different political and social systems, economic levels, and cultural background. The idea of reaching a PCA between the EU and China is aimed at coordinating each other's goals and means so as to strengthen cooperation and partnership. However, as mentioned earlier, the negotiations are progressing slowly. Since the beginning of 2007, three years have passed, but there is no timetable yet for when the negotiations will be concluded.

Against such background, we organised an international workshop in April 2008 at the College of Europe in Bruges to examine the EU-China PCA from different perspectives. The PCA has the objective of providing a more appropriate and updated framework to "encompass the full scope of their bilateral relationship," which have significantly expanded and deepened in the last thirty years.[17] The participants discussed together the prospects of the PCA, the influence that the PCA that will bring to EU-China relations, the divergence and convergence between the EU and China in their negotiations of the PCA, and the major concerns and core interests of both sides. Based on the successful organisation of the workshop, we selected 9 papers and edited them into this book so that our readers can share with us the research results of experts and scholars in the field of EU-China relations.

---

16 Author's interview with Chinese diplomats, July 2006.

17 Joint Statement of the 10th China-EU Summit, Beijing, 28 November 2007, retrieved on 15 July 2009, http://www.eu2007.pt/UE/vEN/Noticias_Documentos/20071202CHINA.htm.References.

Chapter Outlines

In each chapter, the authors present the state of the art of EU-China relations in a specific field. At the same time, they critically address the main challenges, which confront the EU and China at present. Drawing from these analyses, the authors then elaborate on the prospects for EU-China relations and offer recommendations and policy suggestions. Therefore, this book presents a combination of academic research and policy proposals, which are valuable for university teachers and students in the fields of European and Chinese Studies, Political Science and International Relations as well as EU officials, policy practitioners and the wider public interested in EU-China relations.

In Chapter 1, Andrew Cottey and Joern-Carsten Gottwald examine the EU-China Partnership and Cooperation Agreement (PCA) in the context of the new global economic and political order created by the rise of Asia and the non-Western world, the (relative) decline of the West and the 2008 financial crisis. After briefly accounting for the evolution of EU-China relations and describing the major changes in the international order, the authors sketch five alternative future scenarios for EU-China relations: (i) status quo; (ii) Chinese assertion, European acquiescence; (iii) European assertion, Chinese acquiescence; (iv) confrontation; and (v) true partnership. Cottey and Gottwald also identify the policy choices facing the EU and China as they proceed in negotiation of the PCA. The authors conclude that the PCA may help address some bilateral issues and further institutionalise EU-China relations, but point out in the meantime that the PCA will not dramatically change EU-China relations, which in the foreseeable future are likely to maintain the present "status quo," characterised by "extensive economic relations, a highly institutionalised diplomatic-political relationship and ongoing efforts to develop substantive cooperation in a range of areas." For the time being, the EU-China partnership will remain "constrained by divergent political systems and limited convergence on many important bilateral and global issues."

In Chapter 2, Kim Van Der Borght and Lei Zhang analyse the institutionalisation of EU-China relations in the last thirty years and examine the shortcomings of the present legal framework. Van Der Borght and Zhang point out that while EU-China relations grow out of the 1985 Trade and Economic Cooperation Agreement, the several legal instruments that have been set up to regulate the expansion of relations are presently too incoherent to provide an effective basis to build future relations. Therefore, the authors appreciate the importance of the ongoing negotiations for a comprehensive PCA and they provide interesting scenarios and suggestions as their conclusion. In particular, Van Der Borght and Zhang suggest that for sensitive issues, "the two parties need mutual trust and substantial communication to resolve conflicts. It is not wise to regulate these issues by hard legal clauses." As for the less sensitive issues, the authors suggest that the two parties, on the basis of mutual respect and equal consultation, "may look for an effective and efficient means to settle down these matters in the form of clauses."

In Chapter 3, Frauke Austermann analyses the significant issue of Corporate Social Responsibility (CSR) and how the European model of CSR can help improve labour standards in China, and thereby contribute to a sustainable development of the country's economy. Austermann presents the three main characteristics of European CSR, namely its inherently stakeholder-focused model, its integrated strategies and its voluntary character. After briefly presenting the Chinese business context, she then elaborates on the two possible ways of transplanting European CSR to China: learning from European business practice in China and learning from European governments. In both cases, Austermann demonstrates that European CSR has the potential to contribute to improve labour standards in China, notwithstanding China's different stage of economic development and its political system. Austermann suggests that in the ongoing PCA negotiations, the EU should use CSR as a strategic tool in order to "support China's transition to an open society based on the [...] respect for human rights," which is one of the EU's main declared aims towards China.

In Chapter 4, Antoine Sautenet assesses the content and implementation of the PCA for EU-China trade. More specifically, Sautenet provides an insightful and technical discussion of two major issues under consideration in the PCA, (i.e. intellectual property rights and investments). The author contextualises the ongoing negotiations for the PCA within the Chinese economic environment and the evolving European approach towards China, which also involves political and economic dimensions. In this way, Sautenet highlights the major points of friction between the EU and China, the European *desiderata* in IPR protection and investments and the Chinese internal legal situation with regard to these two issues. Sautenet points out the inherent risks and opportunities for the conclusion of the PCA and suggests that the EU negotiators should try to find a balance between their political and economic ambitions in order to avoid a fragile agreement at the commercial level.

In Chapter 5, Nayia Pyridi deals with the issue of investments in EU-China relations and she reflects upon how the PCA could grant a mandate for the EU to negotiate a European bilateral investment treaty. Pyridi approaches the issue by discussing in detail the evolving legal competences of the EU in investment matters. In particular, she highlights the power that the EU will gain with the coming into force of the Lisbon Treaty. At present, 25 out of 27 EU member states have signed bilateral investment treaties with China. As the latter grants different commitments to different member states, it creates a patchy and confusing situation. A European bilateral investment treaty with China could thus provide a clearer framework for European investors in China. In order to obtain such a goal, Pyridi explores from a legal viewpoint how the combination of the Lisbon Treaty and the possible conclusion of the PCA could provide a clear mandate to the EU to draft a European bilateral investment treaty with China. The author concludes by providing useful recommendations to European negotiators on how to include in the agenda of the ongoing negotiations for the PCA, the possibility to establish an investment mandate for an EU bilateral investment treaty with China.

In Chapter 6, Jappe Eckhardt deals with the evolution of EU-China trade relations and analyses a specific and significant sector, (i.e. the clothing and textile industry). Eckhardt distinguishes three major historical periods, namely 1978-1994, 1995-2005, 2005 to date, and for each period he provides an analysis of the European trade preferences and policy towards China. The author points out that in the clothing and textile sector until the mid-1990s, protectionist forces ruled the scene in Europe and they had enough political clout to impose very tough measures towards China's exports. However, in the ensuing two periods, the restructuring of the clothing and textile sector in Europe, the relocation of some European companies in China, and the increasing market concentration of retailers slowly allowed anti-protectionist forces in Europe to gain the upper hand. This determined a more balanced EU policy towards China on trade in clothing and textile. Eckhardt's findings from the case of textile and clothing can be generalised to other trade sectors in EU-China relations. However, as Eckhardt also maintains, this does not mean that European protectionism has disappeared. Although the quota system is already history, more subtle measures could still be put in place in the EU and legal battles over EU-China trade will resurface despite the establishment of the PCA.

In Chapter 7, Edward Cameron and Hilary McMahon investigate how the EU-China partnership can forge a new space for climate change policy. The authors study the environmental problems facing the EU and China at present, the differences and similarities between the EU and China in their environmental policies and the possibility to forge an effective partnership to fight climate change worldwide. Cameron and McMahon point out that the EU and China have recognised the effects and damages of climate change and both are aware of the need to construct a global framework on mitigation, adaptation, technology and finance to fight climate change. Considering the economic and political clout of both the EU and China in international affairs, Cameron and

McMahon maintain that the two partners have the potential to steer the global community from principle to practice. In order to translate rhetoric into practice Cameron and McMahon propose that the EU and China develop a common understanding of each other's needs and capacities, a common vision for new commitments, promote equity and enhance financing, build better governance both at international and internal level, and expand their practical collaboration.

In Chapter 8, Katrin Kinzelbach discusses the issue of human rights in EU-China relations and its relevance for the PCA. In order to do so, Kinzelbach offers analyses of one of the key instruments applied by the EU to promote human rights in China: the EU-China Dialogue on Human Rights. Few authors have attempted to do so, due to the high level of confidentiality that governs the Dialogue and the lack of transparency that characterises it. Kinzelbach provides a wealth of information and data on the Dialogue process, which are the fruit of extensive interviews among European and Chinese officials and of her active participation in several EU-China academic dialogues. Kinzelbach attempts to invest-tigate whether the Dialogue represents "a normative partnership or antagonism in disguise." In the author's opinion, a normative partnership has to respond to three main criteria: equality of partners, good faith, and agreement on modality and goals. However, through the analysis of the Dialogue process, Kinzelbach points out that the Dialogue does not meet any of these three criteria yet. As a conclusion, the author puts forward some important suggestions for the ongoing negotiations on the PCA to substantially redesign the EU's approach to human rights in China and establish a genuine partnership on human rights.

In Chapter 9, Carmen Amado Mendes questions whether the PCA will represent a concrete and substantive step forward in EU-China relations, or will it instead represent just a more advanced institutional framework to regulate the ongoing relations. This question stems from the analysis of the Sino-Portuguese Comprehensive Partnership Agreement, which, according to the author, has been unable to provide any substance to Portugal-China relations. In order to answer this question, Amado Mendes provides an insightful review of EU-China relations and investigates three major contentious issues, namely, human rights, the arms embargo and the WTO. The author proves that although these issues show ideological differences and ongoing challenges, "Brussels and Beijing perceive themselves as partners and are willing to improve cooperation." However, to what extent such cooperation can be considered "strategic" remains doubtful for Amado Mendes. While the PCA could soon be reality, its strategic dimension may take some time to materialise.

CHAPTER 1

EU-China Relations in a New World Order

Status, Dynamics, Scenarios

Andrew COTTEY & Joern-Carsten GOTTWALD[1]

Since the 1980s relations between the European Union (EU) and China have deepened significantly. Bilateral trade has expanded dramatically and a web of institutionalised diplomatic and technical ties has been established. Leaders on both sides have referred to the EU-China relationship as a "maturing partnership,"[2] a "comprehensive strategic partnership"[3] and an "all-around strategic partnership."[4] It was in this context that negotiations began in 2007 for a Partnership and Cooperation Agreement (PCA) to replace the 1985 Trade and Economic Cooperation Agreement (TECA) which remains the legal basis for relations. In late 2008, however, relations suffered something of a setback when China unexpectedly withdrew from the annual EU-China summit in protest at French President Nicolas Sarkozy meeting with the Tibetan spiritual leader (France also at this point held the EU's rotating Presidency, leading the Chinese to argue that Sarkozy was *de facto* acting on the EU's behalf). Furthermore, in 2009, a widely noted report from the European Council on Foreign Relations (ECFR) argued that the failure of EU member states to develop a truly common policy and their reluctance to confront difficult issues resulted in a China policy that amounted to

---

1 Research for this chapter was supported by an Irish Research Council for the Humanities and Social Sciences (IRCHSS) Government of Ireland Small Research Project Grant (2008-09) entitled 'China, Ireland and the European Union: Distant Partners, Global Competitors?'.

2 Commission of the European Communities, *Commission Policy Paper for Transmission to the Council and the European Parliament: A Maturing Partnership – Shared Interests and Challenges in EU-China Relations*, COM(2003) 533 final, Brussels, 10 September 2003.

3 'Wen Stresses Importance of Developing Comprehensive Strategic Partnership,' *People's Daily Online*, 7 May 2004, retrieved on 26 June 2008, http://english.people.com.cn/200405/07/eng20040507_142556.html.

4 'Chinese President Calls for Enhanced Dialogue with EU,' *People's Daily Online*, 25 April 2008, retrieved on 26 June 2008, http://english.people.com.cn/90001/90776/90883/6399429.html#.

nothing more than "unconditional engagement."[5] Although the diplomatic waters of EU-China relations subsequently settled, these developments suggested that the relationship between Europe and China was more problematic than implied by the rhetoric of strategic partnership.

This chapter assesses EU-China relations and explores their future prospects. The first part reviews the current status of bilateral relations. The second part analyses the changing global context of EU-China relations, including the impact of the 2008 world financial and economic crisis. The third part sketches five alternative scenarios for the future development of relations: status quo; Chinese assertion, European acquiescence; European assertion, Chinese acquiescence; confrontation; and true partnership. The conclusion summarises our argument and discusses the implications for a possible EU-China PCA. We argue that while ties have expanded significantly since the 1980s, the EU-China relationship is constrained by the EU's member states' divergent political systems (liberal democracies) and China (a one-party communist system), which inevitably produce significant differences over human rights and democracy. Furthermore, the divergent historical experiences and political paths of European states and China also creates significant differences on important international issues, in particular on questions of state sovereignty and sharing the burden of addressing global challenges. Neither the EU nor China, however, poses a significant direct threat to the other, nor is either side inclined to challenge the other's major strategic interests. As a consequence, we conclude that, while a major breakdown in EU-China relations cannot be entirely ruled out (for example, as a result of large-scale unrest in China and a government response on the scale of the 1989 Tiananmen Square massacre or violent conflict over Taiwan), three of our scenarios – Chinese assertion, European acquiescence; European assertion, Chinese acquiescence; and confrontation – are reasonably unlikely. At the same time, the development of a true partnership involving much more substantive cooperation will prove difficult, given the systemic differences that exist between the EU and China. The most likely scenario for the future development of EU-China relations therefore is status quo: an extensive economic, especially trade, relationship; the maintenance of a dense network of institutionalised political ties; but real differences over a range of bilateral and global issues which will continue to limit the substance of the putative partnership.

---

5 John Fox & Francois Godement, *A Power Audit of EU-China Relations*, London, European Council on Foreign Relations, 2009, retrieved on 12 May 2009, http://ecfr.eu/content/entry/china_power_audit_ecfr_fox_godement_eu/.

EU-China Relations: The State of Play

Relations between the EU and the PRC expanded greatly in the 1990s and early 2000s. The EU officially recognised the government of the PRC in 1975, accepting its claim to be China's sole legitimate representative (and thereby *de facto* agreeing not to maintain formal diplomatic relations with Taiwan). At this point, however, China was still recovering from the "cultural revolution," maintained a largely isolationist foreign policy and was not a significant political or economic partner for the EU. Equally for China, the EU was not a major strategic interlocutor, especially compared to the Soviet Union and the United States (US). Economic and political relations expanded gradually and in 1985 the EU and China concluded the TECA. At this point, however, China had not begun its dramatic economic rise and integration into the global economy and EU-China ties remained a "secondary relationship," in terms of their significance for both partners or any wider global impact.[6] Sino-European relations were also disrupted by the 1989 Tiananmen Square incident: in response to the Chinese government's use of force to crush dissent, the EU imposed an arms embargo (which remains in place to date) and some limited diplomatic and economic sanctions. In the 1990s and 2000s, however, economic ties between Europe and China expanded dramatically: the EU became a major market for China's export-oriented economy, Europe became a major source of investment and technology for China, with China simultaneously becoming a significant market for Europe. By the early 2000s, the EU and China both figured as leading trading partners, in their respective economic relationship, that continued to expand rapidly. The 1990s and early 2000s also witnessed a parallel expansion of political relations. The first EU-China summit was held in 1998 and such summits – that brought together the Chinese Prime Minister and other Ministers, the Presidents of the EU Council of Ministers, the European Commission, the EU High Representative for the Common Foreign and Security Policy, other Ministers and European Commissioners – have been held annually since then. During the same period a large number of roundtables, dialogues and other regular meetings between experts, technocrats and other representatives of both sides were established. China and the EU also expanded their ties by officially incorporating a second track of non-governmental organisations (NGOs) or civil society organisations (CSO) – the latter term reflecting the near impossibility of the existence of truly non-governmental bodies in China's party-state system. By the early 2000s, the EU-China relationship was substantial

6 Michael B. Yahuda, 'China and Europe: The Significance of a Secondary Relationship,' in Thomas W. Robinson and David L. Shambaugh (eds.), *Chinese Foreign Policy: Theory and Practice*, Oxford, Oxford University Press, 1994, pp. 266-282.

and growing: a major economic relationship based on mutual trade and investment; a relatively strong institutionalised political relationship; a multi-faceted relationship involving engagement across a wide range of issues (including economics, politics, the environment, social challenges and human rights); a relationship which drew the EU into China's on-going process of domestic reform (through the provision of advice, assistance and various dialogues); and a relationship which might have a bearing on how wider global challenges were addressed. Although there were differences and disputes – over trade, human rights and the EU's arms embargo against China – these appeared to be limited in scope and manageable. Both China and the EU began to use the rhetoric of "strategic partnership." It was in this context that the agreement was reached on the initiation of negotiations for a PCA to replace the 1985 TECA and provide a formal framework for the new relationship. American observers also took note of the new EU-China relationship, with some describing it as an "emerging axis" likely to become a significant additional factor in global affairs.[7]

In the latter 2000s, however, Sino-European relations suffered a downturn, leading observers on both sides to question the so-called "strategic partnership." In 2004, the EU agreed in principle to move towards lifting the arms embargo against China. However, after strong US opposition and much diplomatic manoeuvring, the EU abandoned plans to lift the embargo and the issue is now shelved for the foreseeable future. For China, this was a significant disappointment: politically it represented a "slap in the face" – strategically it indicated that when pressed, Europe was likely to defer to the US ahead of China. In Europe, the focus of concerns was predominantly economic: a growing trade deficit with China, the impact of Chinese imports on particular sectors within European economies (such as textiles and footwear), China's failure or inability to take action to protect intellectual property rights (IPR) and market access issues in China.[8] When Chinese and EU leaders met for the 10th EU-China summit in Beijing in November 2007, economic problems were generating friction. Tough words between EU Trade Commissioner Peter Mandelson and China's Grande Dame of foreign trade Wu Yi set the tone for a meeting that praised the progress in

---

7 David Shambaugh, 'China and Europe: The Emerging Axis,' *Current History*, Vol. 103, No. 674, 2004, pp. 243-248.

8 European Union Chamber of Commerce in China, *European Business in China Position Paper 2007-2008: Executive Summary*, European Union Chamber of Commerce in China, Beijing, 2007, retrieved on 4 August 2009, http://www.europeanchamber.com.cn/images/documents/marketing_department/beijing/publications/past_pp/excecutive_summary_en.pdf.

relations but barely disguised tensions below the surface.[9] Protectionist measures within Europe against China were extended in 2008, indicating that from Brussels' perspective the Beijing leadership failed to address European concerns.[10] In addition, growing Chinese outward investment in Europe generated concerns in Brussels and European capitals that Beijing might be gaining an unwelcome degree of influence over strategic sectors of the economy. By the late 2000s, it was also becoming clear that although a multitude of bilateral sectoral dialogues had been established since the 1990s, the substantive impact of these dialogues was limited at best.

Relations were disrupted further in 2008 by tensions over Tibet and the Olympics. In spring 2008, demonstrations in Tibet against Beijing's harsh suppression of human rights and independence movements led to an intervention by Chinese security forces that shocked European public opinion. Only months before the opening of the Beijing Olympic Games, the Chinese government found itself facing global criticism for what it defines as defending national unity against a "splittist" movement. When the Olympic torch relay reached European capitals, governments found themselves caught between the need to ensure the safe staging of the relay and defending the right to free political protest – a fundamental principle for European democracies – against China's actions in Tibet. Demonstrations in Paris, London and other capitals further increased tensions between the Chinese leadership and European governments and spread into the wider communities of Chinese living in Europe and Europeans living in China. In the wake of the violence in Tibet, European leaders were torn over how far to boycott the Olympic Games' opening ceremony in response to the Chinese government's actions. After some debate, most European leaders, including French President Nicolas Sarkozy, as President of the European Council, attended the opening ceremony. The issue escalated again in late 2008 when Sarkozy's willingness to participate in an event that included the Tibetan spiritual and political leader – the Dalai Lama – on its guest list, led China to unexpectedly cancel the 11th EU-China Summit in Lyons at the last

9 Commission of the European Communities, Press Release IP/07/1753, 'EU Trade Commissioner Mandelson in China November 23-28,' Brussels, 23 November 2007, retrieved on 4 August 2009, http://europa.eu/rapid/pressReleasesAction.do?reference=IP/07/1753&format=HTML&aged=0&language=EN&guiLanguage=en and Peter Mandelson, Speech, 'Growing Trade, Shared Responsibilities,' *Speech at the EU-China Business Summit*, Beijing, 27 November 2007, retrieved on 4 August 2009, http://trade.ec.europa.eu/doclib/docs/2008/january/tradoc_137537.pdf.

10 Jonathan Stearns, 'EU Threatens to Renew Tariffs on Footwear from China, Vietnam,' *Bloomberg.com*, 3 October 2008, retrieved on 4 August 2009, http://www.bloomberg.com/apps/news?pid=20601080&sid=ad9olwZ1OK00&refer=asia.

moment and exclude France from a tour of European states by Chinese Prime Minister Wen Jiabao in January-February 2009. Sino-European relations appeared to have reached a low point. The tensions over Tibet, not only further reflected short-term diplomatic problems but deeper differences over fundamental questions of state sovereignty and human rights. From the Chinese perspective, European criticisms of its action were an unjustified infringement of Chinese sovereignty, especially when Beijing viewed itself as taking action vital to maintaining the unity of the Chinese state. From the European perspective, China's actions in Tibet were excessive and reflected an underlying failure to respect international human rights standards.

EU-China relations took a turn for the better in 2009, with the cancelled 2008 summit being re-convened in Prague, under the Czech Presidency of the EU, in May 2009. China's participation in the reconvened summit partly reflected the fact that the Presidency of the EU had shifted from France to the Czech Republic, but it also suggested a recognition in Beijing that its response to European criticisms over Tibet risked long-term damage to a relationship that was important to China. At a minimum, the reconvening of the summit indicated that the relationship had not been fundamentally de-railed by the tensions over Tibet and the Olympics. Nevertheless, while EU-China relations have expanded dramatically since the early 1990s, the tensions of the late 2000s indicated that there remain substantial differences between the EU and China, including over fundamental issues of state sovereignty and human rights, and represented a turning point compared to the sometimes naïve optimism of the preceding decade.

The Changing Strategic Context of EU-China Relations

Until quite recently, the strategic context of EU-China relations was defined by a number of features which allowed the two partners to develop a burgeoning economic relationship relatively free from the sorts of geo-political tensions which often characterise relations between major powers. China was primarily a regional power and after the initiation of economic reforms in the late 1970s, it was focused on its own internal development and maintaining a foreign policy which would not disrupt this process. In being an international actor, the EU was primarily a "civilian power," with its global weight felt only really in the economic sphere. In East Asia, the US acted as the main external security guarantor, balancing first the Soviet Union during the Cold War and more recently China. The US' role in East Asia pushed the need for other Asian states, such as Japan, or for external actors (Europe being the only hypothetical candidate) to assume a more prominent military-strategic role within the region. These factors provided a benign strategic context in which neither the EU nor China was likely to threaten or challenge the other's core interests. Overtly political interaction between the two was limited and trade and investment could expand relatively free from political concerns.

Since the 1990s and especially into the 2000s, this strategic context has changed – and continues to change – very significantly. First, China's rise, resulting from its sustained high levels of economic growth for three decades, has become a current political and economic reality, rather than a likely future trend as was arguably the case in the 1980s and early 1990s, and has made China a global power with a major impact in most regions of the world and in virtually all policy areas. Second, the EU's foreign policy ambitions have expanded significantly since the early 1990s, with the Union formally adopting a Common Foreign and Security Policy (CFSP) and common European Security and Defence Policy (ESDP), enhancing its "bilateral" ties with many states and regions and assuming a more prominent global role in areas such as environmental policy (the Kyoto and post-Kyoto negotiations) and international law (the International Criminal Court). As a consequence of these developments, the EU and China find themselves interacting across a growing range of political, economic, environmental and security issues which are part of the larger global agenda rather than a narrowly defined bilateral relationship. At the United Nations (UN), both the EU and China have been significant actors in the debates relating to reform (for example, of the Security Council and over the recently established Human Rights Council). In the area of climate change, the policies of both the EU and China will be significant determinants of the extent to which it is possible to avert the most severe consequences of global warming. In relation to nuclear proliferation, the EU and China have played a central role in shaping policy towards Iran. In WTO negotiations, China is now a central actor alongside the EU, the US and Japan.

One example of the impact of these two trends is the area of energy and commodity prices. Soaring oil prices hit the global economy in 2006. Other commodity prices soon followed. A key cause of rising energy and commodity prices has been the dramatic economic growth – and hence increasing demand for energy and raw materials – of the larger developing economies, in particular China. The effects on Sino-European relations were twofold: first, China's expansive economic and energy security policy provoked concern in Europe; secondly, the intensifying activity of Chinese enterprises and government in Africa began to receive increasing attention, with the high profile China-Africa summit held in Beijing in 2006 underlining the growing influence of the PRC. China's expanding ties with resource-rich but politically unstable countries, such as Angola, Sudan and Zimbabwe, have led to diplomatic rivalry with the EU and the US. In the eyes of many observers in Europe and the US, the actions of the PRC government reflect the assertive policies of an emerging power contesting the status quo. As a consequence, there are clear tensions between the EU and China over Africa and elements of a strategic competition between the two may be emerging – although it is too soon to assess how far and in what ways this trend will develop.

The global financial and economic crisis which has emerged since 2008 is further altering the strategic context of EU-China relations. The long-term consequences of the global financial and economic crisis remain to be seen and will depend on how quickly and how well different countries recover from the crisis and the resultant impact on the global balance of economic and political power. Nevertheless, a number of implications seem reasonably clear. The Anglo-Saxon neo-liberal economic model which had dominated global economics and politics since the 1980s has been decisively discredited. A new consensus has emerged in favour of greater state involvement in economies and stronger regulation of markets. For many in the developing world, the Chinese model of political and economic development – the so-called "Beijing Consensus" – appears more attractive than the neo-liberalism of the "Washington Consensus." The global financial and economic crisis has also accelerated long-term shifts in the global balance of economic and political power, specifically the rise of the non-Western countries, especially China, and the decline of the West, especially the US. Although China (and other major developing economies such as India) has been hit by the global financial and economic crisis, they have been relatively less severely affected than the US (and other developed economies, including Europe) and appear to be recovering more rapidly. As Philip Stephens has argued, "the big lesson is that the West can no longer assume that the global order will be remade in its own image. For more than two centuries, the US and Europe have exercised an effortless economic, political and cultural hegemony. That era is ending."[11]

The impact of these shifts can be seen in a range of global financial dynamics. Western governments increasingly view China as central to global economic recovery and stability. China's large national economic stimulus package is seen as important not just for the Chinese economy, but for the world economy as a whole. Plans within the Group of 20 (G20) and the International Monetary Fund (IMF) to develop international funds to support global recovery depend to a significant degree on

---

11 Philip Stevens, 'The Financial Crisis Marks Out a new Geo-Political World Order,' *The Financial Times*, 10 October 2008, retrieved on 4 August 2009, http://www.ft.com/cms/s/0ed4a750-961e-11dd-9dce-000077b07658,Authorised=false.html?ilocation=http%3A%2F%2Fwww.ft.com%2Fcms%2Fs%2F0%2F0ed4a750-961e-11dd-9dce-000077b07658.html&ireferer=http%3A%2F%2Fwww.ft.com%2Fhome%2Feurope.

China's ability to contribute to the necessary finances. Whereas leaders in Europe and the US were observing the growing influence of Asian and Middle Eastern sovereign wealth funds and state controlled enterprises – with growing alarm in the years leading up to the global financial crisis – they are now courting them as one of very few available sources of new capital. In her first visit to China in March 2009, the new US Secretary of State Hilary Clinton stressed the importance of Chinese investment in US bonds and declared the financial relationship between China and the US "the most important one in the world."[12] These altered global financial and economic relations will surely have political repercussions: US and European governments, for example, are likely to tone down criticisms of China over human rights and may be more constrained in how they approach issues such as Taiwan, North Korea's nuclear activities and the crisis in Darfur.

One long-term strategic uncertainty with particular consequences for EU-China relations is the extent to which the US will decline as the world's leading power. In the 1990s and early 2000s the world could reasonably be described as unipolar, with the US clearly being the leading global power. The Iraq war, however, illustrated the limits of US power and imposed a significant economic burden on the US. The global financial and economic crisis has accelerated the relative decline of the US and by the late 2000s the US, while still the world's leading power, is now one of a group of major powers in a multipolar world, alongside China, India, Japan, Russia and the EU. What remains uncertain is how far the US' unipolar status will continue and what this will portend for American foreign policy. In one scenario, while other powers may slowly catch up to American dominance, the US will nevertheless remain the world's most powerful state for some decades and be able to maintain its existing global commitments. In a second scenario, domestic economic decline and/or the continuing demands of its global role could force the US to retrench significantly.

Strategic uncertainty over the US' future global role has important consequences for EU-China relations. Since the founding of the PRC in 1949, European states (and eventually the EU) have in effect been able to free ride on the US in East Asia: the US has guaranteed the security of Taiwan and Japan and more generally counter-balanced China; in this context, the EU and its member states have been able to pursue the development of economic and political ties with China and other East

---

12 David Shambaugh, 'China and the US: A Marriage of Convenience,' *International Herald Tribune*, 6 January 2009, retrieved on 13 March 2009, http://www.brookings.edu/opinions/2009/0106_china_shambaugh.aspx.

Asian states, while contributing little to the region's military security.[13] Further American decline could result in the US reducing or even abandoning its security commitments in East Asia, potentially triggering demands for others to step in, such as Japan but also perhaps Europeans countries, to take up more of the military burden in East Asia, or alternatively creating a security vacuum which might draw in other actors, including the EU. At a minimum, such a shift in US policy would raise difficult questions for the EU and its members over how far they could and should take on a greater military security role in East Asia. At present, such a shift in US policy does not appear likely – but considering its implications, this highlights the extent to which the US military presence in East Asia, is a central part of the strategic context that underpins EU policy in the region, and EU-China relations. In this sense, US policy is the largest potential "wild card" in East Asia and any major shift in that policy would imply in that sense that "all existing bets are off."

Five Future Scenarios of EU-China Relations

In light of the trends discussed so far, what are the future prospects for EU-China relations? In developing our argument, we make a number of assumptions about likely future developments within China and within the EU. These assumptions can be questioned, but they represent a reasonable assessment of the most likely scenarios for the development of the two parties over the next two decades. We assume that China will not disintegrate (as the Soviet Union did), equally that it will not (any time soon) make a transition to a Western style liberal democracy, and that although China faces major domestic challenges, these will not fundamentally de-stabilise the existing political and economic system. In the case of the EU, we assume, not withstanding the impact of the global financial crisis, that European economies will remain strong enough not to trigger major social or economic disruption, that the EU member states will remain liberal democracies and that the process of European integration will not be fundamentally disrupted or undermined (even if significant further deepening, beyond existing treaty and policy arrangements, does not occur). Against this background, we suggest the five following possible scenarios for the development of EU-China relations.

---

13 'Zhuanjia: Wen Zongli Ouzhou zhi Hing Biaoming ZhongOu Guanxi Reng zai Xiangqian Fazhan,' *Xinhua News Agency*, retrieved on 24 February 2009, http://news.xinhuanet.com/world/2009-01/20/content_10692280.htm.

Status Quo

In this scenario, the basis of the EU-China relationship remains economic, in particular Europe and China's respective roles as major trading partners for one another. The EU in particular remains a key market for Chinese consumer goods, while China is a growing market for EU exports and for European Foreign Direct Investment (FDI). Disputes on core bilateral issues between the EU and China are successfully managed – not in the sense that they are resolved or completely overcome, but rather that they do not result in significant punitive economic or political measures by either party or disrupt the overall political and economic relationship. In this scenario, the EU would likely continue to criticise Chinese policies on market access, the Renminbi's exchange rate and IPR, but would not introduce significant retaliatory measures (such as general charges or limits on Chinese imports or new restrictions on the ability of Chinese companies to operate within the EU). The EU would also continue to criticise China over human rights issues, but, such criticism would remain moderate in tone and the EU would not put into practice diplomatic or economic sanctions in relation to human rights issues. Similarly, the Chinese response to European criticisms over human rights issues would remain moderate in tone and China would not introduce retaliatory diplomatic or economic measures beyond the occasional cancellation of high level meetings. Differences over wider global issues – in particular, climate change, non-proliferation, human rights, humanitarian crises (as in Myanmar, Sudan and Zimbabwe) and development policy (especially in Africa) – would be similarly managed, with both the EU and China moderating their positions to a limited degree in response to the other partner's policies and concerns, but also with a significant element of "agreeing to disagree." The institutionalised ties established since the 1990s would continue, with dialogue and technical cooperation across the range of bilateral and global issues, but the substance behind these ties would remain limited. There are good reasons to believe that EU-China relations may continue along these lines, with the occasional diplomatic encounter, especially with certain individual EU member states. Both partners benefit substantially from their economic relationship – neither side directly threatens or challenges the other's core interests – as two of the world's rising powers, there is a certain logic in attempting to coordinate their positions on global challenges. The differences between the EU and China on both bilateral and global issues are real and substantive, while the ability of either partner to dramatically alter the other's positions or policies is limited. Thus, Prime Minister Wen's January 2009 visit to Europe and Beijing's willingness to re-schedule the cancelled 2008 EU-China summit were explicitly interpreted as signals that cooperation should be maintained, despite the preceding tensions over Tibet and the Olympics.[14]

Chinese Assertion, European Acquiescence

If China's economic, political and military power continues to rise, one consequence could be the emergence of an increasingly assertive China, seeking to reshape global politics and institutions in its own interests and image. Elements of such a trend can arguably be seen in Chinese foreign policy in recent years, although how far and in what way this trend may evolve remains to be seen. In this scenario, Europe responds by largely acquiescing to China's new global assertiveness. The EU and its members would conclude that China's continuing rise is inevitable, that their ability to shape China's policies is negligible and that the costs of criticising or opposing China are high. Indeed, some critics within Europe (and also in the US) argue that such acquiescence already defines EU policy: although the EU formally criticises China over economic and human rights issues, such criticisms are to some extent *pro forma* statements designed to satisfy domestic critics rather than truly send a strong message to the Chinese leadership; the willingness of some EU leaders to lift the arms embargo imposed on China after the 1989 Tiananmen Square massacre – a policy only modified after strong US opposition – is cited as further evidence of this trend in European policy. As noted in the introduction to this chapter, the ECFR's 2009 "power audit" of EU-China relations argued that the EU's policy is already one of "unconditional engagement."[15] In the Chinese assertion, European acquiescence scenario would however, significantly move European policy further in this direction: the EU would drop its criticisms of China over economic and human rights issues, accept growing Chinese engagement in the European economy largely on Beijing's terms (with, for example, the Chinese sovereign wealth funds discussed above becoming major investors in Europe without significant changes in terms of the funds governance or transparency), end the arms embargo without significant concessions from the Chinese side and accept the Chinese sovereignty-oriented model of responding to international political and security crises, the "Beijing Consensus" as the model for global economic development efforts and the re-modelling of international institutions along these lines. In effect, the world is modelled from a Chinese perception. In the most extreme variant of this policy, the EU and its member states, pursue an increasingly insular and

---

14 'Zhuanjia: Wen Zongli Ouzhou zhi Hing Biaoming ZhongOu Guanxi Reng zai Xiangqian Fazhan,' Xinhua News Agency, *op. cit.*

15 Fox & Godement, *loc. cit.*

defensive policy, focused on preserving their own democracies in an increasingly inhospitable international environment, perhaps also retreating into economic protectionism (although one could equally well envisage versions of this scenario in which the EU continues to maintain external trade and investment ties), while abandoning the project of advancing democracy and human rights at the global level.

This scenario also raises interesting questions about US (and Japanese) policy. One could envisage situations in which US policy largely mirrors European policy in acquiescing, thus leading to increasing Chinese assertiveness: the US, for example, might abandon its existing security commitments in East Asia, in particular, the American military presence in Japan and its security guarantee to Taiwan – the latter step facilitating a PRC takeover of Taiwan (either peacefully or by military means). Such a US policy would pose particular problems for Tokyo: given the geo-strategic proximity of Japan and China and the two countries' very troubled historical relationship, Japan would likely be wary of adopting a strategy of acquiescence to increasing Chinese assertiveness and might respond by seeking to expand its own economic, political and military power in East Asia and beyond, thereby generating increasing tensions with China. Alternatively, one could envisage situations in which the US maintains its security commitments in East Asia and leads resistance to Chinese global assertiveness: if Europe adopted a policy of acquiescence towards China in this context, transatlantic relations would presumably be weakened.

The degree to and the way in which China seeks to assert global influence remains to be seen, but, even if China adopts a strongly assertive strategy, there are reasons to doubt that Europe will respond with passive acquiescence. The economic relationship between the EU and China is one of mutual economic interdependence, rather than of asymmetrical dependence for either partner: Europe therefore has significant economic leverage over China, constraining Beijing from crudely asserting power over it. The values of liberal democracy and human rights are deeply embedded in European societies and it is difficult to envisage Europe completely abandoning global support for these values. European leaders, further, are constrained by domestic pressures to defend human rights and democracy overseas: President Sarkozy's decision to attend the opening ceremony of the 2008 Beijing Olympics, for example, provoked sharp criticism by human rights activists.[16] While China's global rise has been dramatic in the last few years, it is probably

16 'Sarkozy's Olympic Attendance Triggers Outrage,' *EurActive*, 10 July 2008, retrieved on 20 July 2008, http://www.euractiv.com/en/foreign-affairs/sarkozy-olympic-attendance-triggers-outrage/article-174105.

more accurate to interpret this as China's re-emergence amongst the global powers – one of which will be the EU – rather than the beginnings of a new hegemony. Nevertheless, if China's power continues to rise, it is not impossible to imagine scenarios in which the European response is one of increasing acquiescence to growing Chinese assertiveness.

European Assertion, Chinese Acquiescence

A third scenario is applied in strict opposition to the second one: the EU asserts power globally, in East Asia and China, with both acquiescing to bilateral European demands in the larger regional and global assertion of European power and values. In this scenario, Europe would press its demands more forcefully on economic issues, human rights and global challenges, backing up these demands with the threat of diplomatic and economic sanctions. China would acquiesce to these demands: opening its market more rapidly to European goods, improving IPR protection, further re-evaluating the Renminbi, taking concrete steps to address European human rights concerns and modifying its positions on a range of global challenges (for example, allowing the UN Security Council to mandate stronger action against countries such as Iran, Sudan and Myanmar and agreeing to substantial and binding reductions in its greenhouse gas emissions as part of a new climate change treaty). The logic behind Chinese acquiescence to European assertiveness might be twofold: first, the European market is central to China's economy and Beijing might therefore be willing to acquiesce to European demands in order to maintain its market access; second, despite its remarkable economic rise, China faces major domestic challenges, such as increasing employment opportunities for its expanding population, growing economic inequality within society, corruption and environmental degradation, and might decide to therefore focus its attention primarily on these concerns, rather than developing its international role.

A more radical version of this scenario would see Europe adopting a growing military role in Asia. This might develop either in partnership with the US or alternatively with the EU replacing America as the dominant external military actor in East Asia if the US decided to significantly reduce or abandon its military role in the region. This scenario might, for example, involve Europe (whether in the form of individual European states or the EU collectively) sending aircraft carriers and other forces to the Taiwan Strait to reinforce or replace the US security guarantee, European air forces deployed to Taiwan, Japan or other East Asian states and increased European military assistance to East Asian states. The UK and France would likely be central to any such development, since they are Europe's two leading military powers, in particular in terms of naval forces, and because they retain residual security commitments and military ties with a number of East Asian states. Such a development might also take place in the context of the ESDP, which has provided a framework for collective military planning and the conduct of EU military operations.

The scenario of European assertion and Chinese acquiescence may be unlikely for a number of reasons. Although the EU has made significant advances in foreign policy cooperation since the 1980s and is an increasingly prominent international actor, the EU's foreign policy remains heavily dependent on consensus among the Union's member states. A policy of assertion towards China would be controversial within the EU, since it would risk disrupting economic ties with China and dragging the EU into military conflict in East Asia. More broadly, the EU's general approach to foreign policy – its strategic culture – is based on economic engagement and institutionalised political cooperation with partners, reflecting the Union's internal character. An assertive, even confrontational policy, towards China would mark a major break with EU foreign policy to date, both towards China and more generally. In terms of military power, although the EU has made progress with the ESDP since 1999-2000, it has struggled to meet its own initial target (the Helsinki Headline Goal) of being able to deploy a force of 60,000 troops and its military operations to date have been small in size (the largest, in Bosnia, for example, involved only 7,000 troops) and focused on post-conflict peace-building rather than combat operations. Given the slow development of the ESDP and the general reluctance of European states to become involved in military operations outside Europe, it is difficult to foresee the EU or its member states taking on large-scale new military commitments in East Asia.

Equally, a wholesale Chinese acquiescence in the face of European assertiveness seems unlikely. China's reluctance to move forward rapidly in addressing European concerns about the trade imbalance, market access, the RMB exchange rate and IPRs reflect substantial Chinese economic interests, as well as the broader argument that China is still a developing country. On human rights, significant concessions to European demands, in particular in terms of political freedom, would ultimately represent a threat to the rule of the Communist Party. On global issues such as peacekeeping, the Chinese government's position reflects a deeply held view on the primacy of state sovereignty. In the military sphere, if the EU was to take on a significant new defence role in East Asia, it would be difficult to see how the Chinese government would not view this as at least potentially threatening to its interests. More generally, the historical experience of European imperialism inevitably makes Chinese rulers wary of bowing to anything that may appear to be a new European imperialism.

Confrontation

One can envisage a variety of developments that could lead to a more confrontational EU-China relationship. In terms of trade, if the trade imbalance between the two parties continues to grow and China is viewed as failing to address European concerns, political pressure could grow within Europe for the introduction of protectionist measures against China. The then European Trade Commissioner Peter Mandelson warned of this danger during his November 2007 visit to China.[17] The impact of such measures would depend on their scale and character, on the extent to which China would then feel obliged to retaliate with similar steps and on the degree to which the trade issue would then spill over into the wider political relationship. The outcome might range from a narrow trade war limited to specific industrial sectors, which would not greatly damage the wider economic and political relationship to an all-out trade war, disrupting the entire EU-China relationship.

A second obvious potential source of confrontation between the EU and China is human rights. Were very large-scale political protests and/or violence to emerge in China and the Chinese authorities to respond with substantial use of force and repression, there would be strong pressure within Europe for the EU to impose diplomatic and economic sanctions and downgrade or suspend its various political and institutional ties with China. China might respond with retaliatory diplomatic or economic measures. The response of both the EU and the Chinese regime to the spring 2008 violence in Tibet and summer 2009 violence in Xinjiang, however, illustrates the desire of both parties to avoid an escalation of disputes over human rights. In both cases, the EU's criticism of China was limited and there was little support within the EU for wider diplomatic or economic sanctions. Although most Europeans would probably view Beijing's response to the violence in Tibet and Xinjiang as excessive, the Chinese government arguably exercised a degree of restraint, presumably in significant part because of the desire to avoid sanctions from the West. Nevertheless, should more large-scale human rights related protests, violence and/or repression occur – on the scale of a second Tiannanmen Square massacre – it is difficult to see any outcome other than a substantial EU response coupled with a significant downturn in EU-China relations.

The third obvious flashpoint for EU-China relations is Taiwan. To date, both China and the EU have been able to live with the status quo in relation to Taiwan. From the Chinese perspective, the long-term goal of re-integrating Taiwan into the PRC remains but has been subordinated to

[17] Mandelson, *loc. cit.*

economic growth and the maintenance of relations with the US and the EU. The EU has accepted the "one China" principle while leaving open the future nature of that "one China" and developing economic relations with Taiwan. Were the PRC to attempt to use military force to regain control of Taiwan, the EU and its member states would be placed in a very difficult position: at a minimum, the EU would presumably strongly condemn any such action and impose diplomatic and economic sanctions; member states would also probably come under pressure from the US (and domestically) to support American military action in defence of Taiwan (by deploying air and naval forces and/or by providing direct financial contributions). In terms of the EU-China relationship, the impact of any armed conflict over Taiwan would almost certainly be a major rupture in the relationship that has been built up over the past two decades.

A more confrontational relationship could also emerge if both China and the EU adopted the assertive policies discussed above: even in the absence of an immediate crisis over human rights and Taiwan, if both parties adopt more assertive policies and rhetoric, including over the wider range of global issues on which they are increasingly interacting (peacekeeping, proliferation, climate change, energy security, Africa), one could envisage scenarios in which the relationship becomes increasingly confrontational, descending into a pattern of mutual condemnation, criticism and competition. The potential for this type of outcome is illustrated in Africa, where European governments and EU institutions have been criticised for allowing Chinese influence to grow and are being called upon by some critics to pursue more aggressive efforts to counter that influence. While there is a danger of such an outcome, both the EU and China appear to recognise that they have large stakes in maintaining their economic relationship and in not allowing differences over global issues to disrupt that relationship. The European Commission's 2008 communication on the EU, China and Africa thus specifically calls for an EU-China dialogue in this area.[18]

True Partnership

The final scenario – true partnership – is one in which the EU and China move beyond their current relationship to develop substantial cooperation across the majority of the issues on which their relationship is now based. In terms of the various bilateral economic issues in EU-China

---

18 Commission of the European Communities, *Communication from the Commission to the European Parliament, the Council, the European Economic and Social Committee and the Committee of the Regions: The EU, Africa and China: Towards Trilateral Dialogue and Cooperation*, COM(2008) 654, final, Brussels, 17 October 2008.

relations, this scenario would involve significant progress based on long-term compromises (with China gradually addressing Europe's specific concerns and the EU maintaining openness to Chinese imports). On human rights and Taiwan, the basis for this scenario would be a continuing agreement to disagree but not let differences disrupt the larger relationship. The largest difference between this scenario and the others discussed here might be in relation to wider global issues, where one would see convergence of European and Chinese positions, substantive cooperation and the EU and China emerging as global leaders. On climate change, for example, this would imply an EU-China consensus on the need for major GHG (Green House Gas) reductions, a central role for the EU and China in new multilateral arrangements to reduce GHG emissions and substantial EU-China technical cooperation in making the transition to a low-carbon economy. In other areas, such as economic development policy and peacekeeping, it would imply policy convergence and practical cooperation, for example, around a post-Bretton Woods international financial architecture, a post-neoliberal model of economic development for poorer countries and new models of peacekeeping or nation-building. Institutionally, the rising power and cooperation of the EU and China might be confirmed by the G7/G8 being supplanted by the G20 (with the EU and China playing a central role in this framework) or a new G4 (Group of Four, bringing together the US, the EU, China and Japan). To the extent that the US declines as a global leader and/or is resistant to multilateralism, the EU and China might even emerge as the co-leaders of a new multilateral global order.

Such a vision of the EU-China partnership may be appealing, but the obstacles to it are substantial. So long as China remains a one-party authoritarian state and the EU a collection of liberal democracies, the basic systemic differences between them will be real, substantial and liable to generate a variety of value-based conflicts. The historical perspectives of the EU members as developed Western states and China as a developing country are also deep and impinge significantly on their respective attitudes to many key global issues. On economic development policy, climate change, human rights and peacekeeping, the underlying differences of perspective between the EU and China remain significant and cannot simply be removed by the declaration of a "strategic partnership." This is not to say that the EU and China cannot come to compromises and sometimes bridge their differences, but the experience of the last two decades suggests that this process is slow and the outcome will often reflect the lowest common denominator positions, lacking any real substance.

Conclusion

The five alternative scenarios developed in this chapter are inevitably to some extent caricatures – the reality of EU-China relations will likely continue to include a complex mix of elements of these scenarios. Nevertheless, these scenarios are helpful in that they highlight alternative possible outcomes, the factors that may lead to different outcomes and the policy choices facing both China and the EU. Our central conclusion is that the most likely future trajectory for EU-China relations is the continuation of the status quo – extensive economic relations, highly institutionalised diplomatic-political relations and on-going efforts to develop substantive cooperation in a range of areas, but a relationship constrained by divergent political systems and limited convergence of positions on many important bilateral and global issues. On the European side, economic interests, the EU's limited political and military power, the difficulties of developing a truly common foreign policy amongst 27 member states and the Union's deeply embedded strategic culture of non-coercive engagement, are all intertwined so as to act against a strongly assertive policy towards China or steps that might increase the likely-hood of conflict with China. At the same time, the EU is unlikely to simply back down where important economic interests are involved or to entirely abandon the human rights component of European foreign policy. On the Chinese side, Beijing's core priorities have been and are likely to remain sustaining economic growth and avoiding serious domestic instability. Consequently, maintaining economic ties and avoiding, or at least limiting political conflict are likely to remain central objectives in relations with the EU. Equally, however, China is likely to maintain certain "red lines" in its relation to human rights, Tibet and Taiwan. A more conflictual relationship between China and the EU cannot be ruled out, if only because certain variables – in particular, the possibility of more large-scale unrest and resultant repression in China or unintended escalation of conflict over Taiwan – are not fully under the control of Beijing or European capitals. Nevertheless, the dynamics at play on both sides suggest that the scenarios of Chinese assertion and European acquiescence, European assertion and Chinese acquiescence and confrontation are unlikely. The divergent political systems and perspectives on global politics of the EU and China, however, constrain the degree to which real policy convergence and cooperation is possible – suggesting that the prospects for our scenario of true partnership are limited.

While the identities and interests of the EU and China are deeply embedded and constrain the possibilities for their mutual relations, both the EU (member states and central EU institutions) and China also face political choices. The EU faces choices about how far and in what ways it should confront or take strong economic or diplomatic action in response to elements of Chinese policy it finds problematic. China faces choices about how far it should assert itself as a global actor and the risks that this may provoke: in other words, negative responses from the EU and other major powers. Both face choices over how far they are willing to modify their positions – on issues such as climate change, economic development policy, nuclear proliferation and politically unstable countries including Myanmar and Zimbabwe – in order to facilitate policy convergence and cooperation with one another (as well as other states). While the scenario of true partnership may be unlikely, the stakes still remain high, in terms of the extent of real cooperation between the EU and China.

What are the implications of our analysis for a possible EU-China PCA? Most obviously, even if a PCA is concluded it will not dramatically alter relations between the EU and China: a PCA may help address some issues in bilateral relations and provide a strengthened framework for dialogue and cooperation, but it will not remove important basic differences between the EU and China. Whether and how the PCA negotiations are brought to a conclusion will, however, provide an important indication of the direction of EU-China relations. Furthermore, for both sides, the PCA negotiations raise significant policy choices, especially in terms of conditionality and linkage. As of mid-2009, the situation with regard to a number of key issues relating to the PCA is distinctly opaque: will the EU be willing to sign a PCA if its concerns about its trade deficit with China are not addressed? Will China be willing to sign a PCA if the EU arms embargo is not lifted? If the arms embargo is lifted in the context of the PCA, what will China be willing to concede in return? How far and in what ways will human rights be addressed in the PCA? As with many things in life, the devil is in the detail.

CHAPTER 2

The Current Legal Foundation and Prospective Legal Framework of the PCA

Kim VAN DER BORGHT & Lei ZHANG

This paper examines hard law and soft law as the legal foundation of EU-China relations over the past thirty years, and, based on the analysis of these legal instruments, prospective studies and legal forms of the new EU-China framework agreement.[1]

Diplomatic relations between the EU and China started in 1975. Since the very beginning of bilateral relations, trade and economic cooperation have dominated EU-China relations. The first legal instrument which governed bilateral trade and economic activities was the 1978 Trade Agreement, which was soon replaced by an updated agreement – the 1985 Trade and Economic Cooperation Agreement (TECA). The 1985 TECA is still applicable as the main legal instrument to regulate bilateral trade and economic activities although the contents have already been outdated. In order to adapt to the rapid expansion of bilateral trade, the EU and China entered into several agreements covering specific aspects concerning trade and economic cooperation. After China's accession to the WTO in 2001, the two parties committed to agreements under the WTO framework. EU law and Chinese law, to some extent, have effects on bilateral relations as well. These bilateral and multilateral agreements constitute, with the respective domestic laws, the core of the legal foundation of EU-China trade and economic relations. They represent the hard law component.

Meanwhile, the EU and China established more than 20 sectoral dialogues at different levels to improve mutual understanding and cooperation in economic, trade and even political issues. They hold an annual summit in Europe or Beijing in rotation, in a bid to strengthen mutual understanding on a wide range of bilateral, regional and international issues. Both the EU and China publish policy papers that serve as documents guiding their activities in bilateral relations. These dialogues,

1 See Kenneth W. Abbott & Duncan Snidal, 'Hard and Soft Law in International Governance,' *International Organization*, Vol. 54, No. 3, 2000, pp. 421-456.

joint statements in annual summits and unilateral policy documents constitute another important part of the legal foundation of EU-China relations. This amounts to the soft law component.

To reflect the depth and breadth of today's strategic partnership, and in light of the outdated 1985 agreement, the EU and China began negotiating a new framework agreement which comprises all essential issues of bilateral relations. This paper discusses the essential contents in the framework agreement and sketches the possibilities of the legal forms this agreement may take.

Hard Law: Core of the Legal Foundation of EU-China Relations

1985 Agreement on Trade and Economic Cooperation

Initial contacts between Europe and China after 1945 were characterised by pragmatism. Where the US considered China an enemy, European countries continued trading with China. China supported the move towards integration in Europe, using the opportunity to forge a coalition that could strengthen its position in a world with two superpowers.[2] China established formal diplomatic relations with a number of European countries in the early 1970s (Italy (1970), Belgium (1971), the Federal Republic of Germany (1972), Luxemburg (1972)).[3] The EU and China thus established their diplomatic relation in the Cold War era mainly because the two parties desired to develop economic cooperation and anticipated mutual economic and political benefits.

Spurred by direct economic interests, the two parties also saw a need to develop a more legalised form of cooperation between the European Community (EC) and China and not just between China and the European member states. The Trade Agreement concluded in 1978 was the EC's first trade agreement with a state-trading country.[4]

With the development of bilateral trade partly as a result of the Open-Door Policy – the two parties needed to update China's trade agreement within a wider scope. The 1985 TECA has regulated EU-China commercial and economic relations for more than thirty years.[5]

---

2 See Zeng Huaqun, 'Promoting a New Bilateral Legal Framework for China-EU Economic Relations,' *Chinese Journal of International Law*, No. 3, 2004, p. 191.

3 *Ibid.*

4 *Ibid.*

5 Council of the European Union, *Agreement on Trade and Economic Cooperation between the European Economic Community and the People's Republic of China*, OJ L 250/2 (1985), 21 May 1985.

In European legal terms, the 1985 TECA was established on a double legal basis supported by Articles 133 and 181a of the Treaty establishing the European Community (TEC).[6] The Community has exclusive competence in external trade (Article 133) and shared competence in economic cooperation (Article 181a) to conclude agreements with third countries.

The 1985 TECA lays down the MFN treatment to bilateral trade[7] and a determined number of fields in economic cooperation.[8] Article 10 deals with the following fields – in which the two parties shall endeavour to develop cooperation: industry and mining; agriculture, including agro-industry; science and technology; energy; transport and communication; environmental protection; and cooperation in third countries. It places foreign investment in the scope of economic cooperation, providing that the two parties shall improve the investment climate, and promote and encourage greater investment.[9]

An important element of the 1985 TECA is the establishment of the Joint Committee, which reviews cooperation schemes, examines questions and new opportunities in trade, economic cooperation, monitors and makes recommendations for the implementation of the TECA.

The 1985 TECA constitutes a basic legal framework of EU-China commercial and economic relations, covering issues such as import and export,[10] price and rate,[11] payments,[12] industrial and technical activities,[13] investment,[14] dispute settlement,[15] a joint committee.[16]

---

6 European Union, Article 133 of Title IX Common Commercial Policy and Article 181a of Title XXI Economic, Financial and Technical Cooperation with Third Countries, *Consolidated Version of The Treaty Establishing The European Community*, OJ C 325/90&111, 24 December 2002.

7 Council of the European Union, Article 3 of Chapter I Trade Cooperation, *Agreement on Trade and Economic Cooperation between the EEC and the PRC – 1985.*

8 Council of the European Union, Article 10 of Chapter II Economic Cooperation, *Ibid.*

9 Council of the European Union, Article 12 of Chapter II Economic Cooperation, *Ibid.*

10 Council of the European Union, Articles 3-4 of Chapter I Trade Cooperation, *Agreement on Trade and Economic Cooperation between the EEC and the PRC – 1985.*

11 Council of the European Union, Article 8 of Chapter I Trade Cooperation, *Ibid.*

12 Council of the European Union, Article 9 of Chapter I Trade Cooperation, *Ibid.*

13 Council of the European Union, Article 11 of Chapter II Economic Cooperation, *Agreement on Trade and Economic Cooperation between the EEC and the PRC – 1985.*

14 Council of the European Union, Article 12 of Chapter II Economic Cooperation, *Ibid.*

15 Council of the European Union, Article 6 of Chapter I Trade Cooperation, *Ibid.*

16 Council of the European Union, Article 15 of Chapter III Joint Committee, *Ibid.*

However, the contents of the TECA agreement were too basic to keep pace with the rapidly increased bilateral trade and fastly-expanded economic cooperation.[17] EU-China bilateral trade grew from ECU7.3 bn in 1985 to €303.3 bn in 2007, with the EU becoming the largest trading partner and the largest source of high-tech products for China, and China becoming the second largest trading partner and the largest supplier for the EU. The economic cooperation in the spheres of agriculture, Science and Technology (S&T), finance, transport, environment, and energy developed dramatically as well. Obviously, the 1985 TECA cannot reflect the deep and wide cooperation of bilateral commercial and economic relations. Therefore, the two parties have made efforts to negotiate and conclude sectoral agreements to promote developments and cooperation in specific fields of bilateral relations.

Sectoral Agreements

The EU and China concluded several sectoral agreements, covering a wide range of bilateral relations.[18] Soon after the 1985 TECA, the two parties concluded an agreement in a particularly sensitive sector – trade in textiles: the agreement on trade in textile products (the Multi-Fibre Agreement) initialled in 1988.[19] Later, the concluded agreement on trade in textile products was not covered by the Multi-Fibre Agreement (MFA) bilateral agreement (the Silk Agreement), that took effect in 1995. Both agreements made a major contribution to the orderly and equitable development of trade in textiles between the Community and China for more than a decade. The order in textile trade was changed after the elimination of MFA quota restrictions on 1 January 2005. The surge of Chinese textiles and clothing to the European market in the first three months of 2005 caused panic for the textile manufacturers in some EU member states. They put pressure on the European Commission to take urgent protective measures against the huge amount of Chinese imports. After several rounds of closed-door discussions, then EU Trade Commissioner Peter Mandelson and Chinese Minister of Trade and

17 Rafael Leal-Arcas, 'The European Union and New Leading Powers: Towards Partnership in Strategic Policy Areas,' *Fordham International Law Journal*, No. 32, 2009, p. 400.

18 The bilateral agreements between the EU and China can be found on the website of Commission of the European Communities' External Relations Treaties Office Database, http://ec.europa.eu/world/agreements/searchByCountryAndContinent.do?CountryId=2101&countryName=China. See also Franco Algieri, 'EU Economic Relations with China: An Institutionalist Perspective,' *The China Quarterly*, Vol. 169, 2002, pp. 64-77.

19 See Anna Comino, 'A Dragon in Cheap Clothing: What Lessons Can Be Learned from the EU-China Textile Dispute?,' *European Law Journal*, Vol. 13, No. 6, 2007, pp. 818-838.

Commerce, Bo Xilai, reached an agreement on textiles in the form of the Memorandum of Understanding (MoU).[20] The 2005 textile agreement limited the growth of Chinese textile and clothing exports in 10 categories to the EU for 2005, 2006 and 2007, securing a smooth transition before the complete opening of the European market to Chinese textile products in 2008.

To encourage and develop cooperative R&D activities between the EU and China in the field of S&T, the two parties concluded another sectoral agreement in 1998.[21] The S&T Agreement based on Article 170 of the TECA fosters all R&D activities in several forms and establishes a Steering Committee to promote the different cooperative activities and efficient cooperation. The annex provides for the intellectual property rights (IPRs) created or furnished under the S&T agreement. In the area of technical cooperation, the EU and China went further in 2003. They signed the cooperation agreement on the Galileo programme.[22] China became the first country outside of the EU to participate in the Galileo Joint Undertaking.

Another sectoral agreement is related to bilateral maritime transport.[23] This agreement was signed by the Community and its member states on the one hand, and by China, as the other party because the Community and the member states share competence on the subject of transport. Although the Maritime Transport Agreement was signed in 2002, it entered into force as from 1 March 2008. Before the conclusion of the agreement, the majority of member states concluded their own bilateral agreements with China. The Maritime Transport Agreement replaced those bilateral agreements to reflect the considerable improvement of EU-China maritime transport relations.[24] As the EU is China's largest

---

20 European Community, *Memorandum of Understanding on the Export of Certain Chinese Textile and Clothing Products to the European Union between the European Commission and the Ministry of Commerce of the People's Republic of China*, OJ L 177/19, 9 July 2005.

21 European Community, *Agreement for Scientific and Technological Cooperation between the European Community and the Government of the People's Republic of China*, OJ L 6/40, 11 January 2000. The duration of this agreement was 5 years. It was renewed in 2004.

22 Council of the European Union, *Cooperation Agreement on A Civil Global Navigation Satellite System (GNSS) – Galileo between the European Community and its Member States and the People's Republic of China*, COM(2003) 578 final – not published in the OJ.

23 European Community, *Agreement on Maritime Transport between the European Community and its Member States, of the One Part, and the Government of the People's Republic of China, of the Other Part*, OJ L 46/25, 21 February 2008.

24 According to Article 15 of this agreement, if this agreement is less favourable on certain issues than existing bilateral agreements, the more favourable provisions shall

trading partner and China is the EU's second largest one, they both eventually became important providers of international maritime transport services. Considering further development in the future, the two parties concluded the agreement to consolidate bilateral maritime relations.

The EU and China concluded several sectoral agreements in 2004, including the Approved Destination States (ADS) agreement.[25] Europe is one of Chinese tourists' favourite destinations. To attract a large number of tourists and facilitate personal contact and business exchanges, the EU opened its tourist market to the Chinese. Based on Articles 62 and 63 of the EC Treaty, the Community concluded the ADS Agreement with China, setting out the arrangements for travel organised by Chinese tour operators, organised at their own expense, to the EU. Another agreement was on administrative assistance.[26] To improve cooperation between the administrative authorities responsible for the application of customs legislation, the EU and China take action together against operations in breach of customs legislation, including infringements of IPRs. The two parties, under the Administrative Assistance Agreement, establish channels of communication, assist each other by providing information and expertise to ensure the proper application of customs legislation and facilitate effective coordination between administrative authorities. In the area of energy, the EU and China signed the agreement for R&D cooperation towards the peaceful use of nuclear energy.[27] In the following year, the two parties concluded the Memorandum of Understanding on the China-EU Dialogue on Energy and Transport Strategies.[28] Pressured by the MoU, the first plenary meeting of EU-China Strategic Dialogue on Energy and Transport Strategies was held in March 2006.

We can see through the abovementioned examples and frequency of sectoral agreements that the EU and China have pursued cooperation further in trade, S&T, education, energy, environmental protection,

---

prevail. Provisions of existing bilateral agreements not covered by this agreement shall continue to apply.

25 European Community, *Memorandum of Understanding between the European Community and the National Tourism Administration of the People's Republic of China, on Visa and Related Issues Concerning Tourist Groups from the People's Republic of China (ADS)*, OJ L 83/14, 20 March 2004.

26 Council of the European Union, *Agreement between the European Community and the Government of the People's Republic of China on Cooperation and Mutual Administrative Assistance in Customs Matters*, OJ L 375/20, 23 December 2004.

27 Council of the European Union, *Agreement for R&D Cooperation in the Peaceful Uses of Nuclear Energy between the European Atomic Energy Community (Euratom) and the Government of the People's Republic of China*, COM(2004) 755 final, Brussels, 25 November 2004.

28 Memorandum of Understanding on the China-EU Dialogue on Energy and Transport Strategies was signed in September 2005.

customs assistance, industry, transport and culture. The existing and planned bilateral agreements, in a wide range of areas, constitute the essential part of the legal framework of EU-China bilateral relations.

Multilateral Agreements

Multilateral agreements also constitute a part of the legal framework of EU-China relations. The multilateral agreements which have the largest influence on bilateral relations are the WTO agreements. They regulate EU-China trade in goods, services and IPRs. The EU and China reached an agreement on the bilateral trade issues relating to China's accession to the WTO in 2001. This agreement on WTO accession emphasised the EU's concerns in several aspects.[29]

In the area of telecommunications, the EU required China to open its market for mobile phones, increase the proportion of foreign investment in the Sino-foreign equity joint ventures, and open-up China's leasing market in three years. As for the insurance market, the EU asked for more freedom of establishment of joint ventures and faster expansion of the scope of insurance business, than the US did. Concerning import and exports, the two parties agreed that China's tariff levels are generally around 8-10%. The state monopoly on exporting, such as silk, should be completely removed by 2005. In some sectors where Europe holds a comparative advantage, such as motor vehicles manufacturing, pharmaceuticals and chemicals, the EU required China to eliminate some restrictions and abolish preferential treatment to Chinese domestic producers. Furthermore, the EU required China to improve market access in the fields of banking, legal services, accountancy, architecture, tourism, construction, dredging and market research.

On the implementation of WTO legislation, China needs to enforce the GATT, GATS, TRIPS, TRIMS, SPS, TBT, SCM and other agreements. Despite China's recent experience as a member, and despite the criticism it receives from the EU, the overall assessment of China's implementation of its WTO commitments is positive. China has been serious about implementing the bulk of its WTO commitments on time. It reduced import tariffs on hundreds of European products, such as machinery, ceramics and glass, textiles, clothing, cosmetics, and spirits. It phased out import quotas, licenses and other border non-tariff barriers (NTBs).

But the overall picture is more complex. China is yet to fully comply with all its WTO commitments. China's progress in implementation of the General Agreement on Trade and Tariffs (GATT) is better than that in

---

29 See the 'Highlights of the EU-China Agreement on WTO,' retrieved on 28 February 2009, http://trade.ec.europa.eu/doclib/docs/2003/september/tradoc_113818.pdf.

GATS and TRIMS. In practice, China has long adopted a pragmatic attitude that is influenced little by outside pressures. China protects its key service sectors, such as (non-mobile) telecoms, banking, electricity, air and maritime transport, through restrictions such as the requirements that the proportion of FDI be shared with national enterprises. Worst still is China's implementation of its TRIPS commitments. It is reported that half of the counterfeited goods intercepted at European borders in 2005 were sourced from China.[30]

China did not sign the application for accession to the GPA until December 2007. However, even until now, many procurement markets remain closed to European businesses. After the opening of the government procurement market for foreign suppliers, the situation is expected to change gradually in the future.[31]

Internal Law

The implementation of the WTO agreements relies on the transfer of WTO commitments into domestic law and regulation (and the enforcement thereof). In order to fulfil its WTO commitments and improve its commercial and trade relations with other countries, China has gone through an extensive reform of its internal law. It revised its Foreign Trade Law in April 2004, allowing for trading rights to be granted automatically through a registration process for all domestic and foreign enterprises and individuals.[32] This became effective half a year earlier than the scheduled full liberalisation required by China's Protocol of Accession to the WTO. China abolished some national standards and revised its laws to better protect IPRs in line with the TRIPS agreement.[33]

---

30 See the website of the Commission of the European Communities, *External Trade, Trade Issues, Sectoral Issues, Intellectual Property*, retrieved on 26 October 2008, http://ec.europa.eu/trade/issues/sectoral/intell_property/pr081106_en.htm.

31 A high-level Chinese business delegation visited Germany, Switzerland, Spain and the UK in February 2009 to purchase advanced equipment and technology as well as key products and services worth more than 15 bn RMB. This purchasing move is of great significance in expanding the mutual opening of markets between China and Europe, deepening bilateral commercial and trade cooperation, promoting both sides' economic development, bringing about the early revival of the global economy as well as stemming trade protectionism. See 'Chinese Procurement in Europe Contributes to Bilateral Trade, Commercial Ties,' *Xinhua News Agency*, 24 February 2009, retrieved on 28 February 2009, http://news.xinhuanet.com/english/2009-02/24/content_10886867.htm.

32 Articles 8-9 of China's Foreign Trade Law, amended at the 8th Session of the Standing Committee of the 10th National People's Congress and Promulgated on 6 April 2004 and entered into force on 1 July 2004.

33 China commenced the revision of its Patent Law in 2005, Trade Mark Law in 2008 and Copyright Law in 2008, to adapt the WTO requirements.

It updated the Catalogue for the Guidance of Foreign Investment Industries four times since China's accession to the WTO in 2001, respectively in 2002, 2004, 2006 and 2007, reducing FDI restrictions step by step. China's domestic laws and regulations are widely and continuously amended in accordance with the WTO requirements.

The EU's legal framework consists of a large quantity of treaties, regulations, directives and cases that also play a vital role in regulating external relations. The internal laws in both the EU and China work as the supplement to bilateral agreements in external relations, emphasising the protection of their own interests and governing their internal daily activities. The implementation of domestic law has an important effect on the development of bilateral cooperation. While internal law is the vehicle for implementation of international agreements, the bilateral and multilateral agreements are the extension of internal law in external relations. International (multilateral and bilateral) agreements and internal law together constitute the core of the legal framework of EU-China bilateral relations.

Soft Law: an Important Part of the Legal Foundation of EU-China Relations

Dialogues

From the analysis of bilateral and multilateral agreements and internal law, it is possible to establish the rules that can be derived from hard law, in the legal framework of EU-China bilateral relations. Such an analysis omits an important part of legal reality. Determining, analysing and applying the hard trade rules in the trade reality is impossible without taking full account of political issues that constitute all aspects of EU-China relations. Attempting to codify often highly sensitive political issues would have a debilitating effect. The EU and China have therefore adopted a different path that allows for more flexibility, which is needed to reach common ground. The instruments are called dialogues. These political dialogues offer a platform to the parties to discuss sensitive topics without committing themselves to legal clauses in international agreements. These political dialogues are trust-building instruments that allow for non-binding, largely confidential exchanges.[34] As lack of trust was one of the main problems in the WTO negotiations, the political dialogues between the EU and China are all the more important.

The framework of the EU-China political dialogue includes annual summits at the level of the Heads of States or Government, meetings between the EU Troika Foreign Ministers and their Chinese counterpart,

34 Leal-Arcas, *op. cit.*, p. 361.

annual meetings of the EU Troika Political Directors with their Chinese counterpart, annual meetings between EU Troika Asia Pacific Directors and their Chinese counterpart, meetings at least once a year between EU Troika and Chinese experts on international security, arms control, non-proliferation and export controls issues, meetings every six months between the Chinese Ministry of Foreign Affairs (MFA) and EU Ambassadors posted in Beijing, and meetings every six months between the Minister of Foreign Affairs of the country holding the EU Presidency and the Chinese Ambassador posted in the Presidency's capital.[35]

The EU and China first established the framework of the political dialogue in 1994 and upgraded it in 1998 with the agreement to hold regular EU-China Annual Summits. In 2002, the EU and China decided to formally update the framework of the political dialogue through an exchange of letters, which constitutes the legal basis for the dialogue.[36] The scope of the EU-China political dialogue has gradually broadened to cover issues from arms embargo to non-proliferation, from human rights to international peace and security, from climate change to the fight against illegal migration. After progressing for more than one decade, the two parties appreciated this process for the development of EU-China political relations: "the full and effective political dialogue mechanism established between the two sides had played a positive role in enhancing mutual understanding and trust, and expanding common ground and cooperation, and serves as an important foundation for stronger China-EU political mutual trust."[37] There is great potential to further expand this political dialogue, as on the one hand, China shows more and more interest in a reinforced EU Common Foreign and Security Policy (CFSP) as well as on the consequences of EU enlargement. On the other hand, the EU regards China as a growing economic and political power in the international community that can have a significant influence on global concerns.[38]

The EU and China also structure trade and economic dialogue in the form of annual EU-China Joint Trade Ministerial meetings, Senior Officials meetings, annual Ministerial level meetings of the Joint

---

35 See the website of the Commission of the European Communities' Delegation to China, retrieved on 1 March 2009, http://www.delchn.ec.europa.eu/euch_poli2.htm.

36 See Zeng, *op. cit.*, p. 391.

37 Council of the European Union, Joint Statement, *10th EU-China Summit Joint Statement*, Beijing, 28 November 2007, available at http://ec.europa.eu/external_relations/china/summit_1107/index.htm.

38 See the website of the Commission of the European Communities' Delegation to China, *op. cit.*

Economic and Trade Committee[39] and Director-General level Economic and Trade Working Group meetings. At the 10th EU-China Summit in 2007, a High Level Economic and Trade Dialogue (HED) was established, as well as High Level Dialogues on exchange rate issues and on macroeconomic issues.[40] The HED focuses on the "strategic, forward-looking and plan-setting" issues. It will not "duplicate, replace or weaken" the existing EU-China trade and economic dialogues.[41] The first HED held in April 2008 made tangible achievements. It was the first time that some of the issues, such as energy, were a part of the discussions on bilateral trade and economic relations. The second HED was held 7-8 May 2009. The meeting played an effective and constructive role in bilateral trade and economic cooperation in the context of the global financial and economic crisis and continuous EU-China trade disputes, but failed to make substantive progress on market access and especially on the PCA.

Apart from the political dialogue, and the trade and economic dialogue, the EU and China cooperate in 24 different sectoral dialogues, from social affairs to the environment, from regional policy to education and culture – to meet shared interests, solve problems and promote exchanges.[42] These dialogues are held at various levels, such as the ministerial or working level, and in the forms of conferences, formal annual meetings, working groups, and by informal exchanges. The participants include officials, politicians, organisations, and enterprises. Through sectoral dialogues, the two parties exchange information and experiences on a wide range of topics. For example, China is trying to establish the legal regime of competition in the Chinese market.[43] The EU has a developed competition policy. Through dialogue and exchanges of information in the past few years, China has learned from the EU's

---

39 The EU-China Joint Economic and Trade Committee was established in 1985 through the Trade and Economic Cooperation Agreement between the EU and China.

40 See Council of the European Union, Joint Statement, 10th EU-China Summit, *op. cit.* See also Wei Shi & Robert Weatherley, 'Harmony or Coercion? China-EU Trade Dispute Involving Intellectual Property Enforcement,' *Wisconsin International Law Journal*, No. 25, 2007, pp. 448-449.

41 'Interview: China-EU Trade Talks Promotes Trust and Concrete Progress,' *People's Daily*, 9 May 2008, retrieved on 1 March 2009, http://english.peopledaily.com.cn/90001/90776/90884/6407671.html.

42 For more information about the sectoral dialogues, see the website of the Commission of the European Communities' Directorate-General for External Relations – China, retrieved on 1 March 2009, http://ec.europa.eu/external_relations/china/sectoral dialogue_en.htm.

43 See Robert F. Dodds, Jr., 'State Enterprise Reform in China: Managing the Transition to a Market Economy,' *Law and Policy International Business*, No. 27, 1996, pp. 712-714.

experience on this subject.[44] China is currently updating its comprehensive competition law system that shall bear many similarities to the EU model. The scope and range of sectoral dialogues, have helped to develop a solid foundation for the EU-China relations in many areas. Sectoral dialogues and agreements[45] are expected to play an increasingly important role in building EU-China relations with mutual benefits.

Unilateral Policy

Dealing with EU-China relations, the two parties respectively issue policy documents in which they expose their own guidelines and express their own concerns and expectations. These orientation documents are part of the soft law regulating EU-China relations. The EU's most significant unilateral policy documents are the European Commission's communications and policy papers. The first communication towards China was published in 1995: *A Long-Term Policy for China-Europe Relations*,[46] chartering the long-term path for bilateral relations into the 21st century. The EU recognised China's rise in both the military-political and economic spheres, and expressed its aim to develop a long-term relationship with China. The communication outlined the Commission's policies in political relations, economic and trade relations, and cooperation strategy. In 1998, the Commission issued a second communication to build a comprehensive partnership with China.[47] The EU indicated that its prime objectives were "to see China integrated rapidly and fully into the international community, both politically and economically, and to support its transition towards an open society based upon the rule of law,"[48] to improve the efficiency of EU-funded programs[49] and to raise the profile of the EU in China.[50] In order to fully and efficiently implement the 1998 Communication, the Commission issued a report in 2000[51]

---

44 See Wei Shi & Weatherley, *op. cit.*, pp. 453-456.

45 The sectoral dialogues are established by relative bilateral agreements between the EU and China.

46 Communication of the Commission of the European Communities, *A Long-Term Policy for China-Europe Relations*, COM(1995) 279 final, Brussels, 5 July 1995.

47 Communication of the Commission of the European Communities, *Building a Comprehensive Partnership with China*, COM(1998) 181 final, Brussels, 25 March 1998.

48 See Parts A, B and C of the 1998 Communication.

49 See Part D of the 1998 Communication.

50 See Part E of the 1998 Communication.

51 Report from the Commission of the European Communities to the Council and the European Parliament on the Implementation of the (1998) Communication, *Building a Comprehensive Partnership with China*, COM(2000) 552 final, Brussels, 2000.

and a Communication in 2001.[52] The report reviewed the implementation of the recommendations of the 1998 Communication and demonstrated that although EU-China relations had developed significantly over the past two years, much potential still remained in expanding the relationship further. The latter document reviewed the developments in each of the EU's objectives outlined in 1998 and made concrete short and medium-term action points, for EU policy to progress towards. In 2002, the Commission issued the China Country Strategy Paper covering the 2002-2006 period, analysing the political, economic and social situations in China, providing an overview of past and ongoing EC-China cooperation, defining the EC response strategy and listing work programs to implement its strategy.

In 2003, the Commission published a policy paper updating the 1998 and 2001 Communications on EU-China relations.[53] It set out a framework guiding the EU's policies and actions towards China in the subsequent three years. The policy paper identified six priorities for bilateral relations, including sharing responsibilities in promoting global governance, supporting China's transition to an open society based upon the rule of law and the respect for human rights, including China's promotion of domestic and external economic liberalisation process. The paper also contained a number of concrete proposals to enhance EU-China relations in key areas, such as economic and trade relations and China's internal reform process. With the European Commission's then-President's (Romano Prodi) visit to China for the Annual Summit, in the same year, a comprehensive strategic partnership was established between the EU and China. In 2003, China also made a historical move: it released its first EU policy paper.[54] The paper aimed to "highlight the objectives of China's EU policy and outline the areas and plans for cooperation and related measures in the next five years so as to enhance China-EU all-round cooperation and promote a long-term and stable development of China-EU relations."[55] The intensive issue of policy documents reflected that the development of EU-China political and economic relations had reached its peak. The comprehensive strategic partnership brought the EU and China into the "honeymoon period" in 2003-2004.

---

52 Communication of the Commission of the European Communities, *EU Strategy towards China: Implementation of the 1998 Communication and Future Steps for a More Effective EU Policy*, COM(2001) 265 final, Brussels, 15 May 2001.

53 Communication Policy Paper, *A Maturing Partnership – Shared Interests and Challenges in EU-China Relations*, COM(2003) 533 final, Brussels, 10 September 2003.

54 People's Republic of China, *China's EU Policy Paper*, Beijing, 13 October 2003.

55 See People's Republic of China, Foreword, China's EU Policy Paper, *op. cit.*

The situation changed in 2005, triggered by the textile dispute. After the "honeymoon period," bilateral relations cooled and the two parties started to reflect upon, from a realistic point of view, the common interests and different aspects between the EU and China. In this context, the EU issued another communication[56] and a working document[57] in 2006. The 2006 Communication aimed to reinforce the potential of a dynamic relationship with China based on the EU's values. Although the EU recognised the predominant cultural differences with China, it believed that they could be managed effectively. The rising problems in trade relations spurred the Commission to publish a separate policy paper on EU-China trade and investment, which analysed bilateral economic and trade relations, including the benefits of openness, the impact of competition and obstacles of market access, and defined the EU's response and priorities for action. In 2007, the Commission published a China Strategy Paper for the period 2007-2013, defining its response strategies and budgets in trade, transport, financial services, social protection, sectoral dialogues, environment, energy and climate change, human resources development and higher education.

Although sectoral dialogues and unilateral policy documents are not legally binding on the EU and China, they express the two parties' aims, strategies and ways to implement the objectives. These policies guide the two parties to further develop bilateral relations, solve disputes and draw a blueprint for the future of EU-China cooperation, not only in economic and trade areas, but also in political and social areas. The sectoral dialogues and unilateral policy documents, as soft law, constitute an important part of the legal foundation of EU-China relations.

Features of the Current Legal Framework of EU-China Relations

As previously discussed, we can see that the current legal framework of EU-China relations is built on a parallel basis: hard law and soft law. Hard law establishes the solid legal foundation governing the two parties' activities in bilateral relations while soft law reflects policies and dynamic issues in the development of bilateral relations and supplements hard law in the legal framework. It is noticeable that the contents of hard

56 Communication of the Commission of the European Communities, *EU – China: Closer Partners, Growing Responsibilities*, COM(2006) 631 final, Brussels, 24 October 2006.

57 Commission of the European Communities Working Document Accompanying COM(2006) 631 final: Closer Partners, Growing Responsibilities, *A Policy Paper on EU-China Trade and Investment: Competition and Partnership*, COM(2006) 632 final, Brussels, 24 October 2006.

law and soft law have different emphasis. Hard law mainly regulates bilateral relations and cooperation in the areas of trade and economic cooperation, S&T, energy, and administrative assistance. In contrast, soft law relates to a wider range of fields, such as political dialogue, social reform, IPR and regional security.

One of the reasons behind the differences is that some areas and subjects covered by soft law are more sensitive, like human rights. Although human rights feature prominently in the EU's external relations discourse, the enforcement practice is typified by pragmatism. This attitude accommodates China's position that is insistent on a dialogue based on equality. The consequence is a dialogue that allows for flexibility from both sides. As such, China's EU Policy Paper stressed that China would maintain close contacts and timely communication with the EU at high levels through various means to strengthen the exchange of high-level visits and political dialogue,[58] and provided that the Chinese side:

> stands ready to continue dialogue, exchange and cooperation on human rights with the EU on the basis of equality and mutual respect so as to share information, enhance mutual understanding and deepen cooperation in protecting, *inter alia*, citizens' social and cultural rights and the rights of the disadvantage.[59]

Despite intense criticism from the EU, regarding this degree of flexibility, it has contributed to piecemeal improvements in China's human rights record, thus adding to the EU's commitment to the process.[60]

Another reason behind these differences relates to the Community's competence. The Community has exclusive competence in Common Commercial Policy, including external trade, allowing it to conclude bilateral agreements, for itself with China, concerning trade and economic cooperation and customs assistance. However, in regards to political and social aspects and human rights, member states share competence with the Community in these areas. It is not easy for the Community and different member states to speak with one voice on these sensitive issues, in light of their different interests and separate bilateral relations with China.

The parallel system of legal frameworks plays an effective and efficient role in regulating EU-China relations. Economic and trade cooperation between the two parties grew at a significant pace despite the problems that often occurred between the two parties. In this context,

---

58 People's Republic of China, Part Three I.1, China's EU Policy Paper, *op. cit.*

59 *Ibid.*, Part Three I.5.

60 See Zeng, *op. cit.*, pp. 198-199.

having a separate agreement on trade within the exclusive competence enables the Community to react in timely fashion to these issues by establishing action points and communicating with China with one voice. For China, the Ministry of Commerce, being the sole governmental representative, can react quickly and target the Community rather than negotiating separately with 27 member states. The two parties can thus focus on strictly building-up trade and economic cooperation or solve disputes without delay, due to negotiation on some sensitive issues.

Like two sides of the same coin, the advantages of separate agreements also come with disadvantages. The 1985 TECA is the most important part of the legal foundation of EU-China relations but the single agreement cannot cover all cooperative areas and reflect the depth of the developing relationship between the EU and China. In light of the "ups and downs" felt during the past years of the relationship and of the inevitable future overlaps and conflicts, the EU and China need to build-up stable bilateral relations based on a comprehensive legal foundation. The two parties need a comprehensive agreement to set down the principles and common objectives according to mutual benefits, make long-term strategies to further increase cooperation in different areas, and define various ways to implement a wide range of programmes and projects.

Perspective Contents and the Legal Forms of the Framework Agreement

The two parties affirmed, at the 7th EU-China Summit Joint Statement, to actively explore the feasibility of concluding a new EU-China framework agreement.[61] In 2006, the two parties stated that in order to reflect the full breadth and depth of the current comprehensive strategic partnership, they agreed to launch negotiations on a new PCA which would encompass the full scope of their bilateral relationship, including cooperation in political matters.[62] In January 2007, the EU and China announced the official launch of talks on the PCA at a joint press conference held by Chinese Foreign Minister Li Zhaoxing and visiting EU counterpart Benita Ferrero-Waldner. Ferrero-Waldner explained that: "the agreement will provide a comprehensive basis covering the whole range of the political, economic and trade relationships between China

[61] Council of the European Union, Joint Statement, Point 5, *7th EU-China Summit Joint Statement*, The Hague, 8 December 2004.

[62] Council of the European Union, Joint Statement, Point 4, *9th EU-China Summit Joint Statement*, Helsinki, 9 September 2006.

and the EU."[63] Li said that he agreed with Ferrero-Waldner that China and the EU are not only trade partners, but all-round strategic partners sharing broad common interests and common positions.[64] The negotiations started and the two parties expressed their mutual satisfaction on the successful launch of the negotiations.[65] The successful conclusion of a comprehensive PCA, including political and economic relations, remains a contentious issue for both the EU and China. But there are several contentious matters included in the PCA negotiations. How to deal with these issues has a significant influence on the legal forms of the framework agreement.

Political Issues

The political issues involved in the PCA negotiations contain several aspects: the general principles respected by both the EU and China, the forms of political cooperation, as well as some specific issues concerning the EU and China.

The EU and China have reached a consensus with respect to the general principles and rules of international law, including, for example, the UN Charter. The two parties respect the principles of sovereign equality, good faith, peaceful settlement of international disputes, the illegality of the threat or use of force, and non-intervention in internal affairs.[66] As to these general principles, the EU and China have no qualms over inserting them into the PCA.

The political dialogue at various levels between the EU and China will be strengthened in the PCA because the two parties expressed such ideas on many occasions in the past. For example, they stated on the 10th EU-China Summit Joint Statement that:

> the full and effective political dialogue mechanism established between the two sides had played a positive role in enhancing mutual understanding and trust, and expanding common ground and cooperation, and serves as an important foundation for stronger China-EU political mutual trust.[67]

The two parties will definitely further enhance political dialogue at all levels and continue to maintain consultation and coordination on major

---

63 'China, EU Officially Launch Talks on Partnership and Cooperation Agreement,' *Xinhua News Agency*, 17 January 2007, retrieved on 4 March 2009, http://news.xinhuanet.com/english/2007-01/17/content_5619595.htm.

64 *Ibid.*

65 Council of the European Union, Joint Statement, Point 2, *10th EU-China Summit Joint Statement*, Beijing, 28 November 2007.

66 United Nations, Article 2, *Charter of United Nations*, New York.

67 Council of the European Union, Joint Statement, *10th EU-China Summit Joint Statement*, Beijing, 28 November 2007.

international and regional issues. They will probably agree in the PCA, that the political dialogues will continue to be held regularly and in an *ad hoc* fashion so as to enhance mutual political trust and expand strategic common ground.

The most sensitive and continuous issues relate to certain specific political matters between the EU and China, such as democracy, human rights, the rule of law, Taiwan, Tibet, the arms embargo, non-proliferation, disarmament, and the International Criminal Court (ICC). The EU intends to insert a "democracy and human rights clause" as the standard clause in its agreements with third countries. In the Commission's Communication, it stated that taking account of human rights in contractual relations with third countries was one of the Community's instruments to respect, promote and protect human rights and democratic principles.[68] This Communication also defined the standard expression of the "democracy and human rights clause" in the preamble and in the body of the agreements. In the preamble, general references to human rights and democratic values and references to universal and regional instruments common to both parties should be inserted.[69] In the body of the agreements, two clauses should be inserted. The first clause defines the essential human rights elements:

> Respect for the democratic principles and fundamental human rights established by [the Universal Declaration of Human Rights]/[the Helsinki Final Act and the Charter of Paris for a New Europe] inspires the domestic and external policies of the Community and of [the country or group of countries concerned] and constitutes an essential element of this agreement.

The second clause is a "non-execution clause":

> If either Party considers that the other Party has failed to fulfil an obligation under this Agreement, it may take appropriate measures. Before doing so, except in cases of special urgency, it shall supply the Association Council with all relevant information required for a thorough examination of the situation with a view to seeking a solution acceptable to the Parties. In the selection of measures, priority must be given to those which least disturb the functioning of this Agreement. These measures shall be notified immediately to the Association Council and shall be the subject of consultations within the Association Council if the other Party so requests.[70]

68 See Introduction of Commission of the European Communities, Communication COM(95) 216, Brussels, 23 May 1995 on the Inclusion of Respect for Democratic Principles and Human Rights in Agreements between the Community and Third Countries.

69 *Ibid.*

70 *Ibid.*

The appropriate measures include alteration of the contents or channels for cooperation programmes, reduction of cultural, scientific and technical cooperation programmes, postponement of a Joint Committee meeting, suspension of high-level bilateral contact, postponement of new projects, refusal to follow up partner's initiatives, trade embargoes, and the suspension of arms sales.[71] A clause defining general principles has been inserted in the PCAs between the EU and its member states and East European and Central Asian countries, such as Kazakhstan, Moldova, Kyrgyzstan, Turkmenistan, Georgia, Uzbekistan, Azerbaijan, Armenia, Russia and the Ukraine.[72] Some PCAs also include a "non-execution clause."[73]

The EU, especially the European Parliament (EP), insists on inserting such democracy and human rights clauses in the PCA. The EP considers that human rights should be an essential and integral part of EU-China relations. In the EP's Resolution (5 February 2009), it called on the Commission to insist on strengthening the "democracy and human rights clause" in negotiations with China concerning the PCA.[74] It seems the EP will not approve the PCA without the standard "human right clause."

However, it is not difficult to anticipate China's reaction to these standard clauses and measures. The Chinese government emphasises that human rights in China should combine general principles and the special characteristics of Chinese history, culture and practical situation.[75] Following the traditional position of socialist countries, China prioritises those rights listed in the International Covenant on Economic, Social and Cultural Rights (ICESCR). The Chinese government considers that people's right to subsistence and development is the primary concern for human rights. From the Chinese perspective, human rights are in essence a matter of sovereignty. Thus for China, dialogues and cooperation are the only way to promote the development of human rights internationally.[76] In light of the Chinese government's stand, it will be hard to

71 *Ibid.*, Annex 2.

72 Article 2 of the PCAs between the European Communities and their Member States and the East European and Central Asian countries.

73 For example, Article 95 of the PCA between the European Communities and their Member States and Uzbekistan, Article 98 of the PCA between the European Communities and their Member States and Georgia, Article 95 of the PCA between the European Communities and their Member States and Armenia, Article 98 of the PCA between the European Communities and their Member States and Azerbaijan.

74 European Parliament, Resolution, *Trade and Economic Relations with China*, 2008/2171(INI), Strasbourg, 5 February 2009.

75 'Human Rights in China,' *Xinhua News Agency*, retrieved on 7 March 2009, http://news.xinhuanet.com/ziliao/2003-01/22/content_702907.htm.

76 *Ibid.*

reach an agreement on the insertion of the EU's standard "democracy and human rights clause" and adopt measures for non-implementation of such clauses in the PCA. This does not mean that finding consensus on a human rights clause is unimaginable. On the contrary, a general clause on the promotion of democracy, human rights, the rule of law and good governance would be acceptable to the Chinese government especially if it can reflect, at first hand, some of the six other characteristics of a harmonious society: democracy and rule of law; fairness and justice; good faith and friendship; being full of vigour; stability and orderliness; harmony between human and nature.[77]

As to the Taiwan issue, the EU will continue to oppose any measure that would cause the change of the status quo across the Taiwan Strait.[78] The EU may request China to assure the maintenance of cross-Strait peace and stability. However, the Chinese government adopted the Anti-Secession Law in 2005, clearly stating that the Taiwan issue is within China's internal affairs and not subject to interference by outside forces.[79] It also provides that if the Taiwanese secessionist forces act under any name or by any means to cause Taiwan's secession from China, or cause any major incidents entailing Taiwan's secession from China, or act to exhaust the possibilities for a peaceful reunification, "the state shall employ non-peaceful means and other necessary measures to protect China's sovereignty and territorial integrity."[80]

Due to the riots in Tibet last year, the disputes on this issue between the EU and China became more intensive. The EP criticised the Chinese government's activities of discriminatory treatment of ethnic minorities in Tibet, for example, the gross discrimination in the education system, in which Tibetan children learn their native language as a second language.[81] It called on China to honour its commitments to human and minority rights and to the rule of law.[82] The then EP President stressed that "the European Parliament seeks to be a voice raised in defence of human rights and human dignity. In this respect, Parliament has consistently sought to highlight the human rights of the Tibetan people."[83] The

77 See 'Six Characteristics of A Harmonious Society,' *People's Daily*, retrieved on 7 March 2009, http://politics.people.com.cn/GB/8198/70195/index.html.

78 Communication of the Commission of the European Communities, EU – China: Closer Partners, Growing Responsibilities, *op. cit.*

79 Article 3 of China's Anti-Secession Law, adopted at the Third Session of the Tenth National People's Congress on 14 March 2005.

80 Article 8 of Anti-Secession Law of China, *Ibid.*

81 European Parliament, Resolution, *Tibet*, 2008/2557(RSP), Brussels, 10 April 2008.

82 *Ibid.*

83 European Parliament, Press Release, *Common Human Values, Inner Peace and Tibet: Dalai Lama at the European Parliament*, 4 December 2008, retrieved on 7 February

Commission also stated in its Communication that it would "continue to encourage full respect of fundamental rights and freedoms in all regions of China" and freedom of religion and protection of minorities in all regions of China.[84] Concerning this issue, China exclusively holds the view that the "Tibetan issue" is instigated and created by some Western countries and groups in order to prevent China's rising.[85] Chinese scholars also expressed a similar point of view. For example, Lei Sihai wrote that the "Tibetan issue" does not exist, because the word "issue" in international relations is usually used on major contentious matters. Tibet is a part of China's territory and Tibetan affairs are China's internal affairs. From this perspective, there is no "Tibetan issue" between China and any other countries in the international community. From an EU perspective, there is a "Tibetan issue" but the debate in the EU is often grounded in romantic notions rather than based on an objective assessment. Lei Sihai's view that the riots in Tibet were sensationalised by some Western states with the purpose of interfering in China's internal affairs may therefore hold some truth.[86]

China would like to see an end to the arms embargo as part of the negotiations for the PCA. China is, however, pessimistic based on the EU's reaction to this issue being placed on the negotiation agenda. The arms embargo was triggered due to the Tianenmen Square Incident. Following the establishment of the strategic partnership between the EU and China, they started to discuss the lifting of the EU arms embargo against China in the 2004 Annual Summit Meeting.[87] China welcomed this positive signal and regarded it as a symbol of the EU's recognition of China's progress on human rights and in international affairs, in the last decade. The Chinese government reiterated that the EU's arms embargo constitutes a political discrimination towards China and becomes an obstacle in developing a comprehensive strategic partnership.[88] Consi-

2009, http://www.europarl.europa.eu/news/expert/infopress_page/008-43686-336-12-49-901-20081203IPR43683-01-12-2008-2008-true/default_en.htm.

84 Communication of the Commission of the European Communities, EU – China: Closer Partners, Growing Responsibilities, *op. cit.*

85 Guo Jiping, 'The Mistaken Perception of Tibet Contrary to its Trend of Development and Advancement (Dui Xizang de Cuowu Renzhi Weibei Fazhen Jinbu Choaliu),' *People's Daily*, 2 March 2009, retrieved on 8 March 2009, http://opinion.people.com.cn/GB/8887219.html.

86 Lei Sihai, 'The West Should Stop Creating this "Tibetan issues" (Xifang Ying Tingzhi Zhizao "Xizang Wenti"),' *World News Journal*, 20 February 2009, retrieved on 8 March 2009, http://gb.cri.cn/27824/2009/02/20/2945s2433897.htm.

87 Council of the European Union, Joint Statement, Point 7, 7th EU-China Summit Joint Statement, *op. cit.*

88 Council of the European Union, Joint Statement, Point 7, 7th EU-China Summit Joint Statement, *op. cit.*

dering the economic and political benefits of cooperation with China, the European Commission confirmed its willingness to pursue lifting the embargo[89] but faced sharp internal opposition especially from the EP, and external pressure, especially from the US.[90] The EP adopted a report with 504 votes in favour, 24 against and 34 abstentions, calling for the continuation of the arms embargo against China. The report states that the EP "considers that the embargo imposed on China should not be lifted until there is a clear and lasting improvement in the situation regarding human rights and social and political freedom."[91] The US Department of State released a fact sheet on 17 November 2004, stating that it welcomed the partnership between the EU and China but it did not believe that lifting the embargo contributed to enhancing the partnership. It remonstrated that lifting the arms embargo did not accord to Europe's strategic interests. In a language that recalls the controversy around the Cuban boycott in the Helms-Burton Act, the fact sheet concludes with a closing warning that states that: "lifting the Embargo could negatively impact the Transatlantic Alliance." The section contains a hidden threat that lifting the embargo could lead to a boycott of any defense procurement by the US to the EU.[92] The EU subsequently slowed down the negotiations and imposed preconditions to the lifting of the embargo, which required preparations that immediately avoided a qualitative or quantitative increase in arms sales. The preconditions related to making progress on China's human rights situation, working to improve cross-Straits relations, and improving the transparency of China's military expenditure.[93]

These examples highlight therefore the differences in perspective emanating both from the respective European and Chinese camps. It will therefore be very difficult to insert tough clauses concerning specific political matters in the PCA. Although the general principles of

---

89 Council of the European Union, Joint Statement, Point 7, 7th EU-China Summit Joint Statement, *op. cit.*

90 Lu Yiguo, 'EU Lift of Arms Embargo and Sino-Russia Military Cooperation: Killing Two Birds with One Stone? Gaining Advantage from Both Sides?,' *International Herald Leader*, 18 December 2004, retrieved on 8 March 2009, http://news.xinhuanet.com/world/2004-12/20/content_2357980.htm.

91 European Parliament, 'EP Calls for Tougher Rules on Arms Trade,' *European Parliament Post-Briefing Item*, Strasbourg, 22 January 2007, retrieved on 8 March 2009, http://www.europarl.europa.eu/sides/getDoc.do?pubRef=-//EP//TEXT+IM-PRESS +20070112BRI01902+ITEM-012-EN+DOC+XML+V0//EN&language=EN.

92 EU Arms Embargo against China, *US Department of State's Bureau of International Information Programs*, 17 November 2004, retrieved on 8 March 2009, http://www.america.gov/st/washfile-english/2004/November/20041117181504lCJsamohT0.2211115.html.

93 Commission of the European Communities, Point 3.5, Communication: Closer Partners, Growing Responsibilities, *op. cit.*

respecting democracy, human rights, the rule of law and good governance are accepted by both parties, the clauses on concrete implementation will require negotiations by the two parties over a long period. A realistic way to settle these sensitive political issues is to insert a clause on respect for general principles and a clause, with general wording, on political cooperation that would demand a gradual improvement of the situation in China (in the context of the general principles). Continuing the ongoing dialogues will be key in ensuring that these general clauses are imbued over time with concrete meaning and commitments.

Trade and Economic Cooperation

The importance of the clauses on trade and economic cooperation in the PCA does not need to be reiterated. The contents of such trade and economic issues are largely determined by the updated 1985 TECA. That is to say, the PCA as a comprehensive framework agreement, and the updated 1985 TECA as an agreement specialised in trade and economic issues are two separate agreements. However, the principles and the core contents of the updated 1985 TECA will be incorporated into the PCA.[94] The EU and China held the first round of negotiations on updating the 1985 TECA in October 2007 and reached agreement on many issues after intensive consultations.[95] Although negotiations on trade and economic issues move faster than those on political issues, there are still some contentious matters between the EU and China.

As to trade, the EU's anti-dumping measures, anti-subsidy measures, safeguards, TBT (Technical Barrier to Trade) and other restrictions are among China's main concerns. By April 2007, the EU had initiated 127 anti-dumping cases against China.[96] An official from the Chinese Ministry of Commerce said that the EU has become the WTO member that initiates the most anti-dumping cases against China.[97] At present, the anti-dumping cases initiated by the EU are more than 20% of the total anti-dumping cases launched against China in the world.[98] Furthermore,

---

94 'China-EU Trade Negotiations Move On,' *People's Daily*, 21 February 2008, retrieved on 8 March 2009, http://english.peopledaily.com.cn/90001/90776/ 6358453.html.

95 *Ibid.*

96 Yu Lan, 'The EU is the No. 1 Among the WTO Members that Initiate Anti-Dumping Cases against China (Shang Wiebie: Oumeng yi Chengwei Duihua Fanqingxiao Diaocha Zuidao de WTO Chengyuan),' *The Chinese Ministry of Commerce*, 2 April 2007, retrieved on 8 March 2009, http://business.sohu.com/20070402/ n249149604. shtml.

97 *Ibid.*

98 Zhang Xiue, 'Reasons of the EU's Anti-Dumping Measures against China and China's Countermeasures (Oumeng Duihua Qingxioa Yuanyin ji Yingdui ce Lue),' retrieved on 8 March 2009, http://www.lunwentianxia.com/product.free.9462705.1/.

the affected industries number more than 40, including chemicals, textiles, shoes, and electronic products.[99] Chinese exports to the EU often suffer from the EU's TBT measures as well. The EU's technical regulations are complicated and the requirements are strict and frequently revised. Green barriers and social responsibility are also used by the EU to restrict exports from China. During the PCA negotiations, China made it clear that it would address these "irrational restrictions."[100] However, the EU reiterated that trade defence measures and technical and other standards remain instruments to ensure fair trade between the EU and China. It will continue to use these instruments carefully and rigorously in the future.[101]

The full market economy status (MES) is another key topic in negotiations between the EU and China. The EU has five criteria for MES. In June 2007, the EU presented China with an updated assessment of China's progress towards MES, considering that although China has made progress it had only met one of the five criteria.[102] The EU also considered that the assessment of the MES is a technical exercise relevant to anti-dumping investigations. However, China does not agree with the EU on this point. It has its own perception on the MES criterions. Liu Xiaojuan, deputy director of the Research Office of the State Council, said that China had met the basic requirements to be a market economy as examined on the basis of the rules for Western market economies and on the development of its domestic market.[103] Furthermore, China does not consider that the MES criterions are a purely technical exercise but regards non-recognition as unfair treatment.[104]

China will also request that the EU eases restrictions on high-tech exports and tap the enormous potential for technological cooperation and trade in line with the WTO rules.[105] In response, the EU would stress

---

99 *Ibid.*

100 People's Republic of China, Part Three II.1, China's EU Policy Paper, *op. cit.*

101 Commission of the European Communities, Point 3.4, Communication: Closer Partners, Growing Responsibilities, *op. cit.*

102 'EU-China Trade Ministerial Meeting, Brussels, 12 June 2007,' at the website of the Commission of the European Communities' Directorate-General for External Relations, retrieved on 8 March 2009, http://ec.europa.eu/trade/issues/bilateral/countries/china/ pr120607_en.htm.

103 'China Meets Basic Requirements for Market Economy Status,' *People's Daily*, 22 September 2004, retrieved on 8 March 2009, http://english.peopledaily.com.cn/200409/22/eng20040922_157908.html.

104 Zhang Yi, 'What is the Meaning to Recognise China's Full MES? (Chengren Zhongguo Wenquan Shicheng Jingji Diwei Yiyi Chezai?),' *Xinhua News Agency*, 3 November 2004, retrieved on 8 March 2009, http://www.china.com.cn/chinese/zhuanti/sjdw/ 717415.htm.

105 People's Republic of China, Part Three II.1, China's EU Policy Paper, *op. cit.*

halting forced technology transfers as a compulsory part of the establishment of EU-China joint ventures. The former EU Trade Commissioner Peter Mandelson pointed out that royalty payments from Chinese companies to European companies were not fully guaranteed and there were no fair conditions for technology transfers from the EU to China.[106] IPR infringement in China remains a big concern for the EU because Europe's comparative advantage lies in innovation, design and high-value products. Since China is by far the largest source of counterfeit and pirated products, seized at the EU's borders, the EU will also request China to better enforce the anti-counterfeiting laws and strengthen cooperation in customs and related authorities.[107]

The 1985 TECA does not mention much about investment but the updated version will definitely include provisions to further open investment opportunities both in the EU and China. The openness is beneficial to the two parties as the EU gains low-cost production opportunities and market share in China, and China receives access to capital, goods, knowledge, technology and job opportunities from FDI. However, the EU is not satisfied with the breadth and depth of openness in investment areas in China. The existing Catalogue for the Guidance of Foreign Investment Industries prohibits foreign investors in 39 investment areas in 11 sectors and restricts them in 85 investment areas in 14 sectors.[108] In some sectors, foreign investors are still prevented from setting up wholly owned enterprises and are required to establish joint ventures with Chinese partners. For example, in the manufacturing sector, China continues to maintain investment restrictions on some key industries for Europe such as automobiles, petrochemicals and steel. The approval and examination procedures and the high capital requirements for the establishment of foreign-invested enterprises are also an impediment for EU investors. Notwithstanding, China also complained about the lack of market access to the EU's financial market.[109] Chinese financial institutions are keen to gain access to the EU's market.

---

106 'Mandelson Visits Chinese State Intellectual Property Office – Urges Tougher Chinese Action on Counterfeiting, Technology Transfer, Payment of Royalties, Beijing,' at the website of the Commission of the European Communities' Directorate-General for Trade, 8 November 2006, retrieved on 8 March 2009, http://ec.europa.eu/trade/issues/sectoral/intell_property/pr081106_en.htm.

107 Commission of the European Communities, Point 2.4, Communication: Closer Partners, Growing Responsibilities, *op. cit.*

108 See *Catalogue for the Guidance of Foreign Investment Industries*, issued by the National Development and Reform Commission and the Ministry of Commerce, entering into force as from 1 December 2007.

109 People's Republic of China, Part Three II.2, China's EU Policy Paper, *op. cit.*

Apart from the above-cited examples, other key issues remain between the EU and China, such as the EU's trade deficit, the RMB exchange rate, product safety, climate change, subsidies, government procurement, or regarding the special measures to be taken in the context of the economic and financial crisis. To ensure success in the PCA negotiations, the EU and China should set out rational and ambitious but realistic goals for the trade negotiations. Bearing in mind the tremendous mutual benefits and common interests, the EU and China will make progress much faster in the domain of negotiations on trade, and economic cooperation will progress much faster rather than in the political domain. However, the two parties should make use of their economic and trade interests as a driver to achieve open and frank exchanges on all aspects including the contentious political issues. The possibility of concluding two separate agreements, one on political issues, and the other on economic and trade issues is not very likely, unless the political negotiations come to a deadlock and the two parties agree to move ahead first with the trade and economic section. This could only be defined as a failure for the EU-China partnership.

Conclusion

After the EU and China set up a strategic partnership, comprehensive cooperation in a wide range of areas at various levels has been strengthened and improved. The legal basis of EU-China relations needs to be reinforced. The outdated 1985 TECA, sectoral agreements, separate internal laws, sectoral dialogues, and respective policies obviously cannot keep pace with the fast development of bilateral relations. It is inevitable that the two parties seek to establish a new legal framework based on a comprehensive agreement which regulates all aspects of bilateral relations including political, economic, trade and investment aspects. The PCA negotiations provide a practical mechanism to move this objective forward. However, the negotiations on the contents of the PCA are a hard and time-consuming process. The EU and China, due to different interests, cultures, histories, traditions, and phases of development, hold many differences on a variety of issues. As for sensitive issues, the two parties need mutual trust and substantial communication to resolve conflicts. It is not wise to regulate these issues by hard legal clauses. As to less sensitive issues, the two parties, on the basis of mutual respect and equal footing, may look for an effective and efficient means to settle these matters in the form of clauses.

No matter whether negotiations progress smoothly or are temporarily frustrated, the development of the bilateral relations will be ongoing. This bilateral relationship will continue to create opportunities that will provide incremental improvements in the overall relationship. The political dialogues will be improved by keeping the channels of communication open; export and import will expand; foreign investment will increase in an opening environment. In other areas, there also exists room for improvement: cooperation on international and regional peace and security, climate change, S&T, education, culture, and civil society.

No matter whether the framework agreement is a comprehensive agreement or separated into two agreements, the most important issue in the future is the implementation of the agreement(s). The EU and China still need to establish a mechanism for enforcement and assessment of the legal texts.

To maintain a long-term strategic partnership, the two parties need to seek common interests, respect diversity, comply with commitments in agreements, reflect upon experience and lessons, whilst regularly communicating and exchanging views. It is hoped that the framework agreement will build a better and more comprehensive legal framework to further boost bilateral relations in the next twenty to thirty years.

CHAPTER 3

The European Model of CSR and Labour Standards in China

Frauke S. AUSTERMANN

China's weight in the world economy is increasing at breathtaking speed. Consequently, it is pivotal that Chinese business is pursued in a sustainable way. In order to achieve this, the Chinese government increasingly focuses on long-term environmental and social development, and no longer exclusively on growth rates.[1] Corporate Social Responsibility (CSR) has become a key tool in making businesses operate sustainably. It can be defined as "the continuing commitment by business to behave ethically and contribute to economic development while improving the quality of life of the workforce and their families, as well as of the local community and society at large."[2] Labour standards form a decisive part of CSR – they constitute a major issue within the Chinese economy as they are often insufficiently adhered to.[3]

The importance of CSR for the EU-China relationship is also growing, given the fact that it is included in the most recent sectoral dialogues between the EU and China, and is also considered as an "emerging issue at the European Chamber of Commerce in China."[4] However, since CSR has only recently emerged, it is crucial to research why and how it could

1 Victorien Wu, 'Labor Relations in Focus: The PRC Government's Effort to Better Protect Worker's Rights Spring from Worries about China's Social Stability,' *China Business Review*, November-December 2006, p. 3.

2 World Business Council for Sustainable Development (WBCSD), 'Corporate Social Responsibility. Meeting Changing Expectations,' *World Business Council for Sustainable Development*, 1999, retrieved on 16 April 2008, http://www.wbcsd.org/DocRoot/hbdf19Txhmk3kDxBQDWW/CSRmeeting.pdf, p. 3.

3 Anita Chan, 'A "Race to the Bottom:" Globalisation and China's Labour Standards,' *China Perspectives*, No. 46, March-April 2003, retrieved on 14 July 2009, http://chinaperspectives.revues.org/document259.html.

4 Landis MacKellar *et al.*, Evaluation of the European Commission's Co-operation and Partnership with the People's Republic of China. Country Level Evaluation, European Commission/EuropeAid/Evaluation Unit, 2007, retrieved on 30 October 2008, http://ec.europa.eu/europeaid/how/evaluation/evaluation_reports/reports/2007/1077_vol1_en.pdf, pp. 26 & 98.

fit into the currently negotiated PCA between China and the EU. This chapter tackles this need.

The EU, China's largest trading partner, is a leading force in promoting CSR as a vehicle for sustainability. Over the past decade, CSR strategies have been successfully discussed and implemented at the national and supranational level. Moreover, Europe has a vital interest in improving labour standards in China: firstly, China is Europe's second largest trading partner, and secondly, one fourth of the global workforce is nowadays Chinese, which gives the Middle Kingdom an enormous power to determine global labour standards.[5] It is vital that China improves its labour standards in order to avoid a global race to the bottom.

Given the potential of the EU as a model for CSR, and due to the mutual economic and political importance of China and Europe, the purpose of this chapter is to find out whether the European model of CSR can help improve labour standards in China, and thereby contribute to a sustainable development of the country's economy. This focus strongly links the chapter to the normative dimension of the PCA. As the following outline shows, it also cuts across the PCA's economic and political dimension.

After a theoretical discussion of CSR and its related concepts, the chapter examines whether a European model of CSR can be sketched and what its characteristics would be. To do so, CSR approaches within EU member states and at the supranational level are looked at. Thereafter, CSR is placed in the Chinese context. Based on this, the main research question is examined from the perspectives of two key actors in the CSR debate. Firstly, the potential of European business as a CSR role model for Chinese companies is evaluated. Secondly, the question shall examine how the Chinese government can learn from European governmental policies regarding CSR.

Overall, the chapter shows that although China's road to realise CSR is a long one, there is considerable potential for China to learn from the European CSR model. In this sense, the chapter shall increase the understanding of EU policy makers as to why and how CSR can be used as a strategic tool in order to "support China's transition to an open

---

5 Global Labour Strategies, 'Why China Matters: Labor Rights in the Era of Globalization,' *Global Labour Strategies*, April 2008, retrieved on 28 June 2008, http://laborstrategies.blogs.com/global_labor_strategies/files/why_china_matters_gls_report.pdf, p. 4.

society based on the [...] respect for human rights," which is one of the EU's main aims in the PCA.[6]

Theoretical Foundation

CSR and Related Concepts

As defined by the United Nations (UN), sustainable development means that future generations shall have at least the same possibilities to satisfy their needs as current generations.[7] These needs are of an economic, environmental and social nature and together form the so-called "triple bottom line" of sustainable development.[8] Due to the increasing power of (multinational) companies in the course of globalisation, business affects sustainable development in all these three aspects. The corporate world therefore needs to shoulder its responsibilities accordingly.

As Milton Friedman puts it, the primary responsibility of a company is economic in nature, namely to increase profits.[9] While focusing on their economic responsibility, entrepreneurs create employment so that people earn a living. The profits can be re-invested so that new products are created and societal wealth further increases. Friedman's supporters accept that the organisational culture of a company can be based on certain values. However, a company that is badly run from a business perspective will simply go bankrupt, no matter how honourable its values are.[10] Nevertheless, it is dangerous if entrepreneurs solely focus on profits. They might for instance cause long-term environmental damage for the sake of short-term profits. This is currently a severe problem in China. Numerous firms pollute rivers in order to save recycling costs.[11] In

---

6 Commission of the European Communities, *EU Relations with China, 2008*, retrieved on 30 October 2008, http://ec.europa.eu/external_relations/china/index_en.htm.

7 United Nations World Commission on Environment and Development, *Our Common Future*, New York, 1987, retrieved on 1 July 2008, http://www.un-documents.net/ocf-02.htm#I.

8 John Elkington, 'Towards the Sustainable Corporation: Win-Win-Win Business Strategies for Sustainable Development,' *California Management Review*, Vol. 36, No. 2, 1994, pp. 90-100.

9 Milton Friedman, 'The Social Responsibility of Business is to Increase its Profits,' *The New York Times Magazine*, 13 September 1970, retrieved on 28 June 2008, http://www.colorado.edu/studentgroups/libertarians/issues/friedman-soc-resp-business.html

10 Daniel Franklin, 'A Special Report on Corporate Social Responsibility,' *The Economist*, 19 January 2008, p. 22.

11 Hua Chen, '52 Firms Shut Down From River Pollution,' *China Daily*, 21 June 2004, retrieved on 1 July 2008, http://www.chinadaily.com.cn/english/doc/2004-06/21/content_341049.htm.

the long-term, such behaviour can destroy the environment to an extent that these firms cannot continue their own business operations.

Similarly, if a company decreases labour standards, such as health and safety provisions in order to cut labour costs, its workers can more easily fall ill or even die from work-related accidents. This obviously decreases the company's productivity. Thus, fair labour standards are not only of broader societal interest, as reflected in the Universal Declaration of Human Rights, but also of companies' interests. Thus, companies have vested interests in fair labour standards in order to keep their business operations sustainable. There is thus a "society case" and a "business case" for sustainable development which explains the need for companies to also assume social responsibilities.[12]

In order to realise this, companies need to implement a stakeholder perspective in their business operations.[13] "Stakeholders" shall be understood as any party that can be affected by corporate behaviour, such as investors, employees or consumers.[14] Friedman created a theory of stakeholder management: to maximise both the society and the business case, firms must take the power and legitimacy of their stakeholders and the urgency of the matter into account when taking business decisions.[15] If a company, for example, implements a CSR-strategy because of the recent increase in ethical consumerism, it does not only boost its sales by satisfying the demand for "good" products – it also contributes to society by complying with fair trade standards.

Often enough, CSR-policies are a tool to (re)establish consumers' trust in a brand, especially after corporate scandals (such as sportswear producers using child labourers). It also helps to recruit and retain talent in the labour market: "good" employers are also more attractive to work

12 Marta Cuesta González & Carmen Valor Martinez, 'Fostering Corporate Social Responsibility through Public Initiative: From the EU to the Spanish Case,' *Journal of Business Ethics*, No. 55, 2004, p. 276.

13 Ingo Schönheit, 'Corporate Social Responsibility – Deutsche und Internationale Perspektiven am Beispiel China,' in I. Schönheit *et al.*, *Corporate Social Responsibility. Verantwortung fur nachhaltiges Wirtshaften in China*, Berlin, Beuth, 2006, p. 17.

14 Thomas Donaldson & Lee E. Preston, 'The Stakeholder Theory of the Corporation: Concepts, Evidence, and Implications,' *Academy of Management Review*, Vol. 20, No. 1, 1995, p. 85.

15 Jonathan P. Doh & Terrence R. Guay, 'Corporate Social Responsibility, Public Policy, and NGO Activism in Europe and the United States. An Institutional-Stakeholder Perspective,' *Journal of Management Studies*, Vol. 43, No. 1, 2006, pp. 47-73, as cited in Ruth V. Aguilera & Cynthia A. Williams, 'Corporate Social Responsibility in a Comparative Perspective,' in Andrew Crane *et al.*, *Oxford Handbook of Corporate Social Responsibility*, Oxford, Oxford University Press, 2006, p. 456.

for.[16] Due to these business advantages, CSR has sharply increased in the priority lists of CEOs.[17] Accordingly, CSR could lead to a tournament in upgrading labour standards, since companies are no longer only competing to keep costs low but also to keep up their image.

Despite the increasing importance of CSR, it remains a slippery concept.[18] As the term says, CSR-strategies are supposed to be business-based, in other words, adopted by and for companies. Indeed, business-based codes of conduct represent 84% the most common form of CSR development.[19] Nevertheless, this means that every firm can adopt its own CSR-policy. If CSR is not to become arbitrary, it needs a certain bottom line. Governments – and as well as third sector parties[20] – have therefore attempted to streamline CSR. After all, it is governments that set the basic rules of the game for how companies (should) behave. Therefore, political decision-makers in China and the EU are also considering including CSR in the PCA. However, a single definition does not exist. Furthermore, the different conceptualisations are very broad in nature, and implementation is still limited. This increases the danger of companies "green/blue-washing" their activities.[21]

On the other hand, it is questionable whether a single definition fits all contexts. For decades, a heated discussion has been going on whether so-called international labour standards are universally applicable. Many developing countries reject them for being established exclusively by and for developed countries. The main argument here is that developing countries and countries in transition cannot afford minimum wages, social security coverage, or even prohibiting child labour as such obligations would destroy their competitive advantage, which mainly consists of cheap labour.[22] Similarly, some argue that CSR-strategies, which are

16 Apo Leong & Chan Kawai, 'Critical Reflection on CSR: A Labour's Perspective,' *Asia Monitor Resource Centre*, 2007, retrieved 16 April 2008, http://www.amrc.org.hk/projects/Critical_+Reflection_+on_+CSR; Schönheit, *op. cit.*, p. 14.

17 Franklin, *op. cit.*, pp. 3-4.

18 Leong & Kawai, *loc. cit.*

19 Cuesta González & Valor Martinez, *op. cit.*, p. 277.

20 Since the Chinese third sector is still state-dependent, there is a certain "overlap" between these two actors. Therefore, it is sufficient for this chapter to only cover government and business.

21 Kenny Bruno & Joshua Karliner, 'Tangled Up in Blue. Corporate Partnerships at the United Nations,' *CorpWatch*, 2000, retrieved on 2 July 2008, http://www.corpwatch.org/article.php?id=996.

22 Zyhiyi He, 'Corporate Social Responsibility. Herausforderung und Ansporn für die Chinesische Wirtschaft,' in I. Schönheit *et al.*, *op. cit.*, p. 31.

most advanced in Western Multi-National Corporations (MNCs), are based only on the standards of developed countries.[23]

However, this is not to deny the existence of a certain global common denominator of labour standards that any country should adhere to. Nevertheless, it is also important, for this chapter, to analyse the business case of CSR from a Chinese perspective. Moreover, the applicability of CSR depends on different cultural contexts.[24] CSR scholars have pointed out that Brazil and India have a long tradition of philanthropy. Companies in these countries are therefore more receptive to CSR, whereas the Russian cultural climate is less CSR-prone.[25]

Therefore both arguments are valid: the call for global streamlining of CSR, as well as the context-dependency on economic development, the political/institutional, and the cultural environment. Both arguments will now be further examined by analysing whether the European conceptualisation of CSR can help improve labour standards in China. The answer to that question will give clues as to whether CSR should be introduced in the PCA. To do so, the next section will first answer the following questions: is there a European model of CSR and what should its characteristics resemble?

A European Model of CSR?

European integration has been largely economic in nature, which renders the business environment across the EU relatively homogeneous.[26] Therefore, it is easier to adopt a Europe-wide CSR framework compared to a global one. Indeed, this is what EU decision-makers did. They based their initiatives on the assumption that CSR is "a concept whereby companies integrate social and environmental concerns in their business operations and in their interaction with their stakeholders on a voluntary basis."[27]

---

23 Schönheit, *op. cit.*, p. 22.

24 Doh & Guay, *op. cit.*, pp. 47-73 as cited in Ruth V. Aguilera & Cynthia A. Williams, *op. cit.*, p. 456.

25 Franklin, *op. cit.*, p. 18; Geert Hofstede, *Cultures and Organizations, Software of the Mind*, New York, McGraw-Hill, 2004.

26 Brigid Laffan, 'The European Union: A Distinctive Model of Internationalisation?,' *European Integration online Papers (EioP)*, Vol. 1, No. 18, 1997, p. 6.

27 Commission of the European Communities, *Communication from the Commission: Corporate Social Responsibility. A Business Contribution to Sustainable Development*, COM(2002) 347 final, Brussels, 2 July 2002.

The EU has already moved from the question of why CSR is important to how it can be implemented.[28] Consequently, Kolk observes a "European leadership in CSR"[29] and Welford sees European companies as the world leaders in stakeholder engagement and CSR-reporting.[30] But where does this success come from, and how does the European CSR-model differ from others? In the following section, three main characteristics of this model will be distinguished, which are all reflected in the EU's definition of CSR: firstly, it is described as an "inherently stakeholder-focused" model; secondly, CSR-strategies are supposed to be "integrated;" and thirdly, they should be "voluntary" in character. Just as there are important variations regarding the so-called "European social model" across European countries, such differences also exist for CSR. For analytical purposes, attention must nevertheless be drawn to the broad similarities within Europe – and these become especially visible when compared to the US model of CSR.

Talking about the "inherent stakeholder-focus," comparative CSR-scholarship draws a distinction between a continental European CSR-model and an Anglo-Saxon one.[31] Doh and Guay further specify that, because of historical development, economic efficiency and the need to avoid social unrest, the "European business environment has long been characterised by a presumption that corporations have societal obligations that transcend their responsibilities to shareholders."[32] For Anglo-Saxon companies, corporate economic responsibility is of foremost importance.[33]

On an institutional level, EU-based interest groups have "explicit avenues" with which to influence European policy-making, compared to their American counterparts.[34] This stakeholder-focus is likely to stem from the differing political traditions of corporatism in Europe versus pluralism in the US. Licht outlines this difference by calling the European CSR-model an "insider system" in contrast to the Anglo-Saxon "outsider system" of CSR.[35]

---

28 Vladimir Spidla, Speech, 'China-EU CSR International Forum,' Beijing, 7 September 2005, retrieved on 2 July 2008, http://ec.europa.eu/employment_social/speeches/2005/vs_070905_en.pdf.

29 Aguilera & Williams, *op. cit.*, p. 465.

30 Richard Welford, 'Corporate Social Responsibility in Europe, North America and Asia,' *Journal of Corporate Citizenship*, Vol. 17, 2004, pp. 33-52.

31 Aguilera and Williams, *op. cit.*, p. 453.

32 Doh & Guay, *op. cit.*, as cited in Aguilera & Williams, *op. cit.*, p. 456.

33 *Ibid.*

34 *Ibid.*

35 Aguilera & Williams, *op. cit.*, p. 457.

Secondly, CSR-policies in Europe tend to be more *integrated.* Taking the firm-perspective, CSR is supposed to be integrated into the core business activities.[36] In many US firms, they tend to constitute a separate set of activities.[37] Furthermore, European governments make efforts to integrate CSR into different policies and across national borders, as will be seen later on. Matten and Moon therefore characterise the European CSR-model as an "implicit" one, in contrast to its "explicit" Anglo-Saxon counterpart.[38] The problem with the explicit CSR-model is that it allows a company to be externally socially responsible whilst internally retaining immoral business practices. A company that donates to anti-child-labour NGOs but uses children as workers itself would surely not be deserving of the "socially responsible" label.

Turning to the third major characteristic, CSR in Europe is meant to be a "voluntary" practice. This is rather similar to its Anglo-Saxon counterpart: here, free market regulation is generally preferred to legal intervention. Apart from market-compatibility, voluntarism is also important for CSR not to become a surrogate for legally stipulated labour standards. In China, for example, labour law is either poorly developed, or not effectively enforced, so that CSR would sometimes have to fill this vacuum.[39] However, European decision-makers insist that CSR should not replace legislation, but constitute a complementary tool.[40] This is because CSR is aimed at companies and therefore only covers the workers of a particular firm or plant. If CSR replaced legally stipulated labour standards, labour standards would be privatised for the employees of good CSR-performers. To avoid this, CSR must embrace business practices *on top of* a bottom line of legally enforceable labour standards.

This point brings us closer to the question whether the European CSR-model is also applicable in China. Apart from being distinct from the Anglo-Saxon model of CSR, it should not be forgotten that the EU consists only of industrialised countries. Therefore, its CSR-model is

36 EU-China Trade Project (EUCTP), *EU-China CSR Symposium*, 12 July 2006, retrieved on 2 July 2008, http://www.euchinawto.org/index.php?option=com_content &task= view&id=43&Itemid=43.

37 An example is General Electric (GE). On the company's corporate citizenship website, GE advertises for its engagement for better education in the US and health improvement in Africa, rather than good labour practices within GE. One gets a similar impression from Wal-Mart's website.

38 Dirk Matten & Jeremy Moon, "'Implicit' and 'Explicit' CSR: A Conceptual Framework for Understanding CSR in Europe," in André Habisch *et al.*, *CSR Across Europe*, Berlin, Springer, 2004, p. 9.

39 Leong & Kawai, *loc. cit.*

40 Spidla, *loc. cit.*; He, *op. cit.*, p. 30.

clearly based on higher standards compared to developing countries.[41] Although China is now classified as an emerging economy, it still has a long way to go in order to catch up with EU countries in terms of labour standards.[42]

To improve the situation, China is looking more closely at other countries as models in terms of labour standards, and in particular European ones.[43] Apart from the advantages of the European CSR model, another possible reason for this orientation towards Europe could be the following: the EU-model of CSR is quite regulator-driven compared to the rather consumer-driven Anglo-Saxon type, that would more adequately fit the Chinese environment:[44] firstly, the Middle Kingdom's economic and political affairs are still highly regulated by the Communist Party; secondly, although consumerism in China is rising, its ethical forms are only slowly, but surely, gaining ground.[45] The fact that ethical consumerism is on the rise, however, increases the importance of CSR generally, since it is closely linked to the reputation of a given company.

For these two reasons, and because of the EU's own interest in a sustainable Chinese economy, it is important to find out if the European CSR-conceptualisation could serve as a model to improve labour standards in China. Before applying the EU-model in China, it is necessary to determine how far a possible transfer of CSR from Europe to China would be limited by the need to account for local conditions.

CSR in the Chinese Context

The importance of China in the sustainability debate can easily be illustrated with some basic figures about the country. With over 1.3 bn inhabitants, China is the most populous country in the world. Its fabulous GDP growth rates are often-quoted. China reached a new record of 13% in 2007.[46] Although its per-capita GDP is still quite low, and its rich-poor gap has multiplied,[47] China's economic boom has lifted millions of inhabitants out of poverty. China is globally the most sought-after

41 Schönheit, *op. cit.*, p. 16.

42 Chan, 'Race to the Bottom,' *op. cit.*

43 GLS, *op. cit.*, p. 6.

44 Isabelle Maignan & David Allen Ralston, *Business Ethics=Social Responsibility*, 2004, retrieved at http://www.ism.ws/files/Pubs/Procedings/HILallatin.pdf, as cited in Aguilera & Williams, *op. cit.*, p. 462.

45 Jakob Klein, 'Creating Ethical Food Consumers? Promoting Organic Food in Urban Southwest China,' *Social Anthropology*, No. 1, 2009, p. 87.

46 Michael Bristow, 'China's Economic Growth Slows,' *BBC News Online*, 22 January 2009, retrieved on 2 March 2009, http://news.bbc.co.uk/2/hi/business/7843947.stm; This rate shrank to 6.8% at the end of 2008 due to the financial crisis (*Ibid.*).

47 GLS, *op. cit.*, p. 10.

destination for FDI, mainly due to its enormous market potential, but also because of low labour costs and lax social and environmental laws.[48]

In terms of trade, China and the EU have the fastest growing relationship worldwide, with the EU being China's number one trading partner, whereas China is number two for the EU.[49] Despite these impressive figures, there are concerns in terms of the rather unsustainable growth rates, the increasing wage dispersion, and the fact that a one-party state gains such economic and political power, especially when looking at human rights violations, which are often work-related.[50] In order to better understand the current difficulties in implementing (the European concept of) CSR in China, it is necessary to briefly trace back the economic development of the country over time.

From 1949 until 1978, China's business landscape consisted only of publicly-owned enterprises.[51] These state-owned enterprises were all-round social institutions – the so-called "iron rice bowl" – in the sense that they provided lifetime employment, housing, child and health care, education and other benefits to their workers.[52] Decisions were taken by the Communist Party so that all business was dependent on Beijing.[53] However, with Deng Xiaoping's decision to stop China's isolation in 1978, the government gave enterprises more autonomy so that they could focus on economic profits, rather than providing social benefits.[54]

Consequently, the former social responsibility that enterprises assumed – or were forced to assume – was taken over directly by the government,[55] although not always successfully or sufficiently enough.[56] To stick to the example of working conditions, employees in the Chinese toy industry work extremely long hours and are paid below the minimum

48 Schönheit, *op. cit.*, pp. 9-10.

49 Commission of the European Communities, *Bilateral Trade Relations. EU-China*, Brussels, May 2009, retrieved on 12 July 2009, http://ec.europa.eu/trade/issues/bilateral/countries/china/index_en.htm.

50 Schönheit, *op. cit.*, p. 10.

51 Robert J. Rosoff, 'Beyond Codes of Conduct. Addressing Labor Rights Problems in China,' *China Business Review*, March-April 2004, retrieved at http://www.chinabusinessreview.com/public/0403/rosoff.html, pp. 6-7.

52 He, *op. cit.*, pp. 25-26; GLS, *op. cit.*, p. 13.

53 GLS, *op. cit.*, p. 13.

54 Nick Young, 'Three "C"s: Civil Society, Corporate Social Responsibility, and China,' *China Business Review*, January-February 2002, p. 21.

55 *Ibid.*, p. 23.

56 Wendy Chapple & Jeremy Moon, 'Corporate Social Responsibility in Asia. A Seven-Country Study of CSR Web Site Reporting,' *Business and Society*, No. 44, 2005, p. 421.

wage level. They sometimes wait for their salaries several months, and are left with virtually no effective complaint channels.[57]

These conditions persist not because of a legal vacuum in labour standards. Despite the fact that Chinese labour law is poorly-developed, it has recently been reformed.[58] Nevertheless, its implementation is weak, so that one can speak of a *de facto* vacuum of social responsibility in employment matters.[59] Overall, the economic responsibility of Chinese companies seems to have definite priority over social concerns as a result of the former entirely state-controlled business system and the recent "gold-digger" atmosphere.

It is important to mention that China's economic boom has been made possible, in part due to the approximately 140-150 million Chinese migrant workers. They are motivated to leave more remote provinces in order to work in these industries, as they are attracted by the possibility of earning a decent living.[60] Based on a rather discriminatory residence system called *hukou*, migrant workers have only limited access to social benefits and education and they are paid less compared to the local population of these provinces.[61]

Although Asian companies are said to have a lower commitment to labour standards,[62] CSR is still very heterogeneous across Asia.[63] The lack of freedom of association is a very special concern in China, where trade unions are dependent on the Communist Party and strike rights were abolished in 1982.[64] According to the International Labour Organisation (ILO), these circumstances result in China's negative records, such as the highest rate in deaths per capita from work-related sickness and accidents.[65] For entrepreneurs, China may be a "deregulated paradise," but for defenders of global labour standards, it is one of the most important triggers for a "race to the bottom."[66] Both outlooks point to an unsustainable future for the Chinese economy. If every Chinese is to

57 Klaus Piepel, 'CSR in China – Erfahrungen und Herausforderungen am Beispiel der Spielzeugindustrie,' in I. Schönheit *et al.*, *op. cit.*, p. 82.

58 'Accolades for China's New Labor Law,' *ChinaCSR.com: News & Views on Corporate Social Responsibility in China*, 2 July 2007, retrieved on 24 June 2008, http://www.chinacsr.com/2007/07/02/1466-accolades-for-chinas-new-labor-law.

59 Rosoff, *op. cit.*, p. 13.

60 Piepel, *op. cit.*, p. 83.

61 Michael Dillon, *Contemporary China*, Oxon, Routledge, 2009, pp. 63-65.

62 Welford, *op. cit.*, p. 40.

63 Chapple & Moon, *op. cit.*, p. 415.

64 GLS, *op. cit.*, p. 5.

65 *Ibid.*, p. 17.

66 *Ibid.*, p. 6.

further gain from the economic boom, "greater labour rights [are a] prerequisite."[67]

In recent years, Chinese companies and multinationals operating in the Middle Kingdom rediscovered the importance of social responsibility.[68] Also through increasing pressure from the Chinese government, the business sector realised that China must render its economic development sustainable.[69] Nevertheless, the respective CSR-reports of Chinese companies have been dismissed by a Chinese critic as "beautiful books, not much inside."[70] This critique seems valid if one bases it on the EU-definition of CSR in China. However, one must question whether this EU-orientated definition can really be applied in the same context as China?[71]

Thus, it has become clear that the Chinese socio-economic and legal background must be taken into account if CSR is to become a successful tool to improve labour standards, and thus to ensure a sustainable development of this important emerging economy. Despite these cautionary remarks, the European model still has its merits also in the Chinese business environment, especially considering the current plans of the Chinese government to turn China into a high-tech knowledge economy by 2020.[72] Therefore, the applicability of the European CSR-concept in China will now be tested from the perspectives of two key actors in the CSR-debate: business and government.

Transferring European CSR Standards to China: From Theory to Practice

Learning from European Business

The first perspective to be examined will be that of the entrepreneurs, because CSR is concerned predominantly by business interests. Although labour rights violations in China also happen due to the extreme price and time pressure exerted by Western MNCs on Chinese manufacturers,[73] working conditions in Western and especially European-owned plants in China are on average considerably better than in local ones or those

---

67 *Ibid.*

68 Franklin, *loc. cit.*

69 He, *loc. cit.*

70 Franklin, *op. cit.*, pp. 1-24.

71 He, *op. cit.*, pp. 26-29.

72 Xue Lan & Nancy Forbes, 'Will China Become a Science and Technology Superpower by 2020? An Assessment based on a National Innovation System Framework,' *Innovations*, Vol. 1, No. 4, 2006, pp. 111-126.

73 Rosoff, *loc. cit.*

owned by other Asian MNCs.[74] One important reason for the better working conditions is the attempt of European MNCs to include Chinese stakeholders in management processes.

Perhaps the most courageous attempt to do so, given the strict laws on employee participation in China, is the conduct of democratic elections of employee representatives, as they are common in European companies. Reebok, a subsidiary of German market leader Adidas, organised a democratic vote for one of its subcontractors. Supervised by Chinese state officials, the initiative was part of its CSR-strategy with the aim to decrease labour rights violations and induce more loyalty from the workers.[75] As a result, labour disputes are less frequent than in other companies.[76] Thus, it seems that the European approach could help solve fundamental problems in China in terms of labour standards.

Nevertheless, the cultural and political limits should be kept in mind. As Branzei *et al.*, found out by studying 360 Chinese companies, the attitudes of CEOs still influence CSR-strategies much more than in European companies.[77] Such need for strong leadership, which might be rooted in the high-powered structure within Asian companies, is more difficult to combine with bottom-up stakeholder-involvement.[78] Also, company-sponsored union-elections in MNCs with branches in China can easily be interpreted by the Chinese government as a foreign intervention in the country's internal affairs. This is one of the reasons why the impact of such elected representatives remains limited.[79]

In order to implement the second characteristic of the European CSR-model in China, namely the integration of CSR-strategies into core business activities, European MNCs have adopted codes of conduct, including labour standards, which are valid throughout their supply chains.[80] Apart from the general advantages of integrated CSR, this type of integration is probably most crucial to make Chinese business socially responsible: as MNCs focus ever more on brand marketing and sales, whilst outsourcing the actual manufacturing of their products to Chinese suppliers.[81]

---

74 *Ibid.*, p. 7.

75 *Ibid.*, pp. 8-13.

76 Wu, *op. cit.*, p. 5.

77 Aguilera & Williams, *op. cit.*, p. 460.

78 Hofstede, *op. cit.*, p. 211.

79 Anita Chan, 'Recent Trends in Chinese Labour Issues: Signs of Change,' *China Perspectives*, January-February 2005, No. 57, retrieved on 14 July 2009, http://chinaperspectives.revues.org/document1115.html.

80 Rosoff, *op. cit.*, pp. 7-8.

81 Naomi Klein, *No Logo*, New York, Picardor, 2002.

The importance can be underlined by the 2007 Mattel-scandal. Not only were labour standards not complied with in the Chinese manufacturing companies – the US-based toy producer also had to recall millions of products because its subcontractors used lead paint and magnets that children could inadvertently intoxicate themselves with – both of which are life-threatening.[82] One of the reasons for the low quality toys was the pressure to keep production costs low. Mattel initially blamed its contractors for the defect toys.[83] It had a CSR-policy for its own company – however, it did not integrate its suppliers in this policy. Moreover, Mattel intensified price pressures, by keeping a purely short-term price-based relationship with its toy manufacturers instead of developing longer-term relational ties.[84] Consequently, Mattel eventually damaged its own reputation.[85] Although there are still relatively few Chinese multinationals, their numbers are rapidly increasing so that they need to learn from such incidents.[86]

To tackle the unawareness of Chinese workers about their rights at work, Adidas adopted a simple but effective integrative policy. The company summarised the main labour law provisions on posters and hung them up in the plants.[87] Arcandor (formerly Europe's biggest mail order and department store corporation),[88] has been widely promoting integrated CSR, by participating in an initiative for a sector-wide adoption of CSR-codes for its Chinese operations.[89]

Although some scholars have already confirmed the positive influence of this European-style integrated approach on Chinese business,[90] it needs to be recalled that a "one size fits all" approach is

---

82 Geoff Dyer & Tom Mitchell, 'A Boost for China's Product Safety,' *Financial Times Online*, 9 April 2007, retrieved on 7 July 2008, http://www.ft.com/cms/s/0/fbb851da-5b13-11dc-8c32-0000779fd2ac.html?nclick_check=1.

83 *Ibid.*

84 Gary Gereffi *et al.*, 'The Governance of Global Value Chains,' *Review of International Political Economy*, Vol. 12, No. 1, 2005, pp. 83-84.

85 Dyer & Mitchell, *loc. cit.*

86 Andrea Goldstein & Fazia Pusterla, '"Emerging Economies" Multinationals: General Features and Specificities of the Brazilian and Chinese Cases,' *Centre for Research on Innovation and Internationalisation (CESPRI) Working Paper*, No. 223, 2008, retrieved on 4 March 2009, http://ftp.unibocconi.it/pub/RePEc/cri/papers/WP223GoldsteinPusterla.pdf.

87 *Ibid.*, pp. 8-9.

88 Arcandor filed for bankruptcy in June 2009; see Carter Dougherty, 'German Retail Group Arcandor Files for Bankruptcy,' *New York Times Online*, retrieved on 14 July 2009, http://www.nytimes.com/2009/06/10/business/10arcandor.html.

89 Maren Böhm, 'Lieferantenauditierung und Runde Tische in China,' in I. Schönheit *et al.*, *op. cit.*, pp. 70-74.

90 Rosoff, *op. cit.*, pp. 8-9.

unlikely to completely fit, because "what is right in Europe may not be right in China."[91] This becomes evident when examining the third pillar of the European CSR-model: the voluntary character. Franklin explains that the many business-based codes adopted by and for Chinese companies often simply repeat what Chinese labour law already prescribes.[92] If one strictly applies the EU-definition of CSR, namely that it should be something voluntary on top of the law, the Chinese codes would therefore be currently undeserving of being granted the CSR-label.

There are even greater concerns about the fact that critics from the Chinese side perceive CSR as an external, foreign concept that is imposed by the West.[93] For many Chinese companies, CSR-strategies are a regulatory burden that keeps them from lowering costs. In this spirit, CSR in China has been dubbed to be a sort of "corporate policemen responsibility."[94] In fact, many Chinese companies supplying Western MNCs with manufactured goods try to avoid their buyers' CSR-codes, for instance, by not informing their employees respectively, or by drilling their workers to give "the right answers" to CSR-inspectors that perform audits.[95] Thus, until now, few Chinese entrepreneurs have implemented CSR-strategies on a voluntary basis.

The reluctance to comply with CSR-standards may also stem from the extraordinary "short-term profit orientation," that the Chinese economic boom has created. This orientation, which is intensified by Western buyers themselves (see the Mattel-case), makes Chinese business actors ignore or at least devalue the long-term benefits of CSR more than it is generally the case for outsider entrepreneurs, who are naturally interested in short-term profitability. Others argue that the unwillingness has to do with a lack of Chinese stakeholder-involvement: if they were better integrated in the process of formulating codes of conduct, these codes would be much more readily accepted.[96] This makes clear that the three characteristics of the European CSR-model would need to be implemented simultaneously in order to achieve effective CSR-strategies in China.

---

91 Franklin, *op. cit.*, p. 8.

92 *Ibid.*, p. 18.

93 Piepel, *op. cit.*, p. 88.

94 Mabel Wong, 'What Difference Does CSR Make to Development,' *United Nations Research Institute for Social Development (UNRISD): Corporate Social Responsibility and Development – Towards a New Agenda?*, 17-18 November 2003, Geneva, pp. 18-21, as cited in K. Piepel, *loc. cit.*

95 Rosoff, *loc. cit.*

96 Böhm, *loc. cit.*

Although several authors have observed that China is starting to challenge Western CSR-standards,[97] Chinese companies nevertheless signalled the "will to learn [in particular] from European business."[98] Evidence shows that especially concerning CSR's voluntary character, Chinese business could learn from its European counterpart: in a global comparison, CSR-reporting is most common in European companies.[99] Furthermore, whereas in the US only 3% of these reports are externally verified, 45% are verified in Europe.[100]

Overall, there is potential for Chinese business actors to take European companies as CSR-models. The inherent stakeholder-focus together with the integrated and voluntary character constitutes a formula that would help establish effective CSR-policies in China. However, one must remain cautious about fundamental institutional differences that exist in terms of dependent unions, the lack of law-enforcement or the perception of CSR promoted by the West. Let us now turn to governmental initiatives for CSR and test whether Europe can serve as a model here.

Learning from European Governments

As mentioned in the theoretical part, purely business-based CSR-codes do not constitute a sufficient "respon[se] to social demands."[101] For CSR not to become an arbitrary practice, governments adopt policies to streamline it. To be sure, the call for more government intervention in the CSR-debate must become louder, especially for developing countries and countries in transition.[102]

One must, however, admit that China's economic power makes Western governments ignorant of "corporate irresponsibility" in the Middle Kingdom, more than in others.[103] The EU has, for example, recently "suspended its trade preferences with Belarus" due to the country's non-compliance with the international labour standard of freedom of association. After Burma/Myanmar, Belarus is the only

97 Anita Chan, 'China Says No to Developed Countries' Corporate Social Responsibility,' *Asian Analysis*, February 2005, retrieved on 14 July 2009, http://www.aseanfocus.com/asiananalysis/article.cfm?articleID=816; Franklin, *op. cit.*, p. 20.

98 EUCTP, *op. cit.*

99 Aguilera & Williams, *op. cit.*, p. 465.

100 Ans Kolk, 'Sustainability, Accountability and Corporate Governance: Exploring Multinationals' Reporting Practices,' *Business Strategy and the Environment*, Vol. 17, No. 1, 2006, pp. 1-15, as cited in Aguilera & Williams, *op. cit.*, p. 466.

101 Cuesta González & Valor Martinez, *op. cit.*, p. 279.

102 *Ibid.*, pp. 275-278; Rosoff, *loc. cit.*

103 Aguilera & Williams, *op. cit.*, p. 455.

country ever to face this sanction.[104] China, by contrast, has not been punished – and is unlikely to be punished in the future since its economic might is unlikely to dwindle. Keeping in mind that governments make strategic decisions, politicians in Brussels and in the EU member states nevertheless try to encourage CSR within and outside Europe, including China.[105] Again, it will be tested if this European governmental initiative has a model-character for China by applying the triple European CSR-formula.

Beginning with the inherent stakeholder-focus, the EU bases its CSR-policy on so-called multi-stakeholder forums.[106] The system is less a naming-and-shaming one and more of a positive incentive system. Thus, socially responsible companies get EU-loans more easily than others.[107] Taking into consideration the aforementioned problem that Chinese companies often perceive CSR as something imposed by the West for which they are punished if they do not comply, such a positive incentive-system might be more fruitful in China. It is conceivable to include a reference to such "best-practices" in the PCA.

Another big theme of European governmental CSR-policies is transparency towards stakeholders.[108] An important transparency-related issue is that most CSR-reports from firms and manufacturers are not translated into Mandarin.[109] Here, the Communist Party could take the EU's tradition to translate all official documents into the language of each member state as a model, and oblige companies to make their CSR-reports available in Mandarin. It is generally problematic that many MNCs operating in China try to keep secret the information concerning their supply chains, and consequently also about their labour standards.[110] French companies could serve as an example here since they are most advanced in terms of CSR-reporting.[111] A Belgian law to forbid misleading advertisement on labour conditions in companies is also a good way to address transparency for their Chinese counterparts.[112] A third way to ensure stakeholder-involvement is through the creation of

---

104 'EU Penalises Belarus Over Labour Rights,' *Ergon: Focus on Labour*, Promoting Labour Rights and Governance, 2007, No. 9, p. 10.

105 Cuesta González & Valor Martinez, *op. cit.*, as cited in Aguilera & Williams, *op. cit.*, p. 456; EUCTP, *op. cit.*

106 Cuesta González & Valor Martinez, *op. cit.*, p. 285.

107 *Ibid.*

108 *Ibid.*, pp. 282-283.

109 Leong & Kawai, *op. cit.*

110 GLS, *op. cit.*, p. 20.

111 Cuesta González & Valor Martinez, *op. cit.*, p. 284.

112 *Ibid.*, p. 282.

"governmental labels" for firms based in China, as initiated by the Austrian government.[113] The list of European government-initiatives that would be useful to involve Chinese stakeholders in the CSR-debate could be further extended. But how realistic is it to believe in the Chinese government becoming more proactive in terms of stakeholder-focus?

After the opening of (ex)-communist countries to the world market, is not only known in China, but also in the Central and Eastern European countries (CEEC) that stakeholders in decision-making processes were neglected. In contrast to the CEEC, China has only opened up in economic terms but less so politically and there is so far little leverage for independent stakeholder institutions, such as unions, to enter policy-making negotiations. Despite this fundamental limitation, an important step towards stakeholder orientation was China's latest Five-Year Programme which stresses the need for a "people-centred and environment-friendly approach to development."[114] On a practical level, the Chinese government has taken initiatives to change, for instance, the adverse situation of migrant workers caused by the *hukou* system. The special economic area of Shenzhen, for example, now grants, to the twelve million migrant workers, official residential status.[115]

The implementation of these objectives is, however, far from perfect.[116] Twelve million represents only a small fraction of the overall 150 million migrant workers.[117] Moreover, CSR-activists in China have pointed out that the new residential cards in Shenzhen do not entitle migrant workers to unemployment benefits or "political rights within the local community."[118] Even the most basic labour standards, such as social security coverage or timely payment for employees seem utopian, given that 80% of private sector workers do not have employment contracts.[119] In Europe, such standards would not be part of a CSR-strategy but simply a legislative obligation for companies. This again underlines the character of CSR not being a surrogate for legally stipulated labour standards, which would force the privatisation of labour standards. Overall,

---

113 *Ibid.*

114 EUCTP, *op. cit.*

115 Hong Chen, 'Working Toward a Better Life in the City,' *China Daily*, 1 August 2008, p. 8.

116 EuropeAid, *CSR Challenges in China*, EuropeAid Co-operation Office Asia Invest, 2006, retrieved on 16 April 2008, http://www.csreuchina.cn/documents/CSR%20challenges%20in%20China.pdf, p. 5.

117 Piepel, *op. cit.*, p. 83.

118 Chen, *loc. cit.*

119 EuropeAid, *loc. cit.*

European policy-examples are potentially useful, but their full implementation method is time-consuming.

Turning to the integrated nature of the European CSR-model, one can say that European governments make efforts to integrate CSR across national borders, across different types of firms and across policies. In terms of cross-national integration, the EU "encourages consistency between national approaches."[120] This consistency primarily refers to the EU member states, but beyond that, the EU also involves China in this approach. Through the EU-China Trade Project (EUCTP), it attempts to promote CSR specifically in the framework of its close trade ties with the Middle Kingdom.[121] An example was the EU-China CSR symposium on 12 July 2006, where senior officials from both regions met in Beijing to lay the political basis for technical cooperation activities on CSR.[122] This project is only one of over a hundred in the "EU's [€200 million] co-operation portfolio in China [...] covering social and economic reform, sustainable development and good governance."[123]

Next to such direct support, Europe can serve as a model to integrate CSR across firms, such as by supporting enterprise-networks.[124] This approach is especially important for small and medium-size enterprises (SMEs). It has previously been explained that there is a strong business case for multinational companies to behave in a socially responsible way in order to keep up their reputation and sales. By contrast, for SMEs, "economic survival is [usually] more important than reputation."[125] This is particularly valid for Chinese SMEs, whose biggest competitive advantage is low labour costs and not (yet) a positive brand image.

This problem, although not so much in relation to cheap labour, also exists in Europe. Since the biggest part of European economic strength is based on SMEs, the EU concentrates its CSR-promotion on integrating these types of companies in its CSR-campaigns.[126] A good example of a respective national policy comes from Italy. Here, the regional government of Tuscany took over a part of the costs for SMEs that wanted the

---

120 Spidla, *loc. cit.*

121 EUCTP, 'Introduction,' *EU-China Trade Project*, 2008, retrieved on 2 July 2008, http://www.euchinawto.org/index.php?option=com_content&task=view&id=12&Itemid=26.

122 EUCTP, 2006, *op. cit.*

123 EUCTP, 2008, *loc. cit.*

124 Spidla, *loc. cit.*

125 Burkhard Remmers, 'CSR – ein Mehrwert in China? Chancen und Risiken Eines Mittelständischen Engagements auf dem Chinesischen Markt,' in I. Schönheit *et al.*, *op. cit.*, pp. 62-63.

126 He, *op. cit.*, p. 29.

CSR-standard SA8000 certification.[127] A similar approach in China would help to truly induce all types of firms in China in behaving in a socially responsibly way, not just the large multinational players.

Finally, the EU also aims at integrating CSR across different policies.[128] To genuinely enforce CSR, the EU needs to include it not only in its policy towards enterprises and industry, but also towards environmental, social and employment policy, and even encourages teaching it in the member states' education systems to make sure that (future) managers receive appropriate training to implement CSR.[129] So far, the Chinese government seems to be open to this approach and has issued legislation referring to CSR.[130] However, it must be kept in mind that EU-policies need to be adapted to the Chinese context.[131] This becomes particularly clear when examining the third characteristic of the European CSR-model – its voluntary nature.

As analysed before, the EU prefers market-compatible CSR-strategies that go beyond simply relying on legally enforced instruments. This is mainly due to the EU's highly-regulated environmental and social models.[132] Despite the rhetoric of voluntary CSR-practices, CSR gets a more obligatory character in some EU member states. Since 2006, British companies for instance have had to report on environmental and social issues.[133] In this sense, the Chinese government, which has acted according to the motto "let it [i.e. economic growth] happen, develop rules later" seems to be the more genuine supporter of voluntarism compared to Europe.[134] However, such a statement is only valid if one ignores the fact that even the basic rules, in terms of social responsibility, are rarely implemented in China.

In other words, the country is still far from being as regulated in practice as European countries.[135] In light of a weak regulatory environment, it is therefore a logical consequence that CSR in China is of a lower, less ambitious standard than in a highly regulated environment.

---

127 Cuesta González & Valor Martinez, *op. cit.*, p. 283.

128 Commission of the European Communities, *Communication from the Commission: Implementing the Partnership for Growth and Jobs: Making Europe a Pole of Excellence on Corporate Social Responsibility*, COM(2006) 136 final, Brussels, 22 March 2006, p. 13.

129 *Ibid.*, p. 12.

130 EUCTP 2006, *op. cit.*, p. 25.

131 *Ibid.*, p. 88.

132 Aguilera & Williams, *loc. cit.*

133 Franklin, *op. cit.*, p. 3.

134 Young, *op. cit.*, p. 23.

135 *Ibid.*, p. 14.

From Franklin's viewpoint, such codes might be of thin content.[136] However, considering the lack of legal implementation in China, it is already a step in the right direction.

Taking into account the risks of CSR as a surrogate for employment legislation, what China really needs at the moment is less a voluntary governmental approach and more a properly enforced legal framework, to create the basis for CSR. This is true if we look at institutional theory: laws trigger "social expectations about responsible corporate behaviour."[137] On that basis, the various stakeholders will create incentives for business to comply with the law.[138] In consequence, if the Chinese government properly adopts and enforces social and employment law, the foundation for (European-style) CSR would be laid. For the PCA negotiations, CSR therefore needs to be linked to general efforts of strengthening the rule of law in China.

Interestingly, the Chinese government moulded its newest labour law on European employment legislation in order to "assist companies in improving working conditions."[139] Furthermore, the sustainability standards issued by the Chinese government are similar or even equal to those issued in Europe.[140] One must remain cautious about these developments, since they might exist on paper, but not (yet) in practice. Institutional theory predicts that organisations become "isomorphic" if they operate in a similar environment.[141] Put differently, since the legal frameworks have become more congruent, Chinese companies could become similar to their European counterparts.

In sum, this section has shown that European governmental initiatives for CSR have the potential to improve labour standards in China in terms of both stakeholder-focus and integrated character. Concerning European CSR's voluntary character, the Chinese government has yet to start with the basics, namely a properly enforced labour law. However, since it already copies European employment legislation, the probability that the Chinese government can learn from European CSR-approaches also increases. In this way, there is more reason to refer to the European model of CSR in the PCA.

---

136 Franklin, *loc. cit.*, pp. 1-24.

137 Franklin, *loc. cit.*

138 Kagan *et al.*, 'Explaining Corporate Environmental Performance: How Does Regulation Matter?,' *Law and Society Review*, Vol. 37, pp. 51-90, as cited in Aguilera & Williams, *loc. cit.*

139 GLS, *op. cit.*, p. 6; ChinaCSR.com, *loc. cit.*

140 EuropeAid, *op. cit.*, p. 2.

141 Doh & Guay, *op. cit.*, p. 49.

Conclusion

In order to realise sustainable development in economic and social terms, a global race to the bottom in terms of labour standards must be avoided. Due to its size and increasing economic and political influence, China merits special concern in this matter, and labour standards therefore need to be treated in the current PCA negotiations between China and the EU. In order to do so, attention has been drawn to a relatively new tool called CSR. As CSR is quite developed within the EU, the focus of this chapter was to determine whether the European model of CSR can be applied in China in order to improve labour standards and in this sense contribute to a sustainable development of the Chinese economy.

Based on this main research question, the chapter has sketched a European model of CSR consisting of three stylised characteristics: being inherently stakeholder-focused, integrated and voluntary. Taking the perspectives of two key actors in the CSR-debate, namely business and government, it has been systematically examined whether the three main characteristics of the European CSR-model could be applied in the Chinese context. As a result, a potential European CSR-model has been revealed, to help improve labour standards in China. However, China and Europe are very different in many respects that are decisive for CSR, such as the stage of economic development and the political system. These limitations do not entirely hinder China from learning from European-style CSR. However, the road to realise CSR will be a long one.

A final point worth emphasising for the PCA is that the Chinese government modelled its recently reformed labour law on European employment legislation. This indicates that a learning process is taking course. At least according to institutional theory, China would therefore be more likely to adopt a similar CSR-path. In order to confirm this supposition, the author highly encourages empirical research. At the end of the day, CSR and sustainable development are long-term issues requiring long-term observation.

CHAPTER 4

EU-China Trade and the Future PCA

Intellectual Property Rights and Investments

Antoine SAUTENET

This paper aims to evaluate the content and implementation of the future PCA for EU-China trade. In the absence of a category of "emerging countries" in international economic law, the EU must adapt its foreign policy with regard to this major economic and commercial power. A new dynamic has been set in motion since 2003, with the drawing-up of preparatory documents by both parties and joint declarations at annual summits bearing on the "strategic partnership." The frequent development of bilateral relations has allowed the EU and China to envisage the conclusion of a new framework agreement: this is the origin of the mandate given to the Commission in December 2005 to conclude a partnership and cooperation agreement. With regard to the PCA negotiations, the EU must integrate elements of added-value into the next agreement with China, in order to prevent commercial tensions arising from the WTO and to guarantee Community operators a better presence on the Chinese market. In regards to China's legal environment, Investments and Intellectual Property Rights (IPRs) should be known as the "WTO plus" fields, and inserted into the future agreement, which would then involve a mixed agreement. Given the EU's ambitions, the negotiations run the risk of being fragile at the commercial level.

EU-China Relations in the Context of China's "Re-emergence"

The "EU-China global partnership"[1] was set up during the 10th summit (2007). But the negotiations between the two partners are, in concrete terms, difficult, especially because of the EU's trade deficit with China. Beijing postponed the EU-China Summit due to be scheduled in Lyons, France, in December 2009, due to its displeasure over the Dalai Lama's

---

1 Council of the European Union, Joint Statement, *10th EU-China Summit*, Beijing, 28 November 2007, retrieved on 20 March 2009, http://www.consilium.europa.eu/ueDocs/ cms_Data/docs/pressData/en/er/97355.pdf.

visits to several European countries, including a meeting with French President Nicolas Sarkozy in Poland, and a speech given to the European Parliament (EP) in Brussels. Finally, the 11th EU-China Summit was held in Prague on 20 May 2009,[2] but was very disappointing. As the two sides failed to bridge their differences on a number of contentious issues, including Myanmar, North Korea, Taiwan, climate change and trade liberalisation, China's Prime Minister Wen Jiabao called on the EU to expand "practical cooperation."

Today, the main problem for the EU is the necessity to adapt its policy to a partner who has two faces: a developing country but also a developed country. Father Jean-Baptiste du Halde, whose encyclopaedia on China was to influence Voltaire's favourable comments, noted in 1735 that the trade of the flourishing Chinese Empire was incomparably superior to that of Europe.[3] Seen from a long-term perspective, China is on track to renew its pre-colonial history, and gradually regain the place it held before 1800, when it was one of the powerhouses of the world economy and the first manufacturing power on the planet.[4] In fact, we see not so much an "emergence" of China as a first-rank economic player on the international scene, but rather a "*retour au centre du monde*"[5] in the words of the geographer Pierre Gentelle.

The Economic "Re-emergence" of China

Actually, the process of economic liberalisation and political reform, started in 1978 by Deng Xiaoping and which paved the way for China's accession to the WTO in 2001,[6] has led to the "re-emergence" of China as a major economic and commercial power. Thus, the People's Republic of China (PRC) experienced an average growth of almost 9.5% in the period 1980-2005,[7] becoming in 2006 the fourth economic power after the EU

---

2 Council of the European Union, Joint Press Communique, *11th EU-China Summit*, Prague, 20 May 2009, retrieved on 20 May 2009, http://europa.eu/rapid/pressReleasesAction.do?reference=PRES/09/147&format=HTML&aged=0&language=EN&guiLanguage=en.

3 Jean Baptiste Du Halde, *Description Géographique, Historique, Chronologique, Politique et Physique de l'Empire de la Chine*, Paris, Bibiliothèque Nationale Française, 1735.

4 In 1800, China represented 40% of the world's gross national product (GNP).

5 'Return to the Centre of the World,' Pierre Gentelle, and 'Géo-Histoire: de l'An Mil à l'An 2000, un Centre Bousculé entre le Continent et la Mer,' in Michel Foucher (ed.), *Asies Nouvelles*, Paris, Belin, 2002.

6 World Trade Organization, *Protocol on the Accession of the People's Republic of China to the WTO*, Decision of 10 November 2001, WT/L/432, 11 December 2001.

7 Organization for Economic Cooperation and Development (OECD), *Synthesis: Economic Study of China*, Paris, September 2005.

(seen as an integrated economic region), the USA and Japan.[8] Thanks to these reforms and to the growth which they generated, China saw its gross domestic product (GDP) per person grow from $148 to $1,700 between 1978 and 2005,[9] which, despite increasing social disparities, particularly in the countryside,[10] led to the emergence of a middle class of around 105 million consumers.[11] This growth in power has been, of late, particularly evident, since real GDP has grown by 9% *per annum* between 1998 and 2005 and more than 11% in 2006 and 2007.[12] Since 2001, this growth has rested essentially on manufacturing and comercial power integrated into the world trading system, and is founded principally upon exports and investments. Thus, China has become the third largest global exporter[13] and one of the principal destinations for FDI, a large part of which goes into the manufacturing industry, centred on exports.[14] China's rapid growth is linked to a unique combination of factors, notably a plentiful supply of cheap labour, the low prices of abundant natural resources, the catalyst effect of accession to the WTO

---

8 Horst Siebert, 'China, Understanding a New Global Economic Player,' *Kiel Working Paper*, Kiel Institute for World Economics, No. 1278, 2006, p. 3. China represents 4.7% of global GNP, with a GNP of $2.2 tn.

9 National Bureau of Statistics of China (NBSC), *Key Advancements of the First National Economic Census with New Changes of China's GDP Aggregates and its Structure*, Beijing, 2005 (b), retrieved on 20 March 2009, http://www.stats.gov.cn/ english/ newsandcomingevents/t20051220_402297118.htm. Nevertheless, according to the authorities, the GNP per person was still ranked 107th in the world in 2004. See 'China Remains Largest Developing Country,' 20 December 2005, retrieved on 20 March 2009, http://english.gov.cn/2005-12/20/ content_132456.htm.

10 The inequalities are in fact "deepened in that the distribution of revenue and jobs tends to favor urban and coastal zones at the expense of the rural and less developed regions." See WTO, Report of the Secretariat, *Trade Policy Review – People's Republic of China*, Economic Environment, General Survey, WT/TPR/S/161, 28 February 2006, point 1.

11 See the evaluation of the French Mission to China, which uses the official statistics taking into account the under-declaration of incomes (30% correction) and uses a specific criterion (an annual income of more than 25,000 RMB), Mission Économique de la France en Chine, *La Classe Moyenne Chinoise: Évaluation et Perspectives,* December 2006, retrieved on 20 March 2009, http://www.missioneco.org/Chine/ documents_new.asp?V=1_PDF_127738.

12 World Bank, *China Economic Indicators – Current*, Washington, 3 July 2008, retrieved on 20 March 2009, http://siteresources.worldbank.org/CHINAEXTN/ Resources/chinaei.pdf.

13 The second largest global exporter if one includes Hong Kong. In 2005, the total amount of exported and imported goods represented some 63.9% of GNP, compared to less than 10% in 1978.

14 More than 50% of China's external trade is conducted by enterprises with foreign participation which have set up businesses in China. See General Administration of Customs of the PRC, *Statistics 2005*, http://www.customs.gov.cn.

on domestic reforms concerning direct investment abroad, and export-centred growth. Trade between the EU and China has grown by 70%, reaching €210 bn and representing 9.4% of the EU's entire external trade.[15] Nonetheless, trade between the EU and China is substantially out of balance: Europe's trade deficit in 2008 was €168 bn.[16]

In addition, China is Europe's fastest growing export market. Europe exported €72 bn worth of goods to China in 2007. Exports from the EU to China grew by 75% between 2003 and 2007. Despite the fact that a large consumer market is developing in China, the EU still exports more to the 7.5 million people who live in Switzerland than to the 1.3 bn people who live in China. It is estimated that barriers to trade in China cost EU businesses a significant amount in lost trade opportunities every year (it represents almost one third of current EU exports to China). IPR theft remains a huge problem for European businesses in China. Almost 60% of all counterfeit goods seized at European borders in 2006 originated from China. The Chinese claim that they have been the victims of IPR violations. In 2007, European manufacturers estimated that IPR theft cost them 20% of their potential revenues in China. China is the biggest target of trade defence investigations in the EU. The EU currently has 45 definitive and 3 provisional anti-dumping measures in force against Chinese imports. These cover less than 2% of Chinese trade. European companies invested €1.8 bn in China in 2007 (down from €6.2 bn in 2006). China invested €2.2 bn in Europe in 2006 and withdrew investments worth approximately €0.1 bn in Europe in 2005. European services companies find it very difficult to break into the Chinese market and are often discriminated against. Although China has signed agreements to open its market, since 2001 it has granted 22,000 telecoms licenses in China, only eleven of which have gone to foreign companies. China maintains investment and ownership caps in many sectors such as banking, construction and telecommunications. Foreign law firms in China are not allowed to employ Chinese lawyers and are not permitted to participate in bar exams to gain Chinese qualifications.

Taking all of this into consideration, including at the political and social levels, China remains a developing country,[17] although it can to a

---

15 China was thus the EU's second largest trading partner, after the US (18.5% of the Union's external trade).

16 Commission of the European Communities, *EU-China Trade in Facts and Figures*, 25 May 2009, retrieved on 20 June 2009, http://trade.ec.europa.eu/doclib/docs/2009/january/tradoc_142202.pdf.

17 The Human Development Indicator (HDI) is telling in this regard, since China remains 85th in the world with a HDI of 0.755 (above the HDI average of 0.718). See United Nations Development Programme (UNDP), *World Report on Human Development 2005*, Economica, 2005, p. 236.

large extent be considered as falling under the category of "emerging countries" in economic terms. However, this category does not exist in international economic law, which constitutes a fairness problem between developing countries. This is particularly true at the level of international trade negotiations and in the legal and economic treatment that is reserved for the PRC,[18] but also of all the new leading powers (NLPs) or "BRIC countries," by the industrialised countries.

The New EU Global Policy Regarding China

The EU-China Legal Framework

The EU must equip itself with a solid foreign policy with regard to the PRC, which is adapted to the economic characteristics of its partner. The economic and trading relations between the European Community and China are currently governed by an agreement for economic and commercial cooperation dating back to 1985:[19] a non-preferential agreement of the kind known as "second generation" concluded on the basis of ex-Article 113 of the EEC Treaty (Common Commercial Policy) and of Article 235 of the same treaty (subsidiary competences). The political dialogue takes place informally, on the basis of annual summits, meetings on the troika model,[20] and subject-specific meetings of experts, notably on the topics of non-proliferation and human rights. Apart from the 1985 agreement, the legal framework of relations is completed by a certain number of sector-based agreements. With regard to China's specific characteristics (both a developed and a developing country), China is also a subject of the EU's "Development Policy," in its unilateral aspect. Even if the "Canada" clause[21] allowed contracting parties to enrich the material

[18] The categorisation of developing countries poses a problem, insofar as a certain number of rights are attached to this status by international organisations: systems of aid and international cooperation (OECD, World Bank), application of specific provisions to developing countries in the General Agreement on Tariffs and Trade (GATT) texts, delays on implementation, application of special and differentiated treatment (WTO).

[19] Council of the European Union, *Agreement on Trade and Economic Cooperation between the European Economic Community and the People's Republic of China*, 21 May 1985, OJ L 250/2 (1985).

[20] The troika is the form in which the EU is represented in terms of the Common Foreign and Security Policy (CFSP). According to Article 18(4) of the Treaty on European Union (TEU), "the Commission shall be fully associated in the tasks referred to in paragraphs 1 and 2. The Presidency shall be assisted in those tasks if need be by the next Member State to hold the Presidency."

[21] In terms of what is known (due to its origin) as a "Canada" clause, the member states can, in parallel with the Community, conduct bilateral activities, including the ability to conclude their own cooperation agreements. This possibility, which must not however impinge upon Community competences and requires a consultation

content of their relations, the conventional framework no longer seems adapted to the ambitions of the Community and China in the absence of an "upgrade" clause.[22]

The EU-China "Strategic Partnership"

Consequently, the European Commission drew up in 1995 – signalling the return to political dialogue after the events in Tiananmen Square, which had led to the suspension of bilateral contacts – an orientation document on the "long-term policy for relations between China and Europe"[23] in line with the Asia strategy approved by the European Council at Essen,[24] which takes into account the emergence of China as an economic and political power. The Community strategy has since been regularly updated and re-evaluated in 1998, 2000, 2001, 2003 and in 2006,[25] leading to an evolution of the semantic terms used by the Community: from a "global partnership" in 1998 to a "mature partnership" in 2003, the characterisation of this partnership has been endowed with a strategic dimension. After the attempt to elaborate an

---

procedure to be respected (Decision No. 74/393/EEC of 22 July 1974, OJ L 208, p. 23), reflects a realistic approach and stems from the principle of subsidiarity.

22 The "upgrade clause" stipulates that the parties are able to examine the extension of the agreement to fields which are not included into the agreement.

23 Commission of the European Communities, *Communication from the Commission: a Long-Term Policy for Relations with China*, COM(1995) 279 final, Brussels, 5 June 1995.

24 Commission of the European Communities, *Communication from the Commission to the Council: Towards a New Asiatic Strategy*, COM(1994) 314 final, Brussels, 13 July 1994.

25 Respectively: Commission of the European Communities, *Communication from the Commission: Building a Comprehensive Partnership with China*, COM(1998) 181, Brussels, 25 March 1998; *Report of the Commission to the Council and to the European Parliament on the Implementation of the Communication: Towards a Global Partnership with China*, COM(2000) 552 final, Brussels, 8 September 2000; *Communication from the Commission to the Council and the European Parliament: Strategy of the EU vis-à-vis China: Implementation of the 1998 Communication and Measures to Take to Strengthen Community Policy*, COM(2001) 265 final, Brussels, 15 May 2001; *Orientation Document from the Commission to forward to the Council and to the European Parliament: Common Interests and Challenges of the EU-China Relationship, Towards a Mature Partnership*, COM(2003) 533 final, Brussels, 10 September 2003; in 2006, two orientation documents were published: a political one fixing the global framework, and the second document, on trade and investments questions. *Communication from the Commission to the Council and the European Parliament: EU-China: Closer Partners, Growing Responsibilities*, COM(2006) 631 final, Brussels, 24 October 2006, and *Strategic Document on EU-China Trade and Investments: Competition and Partnership*, COM(2006) 632 final, Brussels, 24 October 2006.

Asia strategy[26] and the implementation of "strategic partnerships" with the other countries or emerging regional groupings of Asia,[27] India[28] and South-East Asia,[29] the 2003 Communication insists for the first time on the fact that "the EU and China have never had so much common interest to collaborate in the framework of a strategic partnership to maintain and encourage sustainable development, peace and stability."[30] Seen from a long-term perspective, this "strategic partnership" helps provide a measure of predictability in relations between the two partners, through combining elements of "soft law"[31] and "hard law." Close legal analysis shows that the "strategic partnership" has developed simultaneously as a *para-legal instrument* which adds dynamism to economic dialogues, which assists the conclusion of sectoral agreements and the integration of the political dimension, and also as a *pre-legal instrument* which allows one to envisage the conclusion of a new framework agreement – an element of hard law indispensable to the reality of the challenges posed by the EU-China relationship that implies difficult negotiations.[32]

---

26 Commission of the European Communities, *Communication from the Commission: A Strategic Framework to Strengthen the Europe-Asia Partnership*, COM(2001) 469 final, Brussels, 4 November 2001. See Catherine Flaesch-Mougin *et al.*, 'Relations de la Communauté Européenne avec les Pays d'Amérique Latine et d'Asie (ALA), Cadres Conventionnel et Autonome,' *Jurisclasseur Europe*, fasc. 2231, 2005.

27 But also with other new leading powers (Russia, Brazil, Mexico), see Joël Lebullenger, 'Relations UE-Amérique Latine – 2007: Chronique d'Actualité,' *Annuaire de Droit Européen*, Vol. V, Bruylant, 2009; Rafael Leal-Arcas, 'The European Union and New Leading Powers: Towards Partnership in Strategic Trade Policy Areas,' *Fordham International Law Journal*, Vol. 32, January 2009; and Antoine Sautenet, 'La Dynamique Juridique du Partenariat Stratégique,' *Revue Économique et Sociale*, Vol. 67, No. 1, 2009, pp. 107-124.

28 Commission of the European Communities, *Communication from the Commission to the Council, to the European Parliament and to the European Economic and Social Committee: An EU-India Strategic Partnership*, COM(2004) 430 final, Brussels, 16 June 2004.

29 Commission of the European Communities, *Communication from the Commission: A New Partnership with South-East Asia*, COM(2003) 399 final, Brussels, 9 July 2003. It should be noted that this communication does not talk about a "strategic partnership," but includes references to a "strategic dialogue" between the EU and the Association of South East Asian Nations (ASEAN).

30 Commission of the European Communities, Communication from the Commission: A New Partnership with South-East Asia, COM(2003) 399 final, *op. cit.*, p. 3.

31 See Francis Snyder, 'Soft Law and Institutional Practice in the European Community,' *The Construction of Europe – Essays in Honor of Emile Noël*, La Haye, Kluwer Academic Publishers, 1994, pp. 197-227.

32 See Antoine Sautenet, 'Europe and China: a Cooperation with Complex Legal Dimensions,' *Asie Visions*, Paris, Institut Français des Relations Internationales (IFRI), No. 3, March 2008, retrieved on 20 March 2009, http://www.ifri.org/frontDispatcher/

It was during the 7th Summit that the will to negotiate a new framework agreement manifested itself: "the two parties declare that the uninterrupted development of relations between the EU and China in recent years leads them to actively study the feasibility of a new EU-China framework agreement."[33] The partners then decided to "begin negotiations on a new framework agreement [...] which will fully reflect the intensity of the strategic partnership between China and the EU"[34] at the 8th Summit. A mandate of negotiation directives was adopted by the Council on 12 December 2005 on a "Project of agreement of partnership and co-operation (PCA) between the European Union and China."[35] This qualification refers to the typology of agreements concluded between the European Community and its member states and certain East European and Central Asian countries, principally the Russian Federation.[36] The qualification is without prejudice to the nature of the act in question, as the legal basis is often defined at the end of the negotiations.

The Balance of the PCA Negotiations

Actually, the negotiations are not working in the EU's favour. In accordance with the requirement of coherence, the EU will opt for a horizontal approach, that is to say a single agreement encompassing both the commercial and political dimensions of the relations. At the political level, the issue of the inclusion, in the new framework agreement, of a clause establishing the existence of a democratic regime as a condition has been raised. The human rights clause is considered an "essential element"[37] clause, which must, *a priori*, be integrated in all types of agreement.[38] Nonetheless, with regard to China's reservations and

---

ifri/publications/asie_visions_1185271858409/publi_P_publi_asievision__1204823178846.

33 Council of the European Union, Joint Statement, Point 5, *7th EU-China Summit* La Haye, 8 December 2004.

34 Council of the European Union, Joint Statement, Point 6, *8th EU-China Summit*, Brussels, 5 September 2005.

35 EU Bulletin, 12/2005, point 1.6.71.

36 European Community, *Partnership and Cooperation Agreement Establishing a Partnership between the European Communities and their Member States on One Hand and the Russian Federation on the Other*, 1997, OJ L 327, p. 1.

37 An "essential clause" (or clause as an essential element of the agreement) allows the EU to suspend, in whole or in part, the agreement in the conditions of the Vienna Convention. See Article 60 (1) of the Vienna Convention on the Law of Treaties (VCLT): "A material breach of a bilateral treaty by one of the parties entitles the other to invoke the breach as a ground for terminating the treaty or suspending its operation in whole or in part."

38 As such, the Commission considers that "including questions of human rights and democracy in the political dialogue more systematically would give a foundation to the

difficulties on the subject of human rights, doubts remain as to the formalisation of such a clause. In addition, a conventional introduction of a political dialogue and the inclusion of political clauses (non-proliferation of weapons of mass destruction (WMD), counter-terrorism, the International Criminal Court) should be requested by the EU. Most of these clauses are called "standard clauses,"[39] but the EU wished to see the WMD clause recognised as an "essential clause."[40] At the economic level, the *Global Europe*[41] Communication from the Commission introduces the necessity to concentrate on the new growth sectors or "Singapore subjects:" IPR, services, investments, public procurement and competition. Therefore, the European negotiator should require that the integration of commitments go beyond WTO rules ("WTO plus") in the future framework agreement. The Commission, in its "commercial" orientation document concerning EU-China relations, clarifies that the new agreement should "focus on the trade exchanges and investments issues."[42] In addition, the European negotiators wished to insert a chapter on employment and social affairs, a dialogue on small and medium-sized enterprises (SMEs), and maybe a clause on tax systems.

On the Chinese side, the MES and the lift of the arms embargo are at the heart of Chinese claims. In addition, the Chinese negotiator could require the integration of a "Taiwan clause" in the preamble of the agreement, stipulating that the Community and the member states oppose Taiwan's independence, including *de jure* independence of Taiwan and

---

clauses on the essential elements and would allow the two parties to list the most effective measures to establish political and economic stability." See Communication from the Commission of the European Communities to the Council and the European Parliament, *Role of the European Union in the Promotion of Human Rights and Democratisation in Third Countries*, COM(2001) 252 final, Brussels, 8 May 2001, p. 10.

39 At the opposite end of the spectrum to "essential clauses," "standard clauses" do not constitute an essential element of the agreement. From a legal point of view, they are part of the commitments of each party, such as the other provisions of external agreements. The integration of theses clauses rely on a Council decision. This commitment is purely political, and only the negotiation directives can force the Community negotiator to set them up.

40 For further informations on the political dimension of the PCA, see Antoine Sautenet, 'The Current Status and Prospect of the "Strategic Partnership" between the European Union and China: Towards the Conclusion of a Partnership and Cooperation Agreement,' *European Law Journal*, Vol. 13, No. 6, 2007.

41 Commission of the European Communities, *Communication from the Commission to the Council, to the European Parliament, to the European Economic and Social Committee and to the Committee of the Regions: A Competitive Europe in a Globalized Economy*, COM(2006) 567 final, Brussels, 4 October 2006, p. 10.

42 Commission of the European Communities, Strategic Document on EU-China Trade and Investments: Competition and Partnership, *op. cit.*

Taiwan's participation in any international or regional organisation whose membership applies only to sovereign states.

That is why, with regard to the asymmetry of the intensions, different scenarios are possible: a single PCA, a double agreement (commercial agreement and global agreement with a number of political provisions[43]), or no agreement. There is still a necessity for the EU to deepen the trade and investment aspects of its relationship, in view of the current multilateral check of the Doha Agenda and regional restructurings underway in the field of free trade, in order to insert the "WTO plus" fields into the new agreement.

Faced with the stalemate of multilateral negotiations, the EU must integrate elements of added-value into the PCA with China, in order to prevent commercial tensions arising from the WTO and to guarantee Community operators a better presence on the Chinese market. It is interesting to note that after the failure of multilateral negotiations, the Commission, in its *Global Europe* communication of October 2006, while wishing *a priori* to re-launch this international effort, also wishes to go down the bilateral route and is envisaging free trade agreements (FTAs).[44] The next agreement with China, even if it is not a FTA, may target trade and investment, with a particular focus on Intellectual Property Rights (IPRs), that is to say, the "new sectors of growth" as identified by the Commission in its *Global Europe* Communication,[45] with a view to obtaining real added-value with a framework agreement: investments and IPRs.

Intellectual Property Rights and the PCA Negotiations

China's Current IPR Environment

Overall, the protection of IPRs is not completely assured[46] in the fields of innovation and high technology. Traditionally, intellectual property is divided into two categories: industrial property, which includes inventions (patents), trademarks, industrial designs, and geographic indications; and copyright, which includes literary and artistic works. These rights are granted to creators and inventors to regulate the use of their products.

---

[43] Which corresponds to the content of the standard and essential clauses.

[44] This is a departure from the "Lamy doctrine."

[45] Commission of the European Communities, Communication from the Commission: Global Europe, *op. cit.*

[46] The report of the Secretariat notes that: "In recent years, China has brought in important modifications to its legal framework for IPR protection."

For more than two decades the PRC has passed laws and regulations covering almost every important area relating to IPRs. China is a member of the World Intellectual Property Organisation (WIPO) and a signatory to all major IP treaties including the agreement on Trade Related Aspects of Intellectual Property (TRIPS), the Paris Convention for the Protection of Industrial Property (Paris Convention), and the Berne Convention for the Protection of Literary and Artistic Works (Berne Convention). It joined the WIPO Copyright Treaty, and the WIPO Performances and Phonograms Treaty in March 2007. In practical terms, the administration of IPRs is organised on two levels in China: administrative bodies under the State Council, and local administrative authorities. The administrative bodies under the State Council are responsible for examining and granting or registering IPRs, while the local authorities administer and enforce them at the local level.

Secret Patent and Technology Violations

Patent rights in China are protected under the Patent Law, its Implementing Regulations, and by rules promulgated by the State Intellectual Property Office (SIPO) to implement the Patent Law. The Patent Law is currently being revised. The authorities state that the purpose of the revision is to further enhance patent protection by improving the "patent agent" system and the management of patent rights; clarifying the criteria for granting patents; and preventing the abuse of patents. Currently, patent rights for inventions are granted for 20 years from the date of filing (and ten years for utility models and designs).

While the objectives of the Chinese authorities are perfectly understandable and indeed welcomed, the means used to achieve this end are not always legitimate. The methods employed by the Chinese government can be either direct or indirect. Direct absorption of foreign IP includes the flat refusal to pay royalties to foreign patent owners and the forced disclosure and dissemination of secret data. The more indirect method on the other hand, relies on the use of government procurement practices where foreign companies are selected initially in order to pass their technological know-how to a joint venture partner and are then excluded from successive rounds.

Counterfeiting of Trademarks and Piracy of Copyright

According to national statistics, Chinese IP owners constitute the large majority of the victims of such violations. And yet, it seems that counterfeiting of trademarks and copyright piracy are not a priority issue for the PRC. Trade marks are protected under the Trademark Law, the Regulations for the Implementation of the Trademark Law, and various rules issued by State Administration of Industry and Commerce (SAIC).

The Trademark Law is also being revised, in a bid to shorten the examination period and enhance trade mark protection. Currently, trade marks are valid for ten years, and are indefinitely renewable for a further ten years. The State Trademark Office, under the SAIC, is responsible for the registration and administration of trademarks and geographical indications. Local enforcement authorities are in charge of the administration of trademarks and geographical indications at the local level. All applicants are required to register their trademarks with the State Trademark Office. Foreigners and foreign enterprises are required to file an application in accordance with any agreement concluded between their country of origin and China, or any international treaty, which both have ratified, or on a reciprocal basis.[47] Copyright protection is granted under the Copyright Law and its accompanying regulations.[48] The National Copyright Administration of China under the State Council administers copyrights on a national scale. However, local copyright administration offices (under the local governments of provinces, autonomous regions, and municipalities directly under the Central Government) are in charge of local copyright registration and administration. Protection of cinematographic and photographic works is granted for fifty years, and typographical designs for ten years.[49] Protection for computer software is granted from the date on which its development was completed, for the lifetime of the author plus fifty years.[50]

---

47 Foreigners and foreign enterprises not domiciled in China or with no industrial or commercial establishments in China may register their trademarks in China through an agency qualified to act as their agent.

48 These include, *inter alia*, the Implementing Rules of the Copyright Law, the Regulations for the Protection of Computer Software, and the Regulation on the Collective Administration of Copyright. In addition, the State Council promulgated the Regulations on Protection of the Right of Communication through the Information Network, which came into force on 1 July 2006.

49 Article 21 of the Copyright Law specifies that, for a work created by a process analogous to cinematography, or a photographic work, the term of protection is 50 years, expiring on 31 December of the 50th year after the first publication of such work – however, any such work is not protected under this Law if it is not published within 50 years of the completion of its creation.

50 Software copyright exists from the date on which its development is complete. For a natural person, protection is provided for the lifetime of the person, plus 50 years. For software developed jointly by two or more persons, protection expires at the end of the 50th year after the death of the last surviving developer. A copyright belonging to a legal entity or other body is protected for 50 years from first publication – however, if it has not been published within fifty years of its development, it is not protected under the Regulations for the Protection of Computer Software.

China's IPR Enforcement System

When it comes to the protection of IPR in China, there is mounting concern among developed countries about China's willingness and genuineness to provide adequate protection of IPRs, which have, over time, evolved into one of the most sensitive issues in the ongoing trade debates with Western nations. China's accession to the WTO in 2001 has directed foreign attention towards the issue of IPRs. In particular, it has been debated whether improvements in Chinese intellectual property laws and WTO commitments to enforce these laws will address these concerns – and if they do, in which way and within what time-scale? In 1998, China established the State Intellectual Property Office (SIPO), with the vision that it would coordinate China's IP enforcement efforts by merging the patent, trademark and copyright offices under one authority. However, this has yet to occur. Today, SIPO is responsible for granting patents (national office), registering semiconductor layout designs (national office), and enforcing patents (local SIPO offices), as well as coordinating domestic foreign-related IPR issues involving copyrights, trademarks and patents.

IP protection in China follows a two-track system. The first and most prevalent is the administrative track, whereby an IP rights holder files a complaint at the local administrative office. The second is the judicial track, whereby complaints are filed through the court system (China has established specialised IP panels in its civil court system throughout the country). Determining which IP agency has jurisdiction for a given infringement can be confusing. Jurisdictional competence of IP protection is dispersed throughout a number of government agencies and offices, each typically responsible for the protection provided by a particular statute or a specific area of IP-related law. Geographical limits may be set or conflicts may arise when an administrative agency takes a case that involves piracy or counterfeiting that also occurs in another region – in recognition of these difficulties, some regional IP officials have discussed plans for creating cross-jurisdictional enforcement procedures. China's courts also have rules regarding jurisdiction over infringement or counterfeit activities, and the scope of potential orders.

In addition, the effectiveness of an IPR regime depends not only on legal structures but also on cultural diversity, economic infrastructure, and technical capacity. Although formal compliance with TRIPs obligations has been reasonably good, related enforcement has been poor. The US Section 301 Report shows that Chinese copyright law, for instance, complies with the requirements of the TRIPs Agreement in terms of both scope and period: however, copyright piracy remains a major problem. Moreover, this is a problem which is worsening in areas such as sound recordings, and is influencing the perception of developed states despite China's accession to the WTO. Theoretically, the TRIPs Agreement covers both substantive and enforcement aspects – however, it is the latter which is essential in ensuring the effective protection of IPR. Thus this paper will focus on the enforcement of IPR.

To summarise, instead of concentrating their efforts on improving the efficiency of their action, Chinese authorities prefer to launch periodic campaigns, thus addressing the symptoms rather than the root cause. The main weaknesses of the IP environment in China include:

- Feeble deterrence aimed at those who infringe IP rules;
- Complexity of the administrative organisational structure: a lack of cooperation between and within enforcement agencies, ultimately leading to competition between agencies; lack of involvement of the right holder;
- Burdensome procedures for right holders to initiate and proceed with a case in court;
- Lack of financial and human resources allocated to administrative enforcement agencies responsible for trademarks (Trade Mark Office and State Administration of Industry and Commerce) and copyrights (National Copyright Administration of China);
- Regulatory framework and enforcement at the local level and local protectionism (i.e. developing economy, maintaining employment, and serving the interests of local consumers), resulting in discrimination against foreign IPR holders.

The lack of business confidence in China's IPR framework "will potentially have a long-term and negative impact on the EU-China trading relationship."[51] Consequently, in its 2006 "commercial" orientation document, the European Commission underlined that "the adequate protection of IPRs such as patents, copyrights and trademarks is central to the exercise of Europe's comparative advantage in innovation, design and high-value production."[52]

Prospective on IPR Provisions in the PCA

EU-China IPR Dialogue

It is therefore of particular significance for the EU to promote a shift in China from the "rule by law" to the "rule of law." In the context of EU-China trade relations involving IPR debates, it may be a daunting task

---

51 Commission of the European Communities, Point 5.7, *Trade Sustainability Impact Assessment of the Negotiations of a Partnership and Cooperation Agreement between the EU and China*, Final Report, August 2008,

52 Commission of the European Communities, Strategic Document on EU-China Trade and Investments: Competition and Partnership, *op. cit.*

for the EU to interfere in the evolution of China's enforcement philosophy, from political manipulation to legal implementation. However, there is no shortcut to mitigating the counterfeiting menace in China. Unlike the US whose coercive approach makes the Chinese more reluctant to implement their commitments, the EU should find ways to identify real problems and resolve specific difficulties without merely displacing their Chinese counterparts elsewhere. In light of the goals and priorities of both sides, the EU-China Economic and Trade Joint Committee was established in 1985. As a bilateral summit between the EU and China in trade and economics, the EU-China Joint Committee provides a platform for high level discussion of bilateral trade issues. The Joint Committee, through periodical meetings, serves EU-China relations in three aspects: economy and trade, bilateral agreements and dialogues between the European Commission and the Chinese government, and the EU-China cooperation programme. However, to achieve these goals, the steering role of the EU-China Joint Committee should be intensified and reinforced so as to address not only the broad issues of trade and cooperation, but also concerns arising from the various sectoral dialogues. Hence, the EU-China Joint Economic and Trade Committee, which was held on 23 September 2008, covered a wide range of topics, including notably IPRs, and prepared the next framework agreement. The two sides sought to conclude an IPR Customs Enforcement Action Plan to be signed at the next EU-China Summit.[53] In fact, this Action Plan was signed on 30 January 2009 during the visit of the Chinese Prime Minister Wen Jiabao.[54]

In addition, a new High Level Economic and Trade Dialogue Mechanism was launched in Beijing on 25 April 2008, with the key aim of addressing the EU's ballooning trade deficit with China. According to the EU, about 80% of fake goods on the world market emanate from China, and measures are needed to "combat the flood of fake goods and counterfeits which come toward Europe,"[55] said Peter Mandelson. He nevertheless underlined that China has stepped up its fight against piracy,

---

53 There was also a commitment to work on resolving issues raised in the EU-China working group on online piracy.

54 Action Plan on Customs Cooperation between the European Community and China with regard to enforcement of IPRs. This Action Plan is intended to strengthen the application of customs controls to combat counterfeiting and piracy on EU-China trade relations and to provide a basis for further actions to combat counterfeiting and piracy. See EC Press Release: EC and China sign nine cooperation agreements and foster dialogue on global solutions to economic and financial crisis and climate change, IP/09/212, retrieved on 20 March 2009, http://europa.eu/rapid/pressReleasesAction.do?reference=IP/09/212&format=HTML&aged=0&language=EN&guiLanguage=en.

55 Peter Mandelson, 'Remarks to the Press on the High Level Economic and Trade Dialogue Mechanism (HLM),' Beijing, 25 April 2008.

saying, as trade commissioner in 2004, "the country has moved from a state of denial to a state of national mobilisation."[56]

In any case, with regard to the IPR environment in China, it remains necessary to reinforce the existing mechanisms, such as the "IPR helpdesk," the "EU-China Project on the Protection of Intellectual Property Rights (IPR2)" or the "network" of information centres in Europe, otherwise known as the "increased sensitivity to IPR questions in the businesses of the EU."[57] In addition, the EU has to monitor the Chinese WTO commitments. On 26 November 2004, pursuant to paragraph 18 of the Protocol on the Accession of China to the WTO, the European Commission and the TRIPs Council conducted reviews of China's implementation legislation as part of China's transitional review mechanism (TRM).[58] In this TRM, the European Commission raised six particular questions for China to clarify. For instance, the Commission requested that the State Intellectual Property Office (SIPO) provide detailed information to shed light on the "National IPR Strategy" that was declared in April 2004. SIPO was expected to answer questions as to whether this new strategy would shortly be launched and would "have for main objective to enhance the competitiveness of Chinese businesses in the global economy;"[59] whether the National Strategy "foresaw more transparency in the decision making process"[60] and "accelerated procedures for the registration of patents and trademarks;" whether the National Strategy "included specific measures to reinforce the combat against counterfeiting and piracy,"[61] and whether the National Strategy included an educational programme to deepen intellectual property knowledge among officials at ministerial and provincial levels. The EU's efforts have begun to bear their fruit at last. The Standing Committee of the National People's Congress in China has recently approved the amendment to the Scientific and Technological Progress Law on 29 December 2007, a move that signals final preparations of the state before the publication of the long-awaited National Intellectual Property Strategy (NIPS).[62]

56 *Ibid.*

57 Commission of the European Communities, Point V, Strategic Document on EU-China Trade and Investments: Competition and Partnership, *op. cit.*, p. 12.

58 World Trade Organization, *Transitional Review Mechanism of China, TRIPs Council, Contribution of the European Communities*, Directorate-General for Trade, Brussels, 26 November 2004, pp. 1-3.

59 *Ibid.*, p. 3.

60 *Ibid.*

61 *Ibid.*

62 Peter Ollier, 'China Gets Ready for National IP Strategy,' *Managing Intellectual Property*, 2008.

"Trips Plus" Provisions in the Future PCA

However, "TRIPs plus" provisions[63] should be integrated in the future agreement in order to export "European standards" to China. Provisions concerning global commitments in the field of IPR (stipulating for instance that "the Parties shall provide suitable and effective protection of intellectual, industrial and commercial property rights, in line with the highest international standards,"[64] or "shall accede to the multilateral conventions on the protection of intellectual, industrial and commercial property, which the EC and its member states are a part"[65]) could be inserted. Specific rules (copyright,[66] patent protection,[67] dispute settlement[68]) could also be inserted, following the models of association

---

63 It is necessary to note that the WTO's TRIPs agreement represents today the most comprehensive multilateral agreement on IPR protection. See Alexandre Thillier, 'Politique Commerciale Commune – Délimitation – Instruments – Contrôle,' *Jurisclasseur Europe*, fasc. 2300, 2007.

64 Article 39 (1): The Parties shall provide suitable and effective protection of intellectual, industrial and commercial property rights, in line with the highest international standards. This shall encompass effective means of enforcing such rights. European Community, *Decision of 24 January 2000 on the Conclusion of the Euro-Mediterranean Agreement Establishing an Association between the European Communities and their Member States, of the One Part, and the Kingdom of Morocco, of the Other Part*, OJ L 70, Brussels, 18 March 2000, p. 1.

65 Annex 7 of the European Community document, *Euro-Mediterranean Agreement Establishing an Association between the European Communities and their Member States, of the One Part, and the Republic of Tunisia, of the Other Part*, OJ L 97, Luxemburg, 30 March 1998.

66 Art. 12: "Reaffirming the great importance they attach to the protection of IPRs (copyright – including the copyright in computer programmes and databases – and neighbouring rights, the rights related to patents, industrial designs, geographical indications including designation of origins, trademarks, topographies of integrated circuits, as well as protection against unfair competition as referred to in Article 10a of the Paris Convention for the Protection of Industrial Property and protection of undisclosed information), the Parties undertake to establish the appropriate measures with a view to ensuring an adequate and effective protection in accordance with the highest international standards, including effective means to enforce such rights." Council of the European Union, *Decision of 28 September 2000 concerning the conclusion of the Economic Partnership, Political Coordination and Cooperation Agreement between the European Community and its Member States, of the One Part, and the United Mexican States, of the Other Part*, OJ L 276, Brussels, 28 October 2000, p. 44.

67 Council of the European Union, *Decision 2005/599/EC of 21 June 2005 Concerning the Signing, on Behalf of the European Community, of the Agreement Amending the Partnership Agreement between the Members of the African, Caribbean and Pacific Group of States, of the One Part, and the European Community and its Member States, of the Other Part*, signed in Cotonou, 23 June 2000, OJ L 209, 11 August 2005, Article 46 (Munich Convention).

68 EU-Morocco Association Agreement, *op. cit.*, Article 39 (2).

agreements or the Cotonou agreement. The integration of a bilateral dispute resolution system could potentially have positive effects, permitting the PCA to go beyond the scope of the WTO commitments. Over the past recent years, the EU has repeatedly urged China to improve its enforcement tool, but China's endeavours do not appear to impress the EU. There are indications that the EU is gradually running out of patience over China's failure in delivering concrete results of its IPR enforcement. The former EU Trade Commissioner Peter Mandelson recently expressed his frustration:

> I am firmly convinced that the most effective solution to effective IPR protection is the legal enforcement that mutual cooperation between the EU and China can and should provide […]. We have been constructive and we have been patient, but the return we have received on that patience has frankly been too low.[69]

Lastly, it should be noted that the EU Trade Barriers Regulation (TBR) includes, since its reform of July 2008, the bilateral agreements' provisions.[70]

Investments and the PCA Negotiations

Foreign Direct Investments in China

Investments are recognised as being the most sensitive field in terms of restrictions, whether they manifest themselves in the industrial sector (cars, semiconductors, the naval sector) or in the form of numerous local restrictions on investment (the problem of deregulation), or in the manufacturing and services sector, or in the requirement to establish joint ventures with Chinese operators, as well as requirements in terms of capital (telecommunications, financial services). The terms of the exchange are thus inequitable. The Chinese government practices a policy of aiding "national champions" (through subsidies and privileged access to the banking sector).[71] In addition, European investment in China

---

69 See 'Mandelson Urges China to Tackle Piracy, Hints at WTO Action,' *EU Business*, 26 November 2007, retrieved on 20 March 2009, www.eubusiness.com/news-eu/1196083921.23/.

70 Regulation (EC) No. 125/2008 amending Regulation (EC) No. 3286/94 laying down Community procedures in the field of the Common Commercial Policy in order to ensure the exercise of the Community's rights under international trade rules, in particular those established under the auspices of the World Trade Organization, OJ L 40, 14 February 2008. Regulation (EC) No. 3286/94 is amended so as to remove the existing prohibition for a Community enterprise to rely exclusively on bilateral agreements to bring forward a complaint.

71 World Trade Organization, Report of the Secretariat, *Trade Policy Review – China*, WT/TPRB/299, 16 April 2008.

dropped again in 2007 to around 2% of all European FDI outflows, despite the fact that, globally, European FDI is in fact growing strongly. European companies invested €1.8 bn in China in 2007, down from €6 bn in 2006 and €6.2 bn in 2005.[72] Former EU Trade commissioner Peter Mandelson has also urged China to act to reverse sliding EU investment rates in China.[73]

On 31 October 2007, the National Development and Reform Commission and the Ministry of Commerce jointly produced an amended version of the Catalogue of Orientation for Foreign Investments (the Catalogue), which classifies foreign investment projects in China into four categories: encouraged; authorised; restricted; and prohibited. Under certain conditions, investment projects which fall in the encouraged projects category can benefit from preferential treatment and advantages, mainly in the realm of taxation. The objective of revising the Catalogue is to bring it in line with the strategic priorities of the development of the Chinese economy, as presented by President Hu Jintao during the 17th National Congress of the Communist Party in October 2007 – at that time Hu also said that growth had occurred at the expense of environmental protection and the safeguarding of natural resources.

A study by the China Council for International Cooperation in the Environment and Development revealed that in 2005, 84.19% of the companies with foreign capital established in China had invested in the exploitation of natural resources or highly polluting industries. Conversely, the share of foreign investment in "clean" industrial sectors was lower than 1.2%.[74]

The new tendencies as outlined in the Catalogue, which govern foreign investment in China have been designed to counteract this problem:

- The rules confirm China's will to modernise its industrial structure by encouraging investment projects that involve advanced or high technologies and by reducing its support for investments in the traditional production sectors.[75]

---

72 'Mandelson urges action to reverse sliding EU investment in China,' Tianjin, 26 September 2008, retrieved on 20 March 2009, http://ec.europa.eu/trade/issues/bilateral/countries/china/pr260908_en.htm.

73 *Ibid.*

74 China Council for International Cooperation on Environmental and Development, Point 2, *General Report of Policy Recommendations – 2005*, Beijing, November 2005, retrieved at http://www.harbour.sfu.ca/dlam/recommendations2005/htm.

75 See *Catalogue for the Guidance of Foreign Investment Industries* (Amended 2007), and see *Catalogue of Encouraged Foreign Investment Industries* (Part I), point II. 4.

- The Catalogue also promotes environmental protection and the natural resources industry[76] while placing clean investments in the category of encouraged investments, and restricting, even prohibiting, investments in particularly polluting sectors or sectors that are high consumers of energy or natural resources.[77]
- Investment projects in clean renewable energy and energy production, research and development, environmental protection, the development of biological agriculture and the production of "clean" components for other producers are encouraged.[78] On the other hand, investments in polluting sectors such as heavy industry, machinery and agriculture are now prohibited or restricted since the projects are harmful to the environment.[79]
- Lastly, certain amendments are aimed at protecting the national economy by restricting foreign investments in sectors important to the Government or of strategic interest. Among those, one finds the production of television or radio shows, the development of new Internet sites, scientific research, engineering and geological exploration.[80]

However, the new Catalogue cannot be analysed exclusively as a measure of distrust by the Chinese government with regard to foreign investments. Indeed, as Prime Minister Wen Jiabao said during the 11th National People's Congress in March 2009, China has the will to restrict, even prohibit, foreign investments that lead to pollution or high energy consumption. These measures conform to the general evolution of the Chinese economy and fit in naturally with the mechanisms set up by Beijing for environmental protection. The 11th National People's Congress was thus the occasion to announce the creation of an environmental protection super-ministry, to which various measures have been added during the last few months, such as green credits that penalise polluting companies that wish to borrow capital or the system of green insurance, intended to compensate victims of environmental accidents.

---

76 See Catalogue for the Guidance of Foreign Investment Industries, *op. cit.*; see notably point IX.

77 *Ibid.*; see *Catalogue of Prohibited Foreign Investment Industries* (Part III), point VII.

78 *Ibid.*; see *Catalogue of Encouraged Foreign Investment Industries* (Part I), point VIII.

79 *Ibid.*; see *Catalogue of Restricted Foreign Investment Industries* (Part II), point I & II; and see *Catalogue of Prohibited Foreign Investment Industries* (Part III), point I, II & III.

80 *Ibid.*; see *Catalogue of Prohibited Foreign Investment Industries* (Part III), point X.

Prospective on Investment Provisions in the PCA

In the field of investments, the European policy is in theory conducted in line with the General Agreement on Trade in Services (GATS)[81] and the OECD Guidelines for Multinational Enterprises.[82] Until recently, the EC had not set up common provisions relating to investments in the framework of its bilateral agreements. It is only over the last ten years that the European Commission has wished to introduce more and more in-depth commitments. Notably, ambitious provisions were integrated into the EC-Chile agreement, concerning the "progressive liberalisation of investments" [83] and stipulating the attribution of the "National Treatment" (NT) and the "Most-Favoured-Nation"[84] (MFN) treatment clause in the field of services and financial services, with an extension of the NT to the other sectors of the agreement.[85] The European Commission already possesses the political will[86] and could use the rules of its agreement with Chile as a template.

In addition, the set up of a minimal platform (i.e. common provisions on investments) integrated in all of the EU's future FTAs,[87] could be potentially extended to China, with regard to the commercial challenges of the relation between the two. The idea of this platform is to establish a form of *Bilateral Investments Treaty*[88] applicable to the whole of the

81 See the website of the Commission of the European Communities' Directorate-General for Trade, retrieved on 20 March 2009, http://trade.ec.europa.eu/.

82 The Guidelines are recommendations addressed by governments to multinational enterprises operating in or from adhering countries. They provide voluntary principles and standards for responsible business conduct in a variety of areas including employment and industrial relations, human rights, environment, information disclosure, combating bribery, consumer interests, science and technology, competition, and taxation. See the OECD website: http://www.oecd.org.

83 European Community, *Association Agreement between the EC and its Member States and Chile*, OJ L 352, Brussels, 30 December 2002, Article 164-2.

84 "National treatment" allows foreign individuals and firms the same competitive opportunities, including market access, as are available to domestic parties. "Most-Favoured-Nation treatment," which requires members to accord the most favourable tariff and regulatory treatment given to the product of any one member, at the time of import or export of "like products" of all other members, is one of the WTO's bedrock principles.

85 European Community, Association Agreement between the EC and its Member States and Chile, *op. cit.*, Article 163.

86 Peter Mandelson, Speech, *Les Échanges et les Investissements de l'UE avec la Chine: Changements, Challenges et Choix*, Bruxelles, 7 July 2006, retrieved on 20 March 2009, http://trade.ec.europa.eu/.

87 Notably the future FTAs with South-Korea, ASEAN and India.

88 The majority of the member states have concluded bilateral investments treaties (BITs), see http://www.bilaterals.org/rubrique.php3?id_rubrique=59.

European Community. In other words, the aim of the proposition (built on the basis of the GATS)[89] will be to cover pre-investments and post-investment[90] (to the question of a dispute settlement state/ investors), with an extension of the scope of the establishment provisions to other sectors than just services. Actually, the shared competences between the EC and the member states present a major difficulty. The EC competence covers only market access and the promotion of investments in the framework of the Common Commercial Policy (CCP). But it does not cover the reciprocal protection of investments, which refers to member states' competences. It entails that the Community's exclusive competence for the regulation of foreign investments is then limited. To the extent that the Community has no explicit exclusive competence (such as the one based on Article 133 (1) to (4) of the EC Treaty) and has not yet exercised its non-exclusive competence in all areas, the member states remain competent with respect to the regulation of foreign investments. In accordance with the European Court of Justice (ECJ) case law,[91] the Community's non-exclusive powers can become exclusive as a result of internal harmonisation. It would thus be necessary, in a concrete case, to ascertain whether the matters covered by the international treaty (free-trade agreement or BIT) are already subject to internal legislation containing provisions on the treatment to be accorded to foreign-

---

89 Refers to the mode 3 of services furniture by a member of a company from one country setting up subsidiaries or branches to provide services in another country, officially known as "commercial presence." See article I (2) (c) of the GATS.

90 The provisions of "pre-admission," define the rights of the foreign investors in entrance and in establishment in certain economic areas of the guest country (market access level). The dispositions of "post admission" correspond to the regulation regime applicable to the foreign investors after their establishment in the guest country. The principles of NT and MFN should be implemented (contrary to the EC-Chile agreement).

91 European Court of Justice of the European Communities, Opinion 2/92, 1995, ECR I-521. The article 133 EC Treaty cannot confer an exclusive competence to conclude the 3rd OECD decision on National Treatment which affects the CCP but also intra-community trade (the internal market). Actually, other aspects of foreign investments can fall under the non-exclusive Community competence and under the internal market legal bases of the EC Treaty (such as Articles 44, 47 and 95). This may in particular be the case to the extent that post-establishment national treatment provisions relate also to the participation of foreign-controlled enterprises in intra-Community trade. According to the ECJ (ECJ: Opinion 1/94, 1994, ECR I-5267), some provisions on foreign investments, which are covered by the GATT and the WTO Agreement on Trade-Related Investment Measures, fall under the exclusive Community competence under Article 133(1) to (4) of the EC Treaty. Only when internal legislation has provided for common rules in the sense of a complete harmonisation does the Community's implied exclusive external competence have to be recognised, in order to avoid such common rules being affected if the member states retained their individual freedom to negotiate with non-member countries.

controlled undertakings, or empowering the institutions to negotiate with non-member countries, or effecting complete harmonisation of the rules governing the right to take up an activity as a self-employed person.

As the provisions of the market access in non-service sectors do not exclude the service sectors mentioned in Article 133(6) of the EC Treaty, and relate at least partially to post-establishment national treatment and MFN treatment, including in sectors where the Community has not yet exercised its internal powers, any agreement including these type of provisions would therefore need to be concluded, with China, by the Community and the member states and would thus be a *mixed agreement*. This mixed agreement would be of a "vertical" nature and imply a double legal basis: article 133 (CCP) and 308 (subsidiary competences) of the EC Treaty.[92] In a prospective approach, we cannot ignore the Lisbon Treaty (which completes and reinforces the CCP) as much as negotiation of the agreement should be spread out over several years. The "FDIs" are now expressly included in the scope of the CCP, defined by article 207 of the Treaty on the Functioning of the EU (substitution to the article 133 EC Treaty), which implies the disappearance of the mixity aspect.[93] However, a new problem could appear: the new CCP (an exclusive competence of the EU[94]) could induce a fight for influence between the new High Representative of the Union for Foreign Affairs and Security Policy and the EU Commissioner for external trade.

Constraints on the Commercial Dimension of the PCA Negotiations

In any case, in exchange for Chinese concessions deemed crucial to the EU balancing the trade deficit, China could demand that the EU recognises its MES. At present, for the EU, the conditions for granting MES to China for anti-dumping investigations are not fulfilled. But the Chinese authorities believe that this treatment is unfair for a number of reasons. First, increasing numbers of Chinese firms – especially those in the export sector – are operating within market environments with inputs purchased at their real cost and finance raised on a commercial basis. Secondly, Chinese trade officials point out that Russia, a country hardly

92 Marianne Dony, 'Les Accords Mixtes,' in M. Dony *et al.*, *Commentaire Mégret, Relations Extérieures*, Bruxelles, Université Libre de Bruxelles, Vol. 12, 2005, p. 167.

93 It will depend on the ECJ's interpretation of the expression "foreign direct investments." Nonetheless, it would seem to fall under the exclusive Community competence.

94 Article 207 (1) of the Treaty on the Functioning of the European Union (TFEU): "The common commercial policy shall be conducted in the context of the principles and objectives of the Union's external action."

known for its transparency and openness, is recognised by Europe as a market economy. For the EU, the MES is a technical question. The EU – unlike the United States – re-classified China as an "economy in transition" in 1998. This means that it considers complaints on a case-by-case basis, using five tests to judge whether the Chinese firm against which the dumping complaint has been filed is operating within a market environment.[95] Now, the main problem is that the longer negotiations last, the more the MES recognition loses its appeal and relative value in the negotiation process.[96]

To add to this, China could object to the EU's demands in their entirety, which would strongly highlight the failure of European diplomacy in light of the commercial challenges at stake in the new framework agreement. Furthermore, the EU would have to set up, as a central objective, a "proactive" systematic surveillance of the implementation of WTO obligations, in other words use effectively the combinations of legal tools and political pressure which constitute the WTO's Dispute Settlement Understanding (DSU). In fact, it may come as a surprise that the EC has requested WTO consultations only three times, on auto parts tariffs[97] (3 April 2006) and on measures affecting financial information services and foreign financial information services suppliers in China (3 March 2008), and on Chinese export restrictions on raw materials (23 June 2009). Concerning the auto parts tariffs case, the EU believed that Chinese tariff laws for spare auto parts were WTO-incompatible. The tariffs in question, aimed at "whole vehicles," were, in virtue of Chinese rules, applied to imported spare parts making up 60% or more of the value of a final vehicle. The EU believed that this may have contravened China's WTO obligations not to impose obligatory "local content" rules: to avoid the "whole car" tariff rates, a car-maker has to source 40% or more of the spare parts by value in China.[98] The EU believed this may have constituted an internal tax on imported goods: the tariff is levied on a finished product constructed with imported parts and the same rates are not applied to cars produced with local spare parts. The WTO issued its first official condemnation of Chinese commercial

95 In fact, whilst some countries such as UK are in favour of a status change, other countries (Spain, Italy) are fundamentally opposed to the recognition of the MES.

96 In its WTO accession agreement, China agreed that other WTO members could treat it as a non-market economy until 2015 (appendix A of the Protocol).

97 World Trade Organization, *Dispute Settlement, Appellate Body and Panel Reports Adopted: China-Measures Affecting Imports of Automobile Parts*, WT/DS339/1, 3 April 2006.

98 Chinese Measures for the Administration of Importation of Automotive Parts and Components for Complete Vehicles (Decree No. 125), entered into force on 1 April 2005.

practices, siding with the United States (US), the EU and Canada in this dispute over car parts.[99] The wishes of the EC (along with the US and Canada) to haul China before the WTO over the country's refusal to allow financial news services to interact directly with customers,[100] is perhaps a change in the European strategy concerning the use of the DSU. In addition, the EU recently requested WTO consultations on Chinese export restrictions on raw materials.[101] For the EU, China applies export restrictions – quotas and export duties – on key raw materials. These restrictions distort competition and increase global prices, as some of these resources cannot be found elsewhere. Downstream industries in China therefore have access to cheaper materials than their competitors outside China. That is not a level playing field, and the EU and the US have asked for consultations with China at the WTO.

The EU will nevertheless have to try to reach a compromise on a new agreement allowing better access to markets for European firms, notably in terms of improvement of the situation of direct investments in China. A bilateral dispute settlement inspired by the EC-Chile System template could be integrated into the future framework agreement – the reform of the Trade Barriers Regulation (TBR) envisages an extension of the regulatory field so as to include the content of bilateral agreements.

Nonetheless, given the current treaties, the inclusion of investments is not the only field which can involve a mixed agreement. In accordance with its traditional external policy, the EU attempts to include a political dimension in all future agreements. This is a field which usually relates to the Common and Foreign Security Policy (CFSP). The CFSP does not dispossess member states of their diplomacy (principle of concerted diplomacy). In other words, the integration of a political dialogue and political clauses will implicate an agreement concluded by both the EC and its member states.[102] Generally speaking, difficulties often emerge as a result of the distrust that surrounds China on numerous political questions, particularly pertaining to human rights, which create a substantial number of obstacles to the conclusion of an agreement.[103]

Finally, it should be noted that the new European bilateral approach to Asia (FTAs with India, South Korea and ASEAN; ambitious PCA with

---

[99] See the Hong Kong Trade Council website, http://marketinfo.tdctrade.com.

[100] See *Europolitique*, 7 February 2008.

[101] World Trade Organization, *Dispute Settlement, Consultations: China – Measures Related to the Exportation of Various Raw Materials*, WTDS395, 23 June 2009.

[102] See Antoine Sautenet, 'Europe and China: a Cooperation with Complex Legal Dimensions,' *op. cit.*, pp. 49-60.

[103] See Jing Men, 'EU-China Relations, from Engagement to Marriage,' *EU Diplomacy Papers*, No. 7, College of Europe, Bruges, June 2008.

China)[104] will be generally difficult to manage.[105] Considering the opposition of the new trading powers to certain types of EU trade provisions, the EU has little hope of concluding a strong FTA with India and with ASEAN, or in reinforcing China's engagement as a responsible stakeholder in the multilateral system. According to Evenett, the EU's bilateral approach "should not distract European trade strategists from the necessary task of establishing a new *modus operandi* for the multilateral trading system."[106]

104 Commission of the European Communities, Communication from the Commission: Global Europe, *op. cit.*

105 See Razeen Sally, 'Looking East: The European Union's New FTA Negotiations in Asia,' *Jan Tumlir Policy Essays*, European Centre for International Political Economy (ECIPE), No. 3, 2007, retrieved on 20 March 2009, http://www.ecipe.org.

106 Simon J. Evenett, 'Trade Policy: Time for a Rethink?,' in André Sapir (ed.), *Fragmented Power: Europe and the Global Economy*, Brussels, Bruegel, July 2007, p. 98.

CHAPTER 5

EU-China Investment Promotion and Protection Rules

Nayia PYRIDI

Under existing EU law, the power to enter into bilateral investment treaties (BITs) with third countries has not been delegated to the European Community, but still remains within the competence of each member state. As a consequence, the regulation of EU-China investment activities is primarily based on 25 heterogeneous BITs concluded between EU member states (with the exception of Ireland and Malta) and China, under the general framework of the 1985 EC-China Trade and Economic Cooperation Agreement (TECA). Although they follow the same general format, each BIT is different from the other on certain important issues. As a result, the network of BITs governing EU-China investment relations introduces elements of confusion, inefficiency and uncertainty – it enhances the fragmentation and overlapping of different regimes applicable to foreign investments – due to the fact that China undertakes different commitments *vis-à-vis* investors originating in the EU. This differentiates the conditions under which such investors establish and operate their activities in the same host country.

The current situation, though, is about to encounter a radical shift when the Lisbon Treaty comes into force. Conscious of the need to harmonise EU external economic relations in the field of promotion and protection of EU investors abroad, the drafters of the Lisbon Treaty transferred the power to conclude BITs from the member states to the EU. Under the new Article 207 of the Treaty on the Functioning of the EU (TFEU), FDI becomes an integral part of the EU's Common Commercial Policy (CCP). Within this context and notwithstanding the pending and thorny issue of the entry into force of the Lisbon Treaty, the purpose of this chapter is to explore how the ongoing PCA negotiations will seize the momentum and grab the opportunity to lay the groundwork for the regulation of legal issues arising out of investment flows between the EU and China. The PCA negotiations will therefore provide a clear mandate for the drafting of an EU BIT with China, which will co-exist with and ultimately replace the existing EU member states' BITs with China.

To this end, this chapter is divided into two sections. The first section investigates the limited competences exercised by the EU on FDI issues under the existing European Communities Treaty (EC Treaty) and overviews the bilateral legal instruments of the regulatory framework and their implications on EU-China investment relations. The second section explores the need to include in the agenda the ongoing negotiations for a new PCA, the possibility to establish an investment mandate with a view to concluding at the EU level, a BIT that will cement the ever enhancing EU-China investment links.

The Current Status of EU Rule-Making Authority on its Investment Relations with China

The rise and intensity of investment activities between the member states of the EU and China constitutes one of the most important aspects of their external economic relations, which compel the parties to include foreign investment in the ongoing negotiations for a new PCA. The legal issues stemming from the investment transactions between the two parties underscore the need for a comprehensive and uniform regime that will address concerns raised by both sides with regard to the promotion and protection of such flows in a consistent and harmonised way for all EU member states.

Under the current EC Treaty, however, foreign investment competences always lie predominantly with the member states due to the absence of an exclusive EU competence on foreign investment policy. The most common instruments used by member states are bilateral treaties for the promotion and protection of foreign investments.[1] The lack of such explicit competence on investment in the EC Treaty does not imply that the EU has not concluded international bilateral agreements relevant to investment issues with third parties. On the contrary, the EU has long embarked on a process of concluding a series of bilateral mixed agreements with non-member countries that address also investment issues (generally referred to as economic integration investment agreements). The investment chapters of such agreements usually complement the extensive bilateral network of cooperation agreements signed with third countries at the member state level.

---

1 Germany (112) and the United Kingdom (94) count the largest number of BITs worldwide, France (65) and Italy (48) have concluded a substantial amount of agreements, but most European countries are party only to around 20-40 agreements. Most BITs have been concluded with developing countries, although several EU member states are also party to around 10-20 agreements with other member states (usually BITs between old and new member states). Only the central and Eastern European countries (CEEC) have concluded agreements with other developed countries, most notably the US.

Although there is neither an established EU common foreign investment policy, nor Commission officials dealing 100% with foreign investment issues, member states' competence is intertwined with EU competences in two ways. *De jure*, the EU's CCP, the internal market and the power to conclude association agreements with third countries cover directly and indirectly certain aspects of foreign investment. *De facto*, due to the increasing use of mixed agreements covering investment as one among several economic sectors, it is apparent that the EU itself becomes a party to a considerable number of bilateral agreements, which include obligations on investment.

The Legal Regime Governing EU Competence on Foreign Direct Investment (FDI) Issues

According to the principle of the attribution of powers ("conferred powers"), the EC has the power to enact policies only to the extent it is conferred by the Treaties (Article 5 EC Treaty). The scope of the CCP as it stands today (Article 133 EC Treaty) is limited to external trade and does not mention FDI.[2] Nonetheless, one cannot dispute the fact that the CCP is closely related to investment issues and has significant implications for FDI activities – most foreign invested companies will import materials or technologies and export their products or services. Furthermore, investment is directly associated to trade in services, whose notion clearly encompasses services delivered by "any commercial presence," may that be a foreign funded company, its subsidiary or its branch. The European Commission and the European Parliament (EP) have long since advocated in favour of such a broad definition of the CCP.[3]

2 According to the internationally acknowledged definitions coined by UNCTAD, the IMF and the OECD, FDI is defined as capital funds provided by a resident natural or legal entity in one economy (foreign direct investor or parent enterprise) to an enterprise resident in an economy other than that of the foreign direct investor (FDI enterprise or affiliate) characterised by a long-term relationship and a lasting interest and control of its activity.

3 See part 11 (2) of the 'Commission Opinion on the 1996 Intergovernmental Conference' where the Commission stated that the CCP should be clarified, so as "to take into account of the radical changes in the structure of the world economy, in which services, intellectual property and FDI play an important role." See also European Parliament representatives' proposal at the Intergovernmental Conference 2000 – Commercial Policy and International Agreements, CONFER 4759/00, Brussels, 11 July 2000, where it was put forward to extend the CCP to cover direct investment, as well as services and intellectual property.

However, in Opinion 1/94 and 2/92,[4] the European Court of Justice (ECJ) adopted a narrow interpretation of the CCP. In its opinion on the WTO's General Agreement on Trade in Services (GATS) – which covers among other services sectors the supply of services by commercial presence – it stated that only economic cross-border relations *unlike trade in goods* fall within the scope of the CCP, while the EC Treaty's specific chapters apply to the free movement of natural and legal persons. As FDI usually entails a lasting establishment in the host country rather than cross-border economic supplies, according to Opinion 1/94, FDI is excluded from the current context of CCP. This is confirmed by Opinion 2/92, where the ECJ ruled that Article 133 EC Treaty is not a sufficient legal basis for the EU to conclude the OECD National Treatment Instrument, a voluntary code granting national treatment to foreign investors from other OECD countries. Although the Treaties of Amsterdam and Nice have extended EU competences affecting in particular investment in the services sector, these changes do have little relevance for policies directed at FDI in general. It is therefore clear that, under the current EC regime, there is no single legal basis that explicitly establishes and justifies the EC's competence on investment matters.

Nevertheless, one can invoke the principle of implied powers to ascertain that several EU competences provide for limited powers for the adoption of measures affecting inward investment to the EU. According to Article 48 EC Treaty, foreign companies incorporated in one of the EU member states enjoy full freedom of establishment.[5] In addition, in some sectors, secondary legislation based on Article 47(2) EC Treaty requires member states to regulate branches of non-EU companies no more favourably than EU companies, and provides for a procedure to ensure reciprocal treatment of EU companies by third states.[6]

The free movement of capital (Article 56-60 EC Treaty) covers transactions both between member states and with third countries.[7] Article 56 EC Treaty prohibits all restrictions on the movement of capital

4 See Opinion 1/94 (Re-WTO), 1994, ECR 1-5267 and Opinion 2/92 (Re-OECD National Treatment Instrument), 1995, ECR 1-521.

5 The European Community's exceptions to the right of establishment are set out in Articles 45 and 46 of the EC Treaty.

6 See EC Directive 2000/12 relating to the taking up and pursuit of credit institutions, OJ L 126/1, Article 24 and the EC Directive 2002/83 concerning life assurance, OJ L 345/1 Article 51-57.

7 See Patrick Juillard, 'Freedom of Establishment, Freedom of Capital Movements and Freedom of Investments,' *15 ICSID Review-FILJ*, 2000, pp. 331-332, where he states that movement of capital shall be interpreted to include foreign investment. See also EC Directive 88/361 for the implementation of Article 67 of the Rome Treaty, which defines movement of capital to cover direct investment.

and payments between member states and third countries.[8] Articles 57 to 60 of the EC Treaty allow for certain exceptions and safeguards. In particular, Article 57.2 EC Treaty directly empowers the Community to adopt measures on the movement of capital to or from third countries to facilitate the flow of direct investment. One can argue that the term used in the aforementioned provision embraces not only the adoption of internal measures for the functioning of the internal market, but also the use of external measures arising from international law.[9] The combined effect of these provisions and the provisions granting national treatment within the EC seem to suggest that not only would most investments from third countries – once established in one European country in accordance with the relevant entry and establishment rules – be allowed to freely transfer capital and related payments in and out of the Community, but also that third party firms would be treated in the same manner as EC companies with respect to EC rules.[10]

What is important in support of the EC's limited investment rule-making power is that in Opinion 2/92, the ECJ confirmed that such power, as mentioned above, confer certain parallel external competences on the EU. According to the principle of implied power, a competence to conclude international agreements may flow from internal power, if the conclusion of an international agreement is necessary to achieve the objectives stated therein. This applies in particular if the power has already been used in order to adopt internal measures, which could be affected by agreements concluded by member states on their own. As the EU had taken measures under the Treaty's chapters on establishment, the Court held that there was a basis for a parallel external competence on the OECD National Treatment Instrument. However, since these measures were far from covering all fields of foreign investment, it decided that the EU was not able to conclude the agreement without participation by the

8 In implementing these articles, some member states were granted extensions to enable them to abolish exchange controls as required, with Greece being the last to liberalise in May 1994. Moreover, member states were asked to remove the most blatant or discriminatory measures, such as the authorisation procedures for FDI in France and the 29.5% equity limitation on foreign ownership in British Aerospace plc. and Rolls Royce plc. in the UK.

9 Such a statement is backed up by the fact that this provision was used by the EC as a legal basis for the conclusion of WTO agreements including the GATS and TRIMS agreements, as well as the Energy Charter Treaty and others.

10 It should be noted, however, that while the EC has specific provisions establishing an Open-Door Policy towards investment from third countries, it does not go as far as creating a complete Community-wide foreign investment regime. Instead, investment relations with third countries are, for the most part, within the purview of the individual EC members' national law. Hence, asymmetries between third-party investment regimes within the EC may, and often do, exist.

member states. This suggests that the EU may participate in the conclusion of international agreements on investment along with member states. As a consequence of the implied external competences recognised by the Court, member states may not conclude international agreements that would affect the few EU measures dealing with foreign investment. Therefore, the EU has certain limited power to adopt measures affecting foreign investment under the internal market provisions. On the basis of implied competence, it may participate in the conclusion of international agreements on investment, but it cannot conclude such agreements without the participation of the member states.

Besides the aforementioned limited implied competences on FDI, the EU may adopt international obligations on investment on the basis of specific power accorded to it, to conclude bilateral agreements.[11] According to Article 310 EC Treaty, the EC may conclude agreements establishing associations involving reciprocal rights and obligations, common action and specific procedure. The ECJ held that association agreements involve the creation of special links with non-member countries allowing them to take part, at least to a certain extent, in the Communities' legal system. According to the Court, Article 310 EC Treaty provides competence to the EC to conclude agreements covering the entire scope of the internal policies governed by the EC Treaty. This implies that such agreements may include provisions on the free movement of capital and the freedom of establishment towards third countries. Furthermore, according to Article 181 and 181a(3) EC Treaty, the Community and the member states may conclude agreements on cooperation with developing countries and other countries. Yet, this applies only within their respective spheres of competence. Those provisions therefore merely provide for specific instruments, but do not create any additional power on foreign investment going beyond implied power in the field of the internal market.

As noted above, several of the EU's agreements establishing a broader economic and political association or cooperation with other countries

---

11 The EU's bilateral agreements have been concluded on the basis of a number of different EU powers. Association agreements have been based on Article 310 EC Treaty. Trade and cooperation agreements have been concluded on the basis of Article 133 EC Treaty (CCP) and Article 181 EC Treaty (development cooperation). As beyond the scope of Article 133, neither Article 181 EC Treaty nor Article 181a EC Treaty establish competences independently from internal EU powers; their legal basis also includes several internal market provisions (Article 44(2), 47(2), 55, 57(2), 71, 80(2), 93, 94 EC Treaty). The same applies to PCAs with non-developing countries, for which recently Article 181a EC Treaty (cooperation with third countries) is used instead of Article 181 EC Treaty. All agreements are concluded jointly by the EU and its member states, mainly since the EU does not have sufficient powers in the ambit of the Common Foreign and Security Policy.

include obligations on foreign investment. This applies in particular to the stabilisation agreements with Balkan countries, the PCAs with former Union of Soviet Socialist Republics (USSR) countries, association agreements with Mediterranean countries and the agreements with a number of single emerging economies (i.e. Mexico, South Africa and Chile). Many agreements covering investment, in particular with Mediterranean countries, are limited to a basic obligation on the free transfer of capital related to direct investment, or related to companies established according to the laws of the host state (i.e. limited to the post-entry stage). Some include (pre-entry) restrictions on capital movements. Furthermore, some agreements grant MFN treatment and national treatment for the establishment of companies incorporated in the other contracting party.

In all agreements, provisions on establishment are subject to sector-specific access requirements, and the parties endeavour not to introduce new restrictions on the establishment and operation of foreign investors. It is worth noting here that the association agreement with Chile is the first agreement with a non-European country, which grants full national treatment at the pre-entry and post-entry stage for both natural and legal persons from the other contracting party. National treatment is limited to the sectors and subject to the limitations listed in an annex (positive-list approach) and subject to an explicit right to regulate in a non-discriminatory way. The agreement also includes a consent to state-to-state dispute settlement by arbitration.

Apart from the EC Treaty, a wide range of other rules and regulations at the EU level have implications for FDI, especially in the broad area of internal trade and factor movement. For example, regulations concerning mergers, acquisitions, and alliances and rules about corporate restructuring, government procurement, privatisation, have obvious implications for FDI. Likewise, other regulations on competition policy, trade and commercial policy, regional and social policy and industrial policy may have an impact upon FDI in various ways.

In addition to the aforementioned EC practice and policy, the EU has adopted measures to encourage Community investors to explore developing markets. In 1988, the Community embarked on a *European Community Investment Partners* program, which was enlarged in 1992 and further strengthened in 1995. The main purpose of this program is to offer financial support for investment in Latin America, Asia and the Mediterranean Region. The European Investment Bank (EIB) has simultaneously extended its financial activities to funding overseas investments in the group of Africa, Caribbean, Pacific (ACP) countries and the Mediterranean Regions. In 1996, the EU decided to grant Community guarantees to the EIB against losses from loans for projects in Latin America and Asian countries (including China), with which it had concluded cooperation agreements. Accordingly, the EIB and the Chinese government signed a framework agreement for financing co-operation and the EIB soon offered a loan of €55 mn to finance an oil development program in China.[12]

The Bilateral Legal Regime Governing EU-China Investment Relations

China is been the second largest FDI recipient in the world and the single largest among developing countries for several consecutive years. According to latest data provided by the World Investment Report 2008, China's FDI inflows rose to US$83.521 mn in 2007[13] and its FDI inward stock amounted to US$327.087 mn in 2007 (accounting for 10% of GDP[14]). In particular, China is a very attractive destination for FDI flows originating from EU member states. On the basis of the statistics compiled in the EU FDI Yearbook 2008, China (including Hong Kong) is the second largest EU FDI recipient in the ASEAN region attracting €8.9 bn inward FDI flows and €113.586 bn inward FDI stock (of which €33.733 bn originates from the UK, €14.614 bn from Germany, €5.604 bn from France and €3.368 bn from the Netherlands) in 2006.[15]

In addition to imported FDI originating from the EU, Chinese outward investment towards the EU is also increasing rapidly and is therefore cementing its role, and its even greater potential, as a rising capital exporting country.[16] Based on the statistics contained in the EU FDI Yearbook 2008, China's FDI outflows to the EU amounted to €2.2 bn in 2006 and Luxembourg accounted for 60% of the total investments from China. Despite the impressive aforementioned figures, there are many deep concerns and worries among EU investors on issues related to the legal protection of their investment in China, especially in light of the fact that China is still a transition economy undergoing a process of constant

12 See the 'Ping Hu Oil & Gas Field, a Gas Transport and Distribution Project in Pudong Financed by the EIB,' retrieved at http://www.eib.org/projects/loans/1994/19942244.htm; See also http://www.eu-in-china.com/euan_mile1.htm.

13 See UNCTAD, *Annex B, Table B.1 of World Investment Report 2008 – Transnational Corporations, and the Infrastructure Challenge*, retrieved at http://www.unctad.org/en/docs/wir2008_en.pdf, p. 255.

14 *Ibid.*, p. 259.

15 See, 'European Union Foreign Direct Investment Yearbook 2008 Data 2001-2006,' retrieved at http://epp.eurostat.ec.europa.eu/cache/ITYOFFPUB/KS-BK-08-001/EN/KS-BK-08-001-EN.PDF, pp. 61-62.

16 According to World Investment Report, in 2007 China's FDI outflows amounted to US$22.469 mn and its FDI outward stock grew to US$95.799 mn (representing 3.0% of its GDP). It is also worth noting here that as of the end of 2006, China had concluded 120 BITs and is the second ranked (after Germany) worldwide in terms of the total number of BITs concluded.

regulatory change, in order to fulfill its domestic needs and its international binding commitments.

The existing regulatory framework governing the investment activities between the EU and China is not sufficient in protecting and promoting mutual investment, because the legal instruments discussed below are deemed incomplete, uncertain and sometimes partially contradictory. In view of the fact that there is no comprehensive international instrument addressing cross-border investment flows, and that the existing multilateral instruments are too specific to offer investment protection in a broad and all-inclusive way, the 1985 TECA is too general and overly simplistic to provide any substantial commitment at the EC level. Furthermore, although one can argue that the BITs concluded between China and most EU member states are adequate for the protection of covered investments, the small coverage and their divergences prevent them from providing a solid and sufficient BIT net, for the protection of mutual investments at the member state level.

1985 Trade and Economic Cooperation Agreement

At the EU level, the bilateral framework for the EU-China economic relation consists of the 1985 TECA. The negotiation for this new agreement on trade and economic co-operation was launched in 1983 and was finally concluded in 1985. It replaced the 1978 Trade Agreement and is still the only framework agreement between the EU and China.

In terms of its legal nature, the 1985 agreement[17] belongs to a category of agreements signed by the EC with third countries or a group of countries that, under different names, seek to facilitate international trade and cross-border movements of factors of production. Such category of agreements is generally referred to as "economic integration agreements" (EIAs), while EU law and practice endorses and employs the term "mixed agreements." The recent expansion of such mixed agreements – covering a variable range of economic transactions – constitutes a phenomenon with potentially profound implications for the EU's external economic relations, and specifically its international normative power on investment issues. An important characteristic of the agreements concluded by the EC is that, while trade remains one of their principal components they have a tendency to increasingly address a much more detailed and

[17] Council of the European Union, *Agreement on Trade and Economic Cooperation between the European Economic Community and the People's Republic of China*, 21 May 1985, OJ L 250/2 (1985).

expansive set of investment issues (that's why they are often characterised as "economic integration investment agreements," namely EIIAs).[18]

Such EIIAs offer reciprocal (and sometimes non-reciprocal) treatment on a preferential basis and are concluded in an effort to expand and deepen their economic relations in a limited and flexible setting. This allows them to move beyond the minimum common denominator established by the existing multilateral system and undertake new and complex policy initiatives that are difficult to broach at the multilateral level. As briefly stated above, the EC's counterparts to these agreements are mostly transition economies, developing and least developed countries (LDCs). There are several different types of EIIAs models entered into by the EC and third countries and there may be numerous variations of each, based on the depth of market integration they seek.

The reduction or elimination of tariffs and other border barriers to trade in goods remains the central component of the 1985 agreement and its economic rationale is driven by efficiency considerations, as larger markets "allow gains from specialisation (division of labour), differences in resource endowments, and from economies of scale in manufacturing and technology."[19] But the removal of barriers to other types of international transactions, including investment, expands the extent and range of such benefits, therefore the economic rationale for dealing with investment is also compelling.

The type of framework agreement signed by the EC with China is an example of the EIIA agreement that addresses investment promotion through cooperation. Such investment promotion provisions are part of a broader framework for economic cooperation addressing a variety of sectors and areas of economic activity. As described below, this agreement spells out specific promotional measures that should be taken by the parties (or by some of them), including in particular the exchange of information. The parties through the establishment of a Joint Committee, agree to hold consultations on trade and investment matters and to identify agreements appropriate for negotiation. Furthermore, the parties

---

18 An EIIA means an EIA that deals with *inter alia* trade and contains at least one provision directly setting out a specific commitment on investment. The investment commitment or commitments in an EIIA may be narrow or extensive, and may address issues related to the promotion, protection, liberalisation and/or regulation of investment. Agreements falling under the broad denomination of EIIAs are given different names, including, for example, free trade agreements, free trade and investment agreements, preferential trade agreements, regional integration agreements, partnership and cooperation agreements, association agreements, economic partnership agreements, and framework agreements on trade and investment relations.

19 See Kobrin Steven, 'Regional Integration in a Globally Networked Economy,' *Transnational Corporations*, Vol. 4, No. 2, 1995, pp. 15-33.

are specifically encouraged to conclude and extend the bilateral protection and promotion investment agreements at the member state level.

The 1985 agreement has four chapters. Chapters 1, 3 and 4 address the issues of trade cooperation, the Joint Committee and final provisions, which are virtually identical to the 1979 Trade Agreement, with slight modifications. The new element in the agreement is the inclusion of Chapter 2 dealing with the various forms of economic cooperation between the contracting parties and also addressing investment issues. According to the agreement, the Sino-EC economic cooperation is extended to every possible sphere, particularly in fields of industrial production and mining, agriculture including agro-industry, science and technology, energy, transport and communication, environmental protection, cooperation in third countries. At the same time, both parties agreed to endeavour to promote and facilitate various forms of cooperation, including joint production and joint ventures, common exploitation, transfer of technology, cooperation between financial institutions, visits, contacts and activities designed to promote cooperation between individuals, delegations, and economic organisations, organisation of seminars and symposia, consultancy services, technical assistance, including the training of staff, continuous exchange of information relevant to commercial and economic cooperation. The agreement also takes into account the different levels of development between the EC and China and requires that the EC be prepared to continue, step up and diversify its development activities in China, within the means at its disposal and in accordance with the rules.

Article 12 of the agreement requires the two parties to promote and encourage greater and mutually beneficial investment. Moreover, the parties undertake to further improve the investment climate, in particular, through encouraging the extension of BITs between China and the EC member states, based on the principles of equity and reciprocity. This investment clause, being adopted as part of an agreement that addresses *inter alia* trade and investment, imposes no substantial obligation on the contracting parties but rather expresses their intention for future cooperation. Thus, it has more symbolic than practical value crafting a preliminary stage, in which the EIIA partners limit their commitments to establishing a cooperation framework, in order to create a policy climate in which investment could flow within the EIIA area. This pattern was followed at a time where the parties' political and economic systems were far apart from integrating their investment policies. Exchange of information, regular contact, commitments to improve the investment climate and technical assistance measures aimed at institution-building provided by the agreement, seek to prepare the way for more mature mutually-beneficial stages of EU-China investment relations. Nevertheless, the agreement lays down a general legal basis that serves as groundwork for future cooperation in this field.

Bilateral Investment Treaties

Within the context of the Open-Door Policy, China made efforts to establish a sound and stable international legal framework for protecting and attracting FDI. To this extent, the EU member states were among the first countries targeted by China with a view to concluding BITs. As early as 1982, China signed its very first BIT with Sweden, followed by BITs with Romania and the then Federal Republic of Germany. Up until recently, China has signed 25 BITs with the current 27 EU member states.[20] Paired to the Trade and Cooperation Agreement signed between the EU and China in 1985, the BITs complement the existing bilateral network of international law that governs and regulates investment flows between the EU and China at the member state level. For the time being, BITs between China and the EU member states are the most important international legal instruments for EU-China investment relations, since they are the only legal instruments that could offer general and substantial protection to European FDI. The main purpose of these BITs, as they state, is to promote and protect mutual investment, particularly investment in China. Therefore all of them contain such fundamental provisions as definitions, admission, treatment standards, expropriation, war losses compensation, monetary transfer, subrogation and dispute settlement.

A comparison of the substantive provisions of BITs concluded between most of the EU member states and China identifies a basket of similar clauses which provide that:

- Each contracting party shall encourage investors from the other contracting party to invest in its territory and shall permit such investment in accordance with its laws and regulations;
- Investments shall at all times be accorded fair and equitable treatment and they shall also be treated no less favourably than investments from any third state (MFN treatment), with exceptions related to customs unions, free trade areas, frontier trade, avoidance of double taxation treaty;
- Investments shall not be expropriated unless it is in the public interest, by process of law, in a non-discriminatory way and with compensation, and compensation shall be equivalent to the value of the expropriated

[20] The full text of all the different BITs between EU member states and China can be found and retrieved from the Investment Instrument Online Database (IIA database) on the official homepage of UNCTAD, retrieved on 20 March 2009, http://www.unctad.org.

investment, and shall be paid without undue delay and shall be effectively realisable and freely transferable;

- Investors of one contracting party whose investments in the other contracting party suffer losses due to war or other armed conflict, revolution, a state of national emergency, revolt or riot in the territory of latter contracting party shall be accorded MFN treatment;
- Subject to its laws and regulations, each contracting party shall permit without undue delay the free transfer in convertible currency of any payment related to investment;
- If a contracting party makes a payment to its investors under a guarantee it has given to its investor, in respect of an investment made in the territory of the other contracting party, the latter contacting party shall recognise the transfer of any right and title of the investor to the former contracting party and its subrogation to such right and title;
- Disputes concerning the interpretation and application of the BIT between contracting parties should be, as far as possible, settled through diplomatic channels and those failing to be settled in this way in six months could be submitted to an *ad hoc* arbitral tribunal upon the request of a party;
- Normal disputes between the host country and an investor shall be settled by conciliation or, in case of failure to settle it this way in six months, by a competent administrative authority or a competent court of law of the host country. As an exception, disputes on the amount of compensation for expropriation can be submitted to an international arbitral tribunal, which shall determine the arbitral procedure with or without reference to the International Centre for Settlement of Investment Disputes (ICSID) rules.

However, the BITs under review vary from each other in one way or another. For instance, early BITs like the Sino-Swedish BIT and Sino-German BIT require that the Chinese investors shall be approved before they make any investment abroad, while the later ones do not have this restriction. Again, the Sino-British BIT has a provision concerning national treatment, which is reiterated in the Sino-Spanish BIT and contained as well in the PRC's new generation BITs with the Netherlands and Germany. In respect of monetary transfers, most BITs subject them to local laws and regulations, while the BITs between China-Britain, China-Germany and China-Austria claim unrestricted transfers without mentioning the limitation by domestic laws and regulations. Finally, as to the settlement of state-investor disputes, some BITs require that contracting parties shall conclude a supplementary agreement on the utilisation of the ICSID mechanism, while most of them do not. However, the practice of new generation BITs concluded between China-Netherlands, China-Germany, and China-Finland acknowledges the right to submit for arbitration any dispute concerning the covered investments.

These factors discriminate among different EU investors from different member states. Moreover, transnational corporations with more than one EU nationality (or so-called European Companies) that want to invest in China are faced with the added complexity of identifying the best applicable BIT. With the current trend in mergers, acquisitions and alliances among EU companies this complexity risks becoming even more prominent. Ireland and Malta as yet present unresolved issues. As neither of them has concluded a BIT with China, their investment in China can by no means be effectively protected. In the context of EU integration and China's transition to a market economy, further coordination, consolidation and strengthening of these investment provisions under a new BIT between the EU and China is highly desirable, as it will contribute to a more mature international legal regime able to effectively protect and promote EU investment in China.

The Benefits and Prejudices of the EU-China Bilateral Framework of Investment Rules

The economic integration and investment agreements signed by the EC, including the 1985 TECA, deal more with furthering the liberalisation of investment flows, than with investment protection. They often confer a right to establishment or, at least, contain a commitment to future liberalisation. Provisions guaranteeing a right of free transfer are also common. Thus, these agreements are concerned more with the flow of capital into and out of the host country. These agreements do not also provide for investor-state dispute resolution. Instead, investment disputes arising out of such EC level agreements are normally dealt with, or subject to, the general dispute settlement provisions that cover all matters and are contained in the agreements at the member state level. The 1985 TECA includes provisions for investment promotion, principally through economic cooperation. However, it does not provide for investor-state dispute resolution.

BITs concluded between the EU member states and China generally provide for the treatment and protection of investments (once they have been placed), but do not provide for a right to establish foreign investment. That is, BITs are usually intended to protect and, thereby, promote investment. In contrast EIIAs, such as the EC-China Cooperation Agreement, seek to integrate economies and thus are more likely to focus on liberalising investment flows, as well as protecting and promoting investment. They are also more likely to regulate the behaviour of investment, at least insofar as uncompetitive behaviour is concerned. With respect to the settlement of investment disputes, this agreement and

BITs differ in one important respect. That is, while recent BITs almost invariably allow for direct settlement of investor-state disputes through international arbitration, certain types of EIIAs – typically those that do not address investment protection issues – do not allow for international arbitration of investor-state disputes, nor do they always address specifically the issue of investment disputes, as noted above. Instead, investment disputes are often dealt with implicitly in these EIIAs under general provisions for the settlement of disputes arising between the contracting parties (at the state-state level) that apply to all (or most) aspects of the agreement.

Thus, one can sustain that BITs provide a higher level of investment protection, while the agreement permits more variation, which in turn leads to a weakening of the protection afforded. However, the ongoing negotiations for the drafting of a new PCA demonstrate that it is possible to obtain a high standard of investment protection and liberalisation that shall be bound upon the contracting parties. The distinction between a BIT and an EIIA is not comparable to the distinction between a strong and a weak agreement.

As mentioned above, EIIAs, like the 1985 TECA, tend to include mechanisms for consultation, follow-up and implementation that are more elaborate and complex than those found in BITs (if any). EIIAs also often contain specific mandates regarding the further expansion of the agreement, or specific aspects thereof, which are largely absent in BITs. It is also common to establish elaborate institutional arrangements, including a permanent secretariat, to deal with the day-to-day administration of the agreement. BITs, on the other hand, have tended to rely on informal exchanges and regular diplomatic channels to address questions related to their implementation. While BITs address a more limited number of issues and tend to be quite uniform in their approach to those issues, the 1985 agreement reflects far more variation in its scope and content. Although the latter addresses relatively few investment issues, it potentially addresses a much larger range of investment-related issues than the BITs, and takes into account the special circumstances of China, as a developing country.

Bilateral legal instruments are now possibly playing an even more important and substantial role in current EU-China investment relations in comparison with related multilateral legal instruments (GATS, TRIPS, the ICSID Convention, the Multilateral Investment Guarantee Agency Convention). The 1985 agreement acts as the general legal framework for the economic relations between the EU and China, that also covers investments. Although its provision on investment matters is quite simple and brief, it lays down a general legal ground for future development. In respect of the substantial protection and promotion of investment, BITs between China and the EU member states are of the most significance. Through determining the treatment, expropriation and compensation, dispute settlement and other crucial investment issues, they provide a legal basis for EU-China investment relations, particularly EU investment in China. Nevertheless, as repeated above, it could be argued that both the 1985 agreement and the BITs are insufficient to protect mutual investment. On the one hand, the 1985 agreement is too simple to provide any concrete protection for mutual investment. On the other hand, the BITs' shortcomings can easily be detected as well.

Developing a Mandate for a EU-China BIT under the PCA

After the Community attained exclusive competence in the CCP, it started to seek a uniform policy on the protection of the Community's private investment in developing countries. However, so far what it has achieved seems to be more symbolic than real. The EU member states retain their full competences in concluding BITs with non-member states, whilst the Community has never managed to conclude a pure investment treaty by itself. Like the 1985 agreement, the normal practice for the EU in this respect is to insert one article into the framework treaties with developing countries, expressing their political willingness to promote and protect mutual investment in the future.

In short, it is clear that for the time being the general authority on FDI issues still largely rests in the hands of member states, although the present division of competence between the EU and its member states remains rather ambiguous and has raised a further concern. One may fear that while the EC Treaty assigns certain powers in the field of foreign investment to the Community, these powers cannot be exercised effectively, while member states continue to conduct national policies on foreign investment. This argument goes back to one of the main rationales for an exclusive EU competence for external economic relations, (i.e. to prevent external trade policy by member states from undermining the uniformity of the internal market). This picture will soon change since the new Lisbon Treaty attributes to the EU exclusive competence on negotiating and signing FDI agreements. Hence, it is time to establish a mandate under the new PCA for the drafting of a EU-China BIT.

The New FDI Competence under the Lisbon Treaty

Taking up former proposals by the European Commission, the Lisbon Treaty, establishes for the first time that the EU's CCP covers FDI. Article 207 reads as follows:

> the common commercial policy shall be based on uniform principles, particularly with regard to changes in tariff rates, the conclusion of tariff and trade agreements relating to trade in goods and services, and the commercial aspects of intellectual property, foreign direct investment, the achievement of uniformity in measures of liberalisation, export policy and measures to protect trade such as those to be taken in the event of dumping or subsidies. The common commercial policy shall be conducted in the context of the principles and objectives of the Union's external action.

The main rationale for including foreign investment into the CCP is to strengthen the EU's position as an actor in multilateral negotiations on foreign investment.[21] This takes up the reasoning of the European Commission, which has made the case for an EU competence on foreign investment for many years, most recently during the Intergovernmental Conferences leading to the Amsterdam Treaty[22] and Nice Treaty[23] and in the European Convention's sessions.[24] The Commission argues that, as foreign investment is an important part of international economic relations today, the current procedures involving both member states and the EU in the conclusion and implementation of international agreements are excessively burdensome. An exclusive EU competence would clarify that the Commission represents the EU internationally, while coordination with national governments would be ensured by the Council of Ministers. Thus, the new EU competence on foreign investment has a twofold objective: to enhance efficiency in international negotiations on investment; and to improve coordination between foreign investment and other EU policies.

Despite the fact that the negotiation of investment protection issues remains vested in individual EU member states through the conclusion of BITs, the European Commission has systematically questioned and refuted the compatibility of certain substantive provisions of the intra-EU BITs with EC law (expressing the view that these treaties have been superseded by EC law and that any overlap between them creates legal uncertainty), up to the point that it has petitioned for an *amicus curiae* status before the arbitral proceedings of ICSID tribunals (where foreign investment claims of European investors were filed against new EU

---

21 European Convention, *Draft Articles Concerning External Action*, CONV(2003) 685, 23 April 2003.

22 Commission of the European Community, *Report on the Operation of the Treaty on the European Union*, SEC(95) 731, pp. 57-60.

23 Commission of European Community, *Commission Opinion in Accordance with Article 48 EU*, COM(2000) 34, Brussels, p. 27.

24 Pascal Lamy, Speech, *Speech to the Convention Working Group on External Action*, 15 October 2002, retrieved on 20 March 2009, http://europa.eu.int/futurum/docinstcomm_2002_en.htm.

member states), in order to submit a statement on the relations between BITs and EC law.[25]

In other cases, where there was a claim of incompatibility with EC law, deriving from a BIT signed between two member states (usually the case of a BIT between a new member of the EU and an old one) at a time when one of the parties was not a full member of the EU, the European Commission called upon the member states to take all appropriate measures to mutually terminate and rescind such actions that conflict and contradict with EC law.[26] Similar questions over the automatic termination of an intra-EU BIT, due to the accession and the later conclusion of the EU treaties by a new member state, were raised before international arbitral tribunals that ruled that the BIT remained in force and that, even after the accession, there was no conflict between the substantive protections offered in the BIT and the terms of EC law.[27]

Finally, while the Commission has called for the termination of intra-EU BITs, it has also warned that certain provisions in the BITs between EU member states and non-EU member states pose a certain problem in the implementation of EU law. In particular, in relation to the cases brought by the European Commission before the ECJ on the failure of some member states to adopt appropriate measures to eliminate incompatibilities of pre-accession BITs – which they entered into with third countries – the ECJ ruled that Austria (Case C-205/06) and Sweden (C-249/06) have failed to fulfill their obligations according to the second paragraph of Article 307 of the EC Treaty by abstaining from taking the appropriate steps to eliminate incompatibilities concerning the provisions of movement of capital contained in the respective BITs. The rulings give new impetus to the ongoing debate as to the relationship between the BIT drafts (entered into by EU member states with third parties) and the demands of EU membership. Indeed, this debate occurs under the shadow of the EU's Lisbon Treaty which, as stated above, would give the European Commission greater authority to negotiate and conclude international agreements on foreign investment.

---

25 Such is the case of two proceedings filed separately by the companies AES and Electrabel against Hungary and the case of a claim of a Swedish company filed against Romania before separate ICSID arbitral tribunals.

26 Commission of the European Communities, Directorate-General for Internal Market and Services, *Note to the Economic and Financial Committee on the Free Movement of Capital*, November 2006.

27 See Partial Award of 27 March 2007 in *Eastern Sugar v. Czech Republic* case retrieved at http://www.iisd.org/pdf/2007/itn_eastern_sugar.pdf; *Investment Arbitration Reporter*, Vol. 2, No. 4, 28 February 2009, on the surface details of the jurisdictional holdings in the *Binder v. Czech Republic* case.

The Rationale for the Establishment of a PCA Mandate for an EU-China BIT

The European Parliament was the first to propose an individual investment and intellectual property treaty at the Community level with China, as early as 1984, although no substantial progress has been achieved so far.[28] However, today, under the new EU competence on foreign investment, the dice has been cast to reconsider such an agreement, since the political and economic climate has been changed significantly and favourably since then.

Within the EU, as observed above, with the establishment of the single market and the launch of economic and monetary union, FDI laws and policies, both at the Community level and the member state level, have been significantly coordinated and further liberalised. At the same time, the EU's competence in external relations has been expanded by the amendments to the EC Treaty, lately encompassing the negotiation and conclusion of agreements on FDI. In China, the establishment of the market economy is under way and the opening to the outside world is to be broadened and deepened by the accession to the WTO. China is reshaping its FDI laws and regulations and reviewing its BIT programme, which means the negotiations of an EU-China bilateral investment treaty may possibly affect the Chinese FDI legal environment as a whole. Furthermore, as pointed out, both the EU and China have been approaching each other rapidly in recent years and have expressed extraordinary interest in furthering bilateral investment relations, essentially facilitating EU investment in China.

Conclusion

At this stage, under the ongoing negotiations for the conclusion of a new EU-China PCA, a BIT between the EU and China is the most practical and probably the most feasible solution when the Lisbon Treaty comes into force. First, both sides will be willing to negotiate and sign such a treaty because bilateral political and economic links have been significantly improved and are ever improving. Secondly, under the new EU competence on FDI, a bilateral treaty shall involve only two parties (the EU as a whole) and, therefore, shall face much less conflict of interest. Moreover, since the bargaining power of any member state could not be comparable with that of the EU as a whole, no member state can expect a better BIT with China than that signed at the EU level. In addition, the existing patchwork of BITs between China and EU member

---

[28] See European Parliament, Resolution, *On Economic and Commercial Relations between China and the EC*, 1984, OJ C 127/210.

states have laid down a solid basis for the future negotiations of a BIT at the EU level. Finally, the Joint Committee mechanism established under the 1985 agreement may serve as the preliminary vehicle for negotiating such a BIT, with its competence to "examine means and new opportunities of developing trade and economic co-operation" and to "make recommendations"[29] in the areas of common interest.

An EU-China BIT could well fit in the current legal framework for the economic relationship between the EU and China. It could take the form of a sub-agreement within the framework of the PCA, or it could constitute an individual sectoral agreement (in the form of an annex) deriving from a specific mandate contemplated in the PCA. Such a mandate could stem from a new clause that could be inserted in the PCA, with a view to modifying Article 12(2) of the 1985 agreement by stating that:

> In light of the EU's exclusive competence in concluding international agreements covering foreign direct investment issues, the two sides undertake to replace the existing individual BITs extended by and to China and EU member states with a EU-China BIT concluded at the EU level.[30]

To this extent, the PCA can serve as a bilateral legal basis for the EU's involvement in such an agreement.

As an alternative to an individual BIT, the EU-China BIT may adopt the form of a "built-in" chapter or section in the PCA, like the one in the Fourth Lomé Convention. In other words, the two sides may negotiate the revision of the agreement and then substantiate the section of investment with details of the potential BIT. This approach may be a bit more complicated as compared with the aforementioned one, since it requires a review of the whole framework treaty. To this end, one can argue that China could be "upgraded" as one of the EU's association agreement (AA) partners and substantial investment rules could thus be included in the future AA. This possibility, however, may be too good to be practical for the time being. Among others, China's human rights record, in the EU's eyes, may prove to be the biggest obstacle for such an association.

Finally, the mandate of the PCA procuring the drafting of an EU-China model BIT shall address the relationship of the BIT at the EU level with the existing bilateral investment agreements at the member state level. One could argue that the BITs in force shall continue

---

29 Council of the European Union, Agreement on Trade and Economic Cooperation between the European Economic Community and the People's Republic of China, 21 May 1985, OJ L 250/2 (1985), Chapter III, Article 15.

30 Council of the European Union, Agreement on Trade and Economic Cooperation between the European Economic Community and the People's Republic of China, *op. cit.*, Chapter II, Article 12(2).

governing the investment relations between EU member states and their counterparts for a certain period of time, until they expire. Since the early termination of such BITs is impractical and the EU cannot wait for all such BITs to terminate in order to exercise its own authority to conclude BITs, another approach must be followed. International investment law has developed specific techniques harmonising the concurrent applicability of multiple investment instruments governing the same investment activity. The Energy Charter Treaty (ECT), which constitutes an important multilateral investment agreement concluded in the energy sector, to which both the EC and its member states are parties, provides useful guidance on how the existing member states' BITs may co-exist with the EU-China BIT to come. Article 16 of the ECT thus provides in relevant part:

> where two or more Contracting Parties have entered into a prior international agreement [...] whose terms in either case concern the subject matter of Part III or V of this Treaty,
>
> - Nothing in Part III or V of this Treaty shall be construed to derogate from any provision of such terms of the other agreement or from any right to dispute resolution with respect thereto under that agreement;
> - Nothing in such terms of the other agreement shall be construed to derogate from any provision of Part III or V of this Treaty or from any right to dispute resolution with respect thereto under this Treaty, where any such provision is more favourable to the Investor or Investment.

A similar technique, incorporated in the EU-China BIT, will allow EU institutions to exercise their power to conclude the BIT, now that the Lisbon Treaty is to enter into force, notwithstanding the fact that a great number of BITs concluded by EU member states will still remain applicable. There is also a possibility that an inconsistency could arise between BITs at the state level and other provisions of the Lisbon Treaty, or secondary EU acts or measures, adopted with a view to implementing the FDI dimension of the new CCP. In such a case, in light of the recent ECJ rulings on the status of incompatibility of the extra-EU BITs with EC law, a member state must ensure, until the expiration or renegotiation of such agreements that it had been concluded before the entry into force of the Lisbon Treaty, to abide by EU law, and remove all existing incompatibilities.

CHAPTER 6

The Evolution of EU Trade Policy towards China

The Case of Textiles and Clothing

Jappe ECKHARDT[1]

The current legal framework under which trade relations between the EU[2] and China are structured – the Trade and Economic Cooperation Agreement (TECA) dates back to 1985. Since the signing of the TECA, the relationship between the EU and China as trading partners has, however, changed considerably. In more than 20 years China has become the EU's second trading partner and its most important source of imports, making China, in the words of the European Commission: "the single most important challenge for EU trade policy."[3] In order to cope with this challenge in the future, both sides have come to realise that revision of the 1985 framework is inevitable, because "tentative trade relations of the 1980s bear little resemblance to the extensive and complex relationship of the 21st century."[4] Consequently, the EU and China launched negotiations for a PCA in 2007, an agreement which should reflect the full complexity of today's relations between the two.

In section one, I intend to analyse, from a European viewpoint, the evolution of EU-China trade relations in general and the EU's trade policy towards China in particular. To this end I will answer the following question: what changes have taken place in the EU's trade policy towards China between 1978 and 2009, and what has spurred these changes? This question will be answered with detailed reference to important bilateral trade negotiations between Brussels and Beijing in the aforementioned period as well as to key trade policy decisions taken by the EU. This will

1 Research funded by the Research Foundation Flanders (FWO).

2 Note that the term EU is used throughout the entire chapter, also when the predecessors of the EU (i.e. the European Coal and Steel Community and later the European Community) are meant.

3 See the website of the Commission of the European Communities' Directorate-General for Trade, retrieved on 6 July 2009, http://ec.europa.eu/trade/issues/bilateral/countries/china.

4 'EU-China Talks Mark Growing Maturity,' *China Daily*, 17 January 2007, p. 11.

be done by using an in-depth case study[5] of one of the most politically and economically sensitive sectors within EU-China trade relations: the textiles and clothing sector.

The remainder of this chapter is organised into three additional sections. In section two, I will present some background information on EU-China trade in textiles and clothing products. Section three is devoted to an analysis and comparison of three phases in the evolution of EU textile and clothing trade policy towards China. In the final section, I will use the information provided in section two and three to draw conclusions about the changes in EU trade policy towards China and the circumstances under which these changes took root.

Background Notes on Trade in Textiles and Clothing

No study of the textile and clothing industry is complete without referring to the trade distortions that dominated the sector for so long. In the first part of this section I will, therefore, pay attention to the most important of these distortions – the quota regime. Besides the trade distortions, another important characteristic of the textile and clothing sector is its relatively complex supply chain. In the second part of this section, I will sketch some of the characteristics of the supply chain and indicate what the preferences of the different type of European firms within this chain are, when it comes to the EU's trade policy *vis-à-vis* China.

The Quota Regime

The quota regime in the textile and clothing sector was formally established with the signing of the Multi Fibre Arrangement (MFA) in 1973 and its first implementation in 1974.[6] Established as a temporary measure, the arrangements' declared goal was an orderly opening of restricted markets in the United States (US), Europe and Canada in order to avoid market disruptions and to overcome the severe crisis that had hit their textile and clothing sectors after Second World War. Given that the crisis appeared obstinate and competition from low-income countries increased considerably, textile and clothing manufacturers in these

---

5 The following methods have been used to gather the data for this case study: a study of secondary literature on the topic in question; a thorough assessment of documents, statistics as well as press releases from governments and interest groups – finally, I have conducted interviews with policy-makers, representatives of interest groups and individual companies in the textile and clothing sector. A list of interviewees is available upon request.

6 The Multi-Fibre Agreement itself was an extension of two earlier quota arrangements: the Short-term Arrangement (1960-1961) and the Long-term Arrangement (1962-1973) for cotton textiles.

advanced industrial economies lobbied policy-makers constantly to keep the protective quotas on cheap imports in place. Their lobbying efforts were successful: the MFA was renegotiated four times (1977, 1981, 1986 and 1991) and every renewal of the MFA amounted to an extension of the number of products and countries subject to quotas. It started with quotas on certain cotton products from a limited number of suppliers and in the end there were quotas on all sorts of textile and clothing products from a wide range of countries. In fact, the MFA came to comprise the bulk of developing country exports of textile and clothing products to the US and the EU.[7]

This is not to say that all developing countries were hurt equally by the MFA-scheme. In the EU context, China – a MFA signatory since 1984 – was subject to quotas, while other important EU textile and clothing suppliers were exempted from quotas. Examples of the latter are Turkey, Romania, Tunisia and Morocco – due to Preferential Trade Agreements (PTAs) – as well as Bangladesh and India – who enjoyed preferential access to the EU market under the General System of Preferences (GSP).[8] It must be noted that China was also a GSP beneficiary, but only for a relatively limited number of products.

Despite the privileged treatment of some countries, the quota arrangements clearly benefited firms in Europe, the US and Canada by giving them protection for a period of time from cheaper imports, mainly from Asia. Consequently, the MFA emerged as a counterargument to the general trend towards a free and multilateral trade system that was set in motion with the signing of the General Agreement on Trade and Tariffs (GATT) in 1947. The MFA, in effect, openly violated the principles of the GATT in two ways: the MFA provided for bilateral quotas instead of tariffs and it fostered discrimination among trading partners, rather than following the Most Favoured Nation (MFN) principle.[9] The latter signifies that quotas on certain imported textile and clothing products could be negotiated bilaterally without the MFA having any consequences for the quotas on imports of that same product from other countries. In

---

7 See Geoffrey R.D. Underhill, *Industrial Crisis and the Open Economy: Politics, Global Trade and the Textile Industry in the Advanced Economies*, London, Houndsmill Macmillan Press, 1998.

8 Kenneth A. Reinert, 'Give Us Virtue, But Not Yet: Safeguard Actions Under the Agreement on Textiles and Clothing,' *The World Economy*, Vol. 23, No. 1, 2000, pp. 25-55.

9 Most Favoured Nation (MFN) is a status which one nation awards to another nation in international trade. In practice it means that the nation receiving MFN status will be granted all trade advantages that any other nation receives as well. All the members of the GATT/WTO accord such MFN-status to each other. There are important exceptions to this rule, such as FTAs and customs unions.

spite of this, the MFA was part of the GATT, creating, to say the least, an awkward situation.[10]

After long negotiations, the EU, the US and Canada accepted the expiration of the MFA in 1993. However, this expiration did not mean the end of the quotas. The MFA was replaced by the Agreement on Textiles and Clothing (ATC),[11] which came into force with the establishment of the WTO in 1995 and accepted that all quotas on textiles and clothing, between WTO-members, would disappear in four steps between 1995 and 2005. The ATC was thus a transitional stage between the MFA and the complete integration of trade in textiles and clothing into the multilateral trading regime, which was supposed to give textile and clothing firms in Europe and North-America time to adjust to the new rules of the game.

The Supply Chain

A typical textile and clothing supply chain includes a number of separate, but interconnected activities consisting of different types of firms. Below, I will give a short description of the EU supply chain and indicate what the different type of firms' trade interests are *vis-à-vis* China. However, I shall start by presenting China's role in the worldwide production of textile and clothing products.

Prior to the Open-Door Policy, the textile and clothing industry in China was not a priority at all. Consequently, the inward-looking policies of the communist planners led to a gradual erosion of China's world market share in this sector. It was only after Deng Xiaoping came to power in 1978 and opened the economy, that China's textile and clothing sector started to grow rapidly. Two crucial comparative advantages in particular made this growth possible. First, China's huge, and relatively well educated, labour force permitted Chinese textile and clothing companies to specialise in the production of cheap labour-intensive export products. A second advantage was the vertically integrated structure of China's textile and clothing sector, enabling it to carry out all stages of production domestically without having to import raw materials like most of its competitors. As a result, Chinese companies gradually started to dominate the global textile and clothing market.[12]

---

10 Claudia Jimenez Cortes, *GATT, WTO and the Regulation of International Trade in Textiles*, Vermon, Ashgate Publishing Company, 1997.

11 Annex 1A-5 of GATT Final Act, MTN/FA, 15 December 1993.

12 Yongzheng Yang, *China's Textile and Clothing Exports: Changing International Comparative Advantage and its Policy Implications*, Working Paper Series, Working Paper No. 3, Asia Pacific School of Economics and Management, 1999.

China's dominance had an impact on all segments of the European textile and clothing industry.[13] Let me start with the textile sector. Traditionally, the majority of the textile firms in the EU produced commodities for the European clothing sector. These traditional producers, which compete with Chinese suppliers, have, since China started exporting its textile products *en masse* to the EU, supported a protectionist trade policy towards China. However, the companies that constitute the textile industry in Europe have increasingly produced a wide variety of end-products, such as household appliances and other industrial fabrics (i.e. for furniture and the car industry) – the so-called technical textiles. This segment of the textile industry is much more research and development intensive than the traditional producers and hence face less competition from China. As a result, these types of producers are not so much interested in shielding their markets from Chinese imports, but mainly defend their interests as exporters. Moreover, given that they are confronted with trade barriers in potential foreign markets (i.e. China), producers of technical textiles lobby for market opening.

Also the clothing sector in the EU is a sector with two faces. The industry of the high-quality fashion market can best be described as modern and highly flexible. The competitive advantage of firms in this segment is not (primarily) related to cost effectiveness, but to the ability to produce cloths that capture or influence tastes of their consumers. Although these types of companies do face some competition from China, their main trade interest towards China is to sell their clothes to the Chinese high and middle classes. The other important market segment within the clothing sector is the mass production of lower-quality and standard products (i.e. men's white dress shirts, underwear, t-shirts and uniforms). The manufacturing of these items is labour intensive and therefore European companies within this segment face harsh competition from China and are traditionally very pro-protectionism.

The final segment of the supply-chain is the retail sector. When it comes to retailers, consumers can either buy their clothes at local department stores or boutiques or they can go to one of the huge shopping malls at the outskirts of the city. Traditionally, both these type of retailers in Europe were the key clients of EU clothing producers. However,

[13] Section based on: Frederick H. Abernathy *et al.*, *Lean Retailing and the Transformation of Manufacturing – Lessons from the Textile and Apparel Industries*, Oxford, Oxford University Press, 1999; Hildegunn K. Nordås, *The Global Textile and Clothing Industry Post the Agreement on Textiles and Clothing*, WTO Discussion Papers, No. 5, Geneva, World Trade Organization, 2004; Gary Gereffi, 'International Trade and Industrial Upgrading in the Apparel Commodity Chain,' *Journal of International Economics*, Vol. 48, No. 1, 1999, pp. 37-70; and interviews conducted by the author.

because of changing consumer preferences (better value for money) and the need to cut costs, retailers (especially the big chains) in the EU increasingly turned to imports, mainly from China. Many retailers thus began to compete directly with their former suppliers and their trade preferences in general (and thus towards China in particular), turned very anti-protectionist. Besides focusing particularly on imports, the retail sector also witnessed a dramatic move towards market concentration: ever larger retail organisations have constantly increased their market share at the expense of smaller companies. This has forced the remaining smaller companies to also turn to cheap imports, which in turn has further increased anti-protection sentiments among retailers.

EU Textile and Clothing Trade Policy towards China: Three Phases, Three Faces

In this section, I will analyse in detail three different phases in the evolution of EU textile and clothing trade policy towards China. For each phase I provide first some key facts and figures, such as trade flows. After that I will indicate what the trade policy interests of the most important actors were during that particular phase. Finally, I will analyse, for each phase, several important trade policy decisions taken by the EU.

1978-1994: Protectionism and nothing but Protectionism

The deep crises that had hit the European textile and clothing sector in the 1970s seemed to level out at the beginning of the 1980s, partly as a result of the adoption of ever tougher trade restrictions. Yet, despite this relatively positive news, import competition was still very intense and imports were on the rise in both textile and clothing. Especially from the end of the 1980s onwards there was a considerable and increasing trade deficit in the sector.[14]

This deficit was mainly due to the clothing industry. The clothing sector had faced a trade deficit ever since the start of the crisis in the 1970s and this continued during the 1980s, with a sharp increase from approximately 1986 onward. In 1986 alone, the deficit of the EU10 doubled and continued to grow between 1986 and 1995.[15] The deficit with China especially showed an impressive growth rate during these years. The share of China's imports, as the percentage of total clothing imports to the EU, rose from 7.3% in 1988 to 12.4% in 1995 (see

14 Werner Stengg, *The Textile and Clothing Industry in the EU – A Survey*, Commission of the European Community's Directorate-General for Enterprise & Industry, Enterprise Papers No. 2, 2001, p. 23.

15 Stengg, *op. cit.*

Table 1). This made China the most important clothing supply country for Europe in 1995.

In the textile industry the situation for European producers was much more positive. The textile sector quickly regained its strength after the crisis and the trade surplus grew substantially in the course of the 1980s. As a result of the increasingly capital intensive and specialised nature of the textile production, the textile sector continued to run a trade surplus with most of its trading partners into the 1990s.[16] China was one of the important exceptions to this rule. Although China's growth figures in textiles trade were much less impressive than for clothing, the EU's trade deficit in textiles with China still more than doubled between 1988 and 1995 (see Table 2 for import figures).

Because of this growing (import) competition, parts of the textile and clothing industry in the EU started to make significant restructuring and modernisation efforts during this period. They did this, for example, through the adoption of new technologies and moving towards the production of more research and development intensive products.[17] The restructuring process also involved the outsourcing of more labour-intensive operations (mainly clothing production) to countries like Poland, Romania, Tunisia and Morocco. A large number of these of operations involved "the export of EU fabric, cuttings or semi-finished garments to low-wage countries, which make them into finished garments for re-import into the EU."[18] This relocation was not surprising given the large wage gap between the aforementioned countries and EU member states. Although wage rates in most Asian countries (i.e. Vietnam, China) were even much lower,[19] EU manufacturers preferred neighbouring countries given their geographical proximity and higher quality standards. By outsourcing to its neighbours, EU-based companies expected to be able to respond faster to changing market demands, and to maintain more control over the management and quality of the outsourced operation.[20]

16 Underhill, *op. cit.*, p. 207.

17 Maurizio Giuli, *The Competitiveness of the European Textile Industry*, Research Papers in International Business, Paper number 2-97, London, Centre for International Business Studies, South Bank University, 1997, p. 6.

18 Stengg, *op. cit.*, p. 4.

19 In 1993, in Germany hourly wage costs were nearly US$ 18, while in Poland (US$2.77), Morocco (US$1.36) and Romania (US$1.04) wages were much lower. Even lower wages were paid in Vietnam (US$0.22) and China (US$0.40). Figures based on Giuli, *loc. cit.*

20 Stengg, *loc. cit.*

The restructuring and modernisation process had two important implications for the textile and clothing sector in the EU. First, the outsourcing of lower value-added and labour-intensive production processes caused a general decline in production in the European textile and (especially) clothing sector from 1988 onwards. Second, Europe saw a further decline in employment because of the outsourcing. In just 15 years (1980-1995) the EU lost as much as 47% of the workforce in textiles and 40% in the clothing sector.[21]

Table 1. Most Important EU Clothing Suppliers, Selected Years (Import Values in Million US$)

	1988	1995	2001	2004	2005	2006	2007
China	991	4,633	7,460	14,255	20,963	23,509	29,609
Turkey	1,163	4,172	5,272	9,527	9,934	10,174	11,964
Bangladesh	125	1,265	2,528	4,624	4,402	5,786	5,992
India	526	2,078	1,977	3,077	4,025	4,759	5,214
Romania	347	1,271	3,029	4,774	4,487	4,397	3,729
Tunisia	570	2,262	2,590	3,235	3,065	3,094	3,517
Morocco	588	2,134	2,372	3,017	2,818	2,970	3,448
Hong Kong	2,349	3,332	2,315	2,430	2,108	3,129	2,265
Indonesia	199	1,188	1,604	1,658	1,483	1,752	1,607

Source: figures for 1988 are in million US$ and are based on Stengg W., *op. cit.*, p. 55; all other figures are in million US$ and are calculations by the author based on Eurostat data. Rankings according to 2007 imports.

Table 2. Most Important EU Textile Suppliers, Selected Years (Import Values in Million US$)

	1988	1995	2001	2004	2005	2006	2007
China	679	1,325	1,968	3,947	4,940	5,961	7,277
Turkey	714	1,358	2,226	3,437	3,572	3,978	4,591
India	613	1,753	1,883	2,431	2,506	2,745	3,235
Pakistan	387	984	1,043	1,746	1,539	1,737	2,092
Switzerland	1,338	1,852	1,158	1,239	1,145	1,163	1,324
US	892	1,632	1,442	1,059	1,096	1,208	1,256
Korea Rep	313	547	1,021	1,031	961	890	1,071
Japan	698	814	692	656	626	654	771
Romania	n.a.	88	201	471	498	611	635
Indonesia	n.a.	781	566	517	470	538	621

Source: figures for 1988 are in million US$ and are based on Stengg W., *op. cit.*, p. 55; all other figures are in million US$ and are calculations by the author based on Eurostat data. Rankings according to 2007 imports.

21 International Labour Organization, *Labour Practices in the Footwear, Leather, Textiles and Clothing Industries*, Geneva, International Labour Organization, 2000.

Trade Preferences towards China within the EU

Given the above mentioned developments, the following trade interests towards China can be identified.[22] Import-competing producers (i.e. the traditional clothing and textile firms) were hit hard by the growing Chinese imports and obviously had a lot to gain from restrictions on Chinese imports. These producers, with their historically intimate relationship with the political elite in Europe, have a long tradition of well-established national and European lobby organisations (i.e. Euratex, Eurocotton) and hence have formed a very powerful and well-disciplined lobby machinery, which they used constantly to lobby at both the national and the EU-level.

On the anti-protection side, some big retailers were of course against restrictions on their Chinese textile and clothing imports. However, since many small retailers were at this stage still buying much of their clothing from European producers, the trade interests of retailers were rather diffuse at this point. As a result, they were by far not as well organised as the traditional textile and clothing producers. They had a few national lobby organisations, but in Brussels they were not yet represented properly, which, in turn, made it difficult to set up an effective lobby that could provide adequate opposition. In effect, this was made all the more interesting, as other potential allies (i.e. exporters and companies with outsourced production) were not really interested in lifting Chinese quotas either. Since outsourcing to China had not fully started yet, import-users were not hurt by protectionist measures against China. Moreover, most European exporters did not see China as a very interesting market at this stage and hence did not push for bilateral talks on mutual trade liberalisation.

What is more, traditional textile and clothing production was still important for the national economies of many EU member states (i.e. France, Italy, Spain, Portugal and Greece). Although it is true that the contribution of the sector to the economies of developed countries relatively declined over the years, it was still a major industry in many EU countries. Consequently, many governments in the EU were still eager to help their domestic industries. In short, the coalition pushing for tough restrictions on Chinese imports to the EU was much stronger than the forces in favour of free trade. I will now turn to a discussion of the most important bilateral negotiations on textile and clothing issues between the EU and China in this period, in order to see whether the pro-protection coalition was indeed able to shape EU trade policy towards China.

---

22 Based on interviews by the author.

EU Policy towards China

Trade in textiles and clothing was without any doubt the most sensitive area in EU-China economic relations in the late 1970s and the 1980s and hence a major source of disagreement between both parties. After all, the sector was China's most important source of exports to the EU and an important source of foreign currency earnings.[23] The EU, on the other hand, pressured by member states and producers, was eager to protect its textile and clothing industry. As a result of this tension, textile and clothing trade was not touched upon in the 1978 Trade Agreement,[24] but both parties agreed to negotiate a special agreement on trade in textiles and clothing products. Unsurprisingly, these negotiations were very difficult, but a 4-year agreement was eventually signed in 1979.[25] The aim of the agreement was clear: restrict Chinese textile and clothing inflows into the EU as much as possible.

The agreement limited China's exports to some extent, but the deal was more generous than the standard MFA-type agreement and it enabled China to double its exports in the first few years. Therefore, producers in the EU lobbied heavily for further trade restrictions on Chinese imports. The lobbying was successful. For one, after long-lasting negotiations, and partly due to the political pressure applied by the EU, China became a MFA-signatory in 1984. As a result, China's bargaining position *vis-à-vis* the EU in the negotiations on the renewal of the Textile Agreement was weakened since the agreement now had to be brought in line with the stricter MFA-rules.[26]

A second consequence of the lobbying efforts was that, in its mandate concerning the negotiations on the new Textile Agreement, the Council of Ministers left the Commission little room for manoeuvre. The mandate set down stringent limits on imports from China, especially for sensitive textile and clothing products.[27] What followed were tough negotiations. Eventually an agreement was signed in March 1984 which renewed the Textile Agreement for 5 more years.[28] Although the agreement did increase the amount of quotas for some products, a new Protocol to the

23 Edward K.Y. Chen, 'China-EC Economic Relations: Experience and Prospects,' in G. Sciavoni (ed.), *Western Europe and Southeast Asia: Cooperation or Competition?*, London, Palgrave Macmilllan, 1989, pp. 174-196.

24 Council Regulation (EEC) No. 946/78, OJ L 123 (11/5/1978).

25 Council Regulation (EEC) No. 3061/79, OJ L 345 (31/12/1979).

26 Philippe De Smedt, 'Legal Aspects of the Economic and Trade Relations of the People's Republic of China with the European Economic Community,' *China Law Reporter*, Vol. 1985-1986, No. 3, 1985, p. 188.

27 *Ibid.*

28 Council Regulation (EEC) No. 2072/84, OJ L 198 (27/7/1984).

agreement was added at the same time, which included all the restrictive demands the Council of Ministers had put forward in its aforementioned mandate. The net result was a further increase of restrictions on Chinese textile and clothing imports.

The following period (1988-1995) was very similar to the previous time-period. With decreasing production, job losses and a mounting trade deficit, European producers sought further protection against Chinese imports and lobbied intensively for a renewal (and toughening) of the agreement. Backed by a majority of the EU member states, a new 4-year agreement was indeed negotiated by the Commission in 1988 which again introduced restrictions on Chinese products which had not been covered by quotas before.[29] In 1992, again another agreement – in the form of an exchange of letters – was negotiated between Brussels and Beijing.[30] This new agreement, which amended the 1988-agreement and took account of the EU's enlargement process, was applicable to the end of 1995 and was as restrictive as its predecessors.

1995-2001: Small Steps towards Liberalisation

On 1 January 1995, the Agreement on Textiles and Clothing (ATC) came into force and it was expected that quotas would gradually be eliminated and that it would ensure a smooth transition to the full integration of the industry into GATT/WTO rules. Yet, the effects of the first two stages (1995-2001) of the ATC on trade to and from the EU were modest at best. On the one hand, the ATC offered all kind of loopholes enabling EU countries to step aside from extensive quota elimination. Moreover, hardly any country in the top ten of the EU's most important textile and clothing suppliers was subject to the ATC during this period. Some countries were, as mentioned earlier, already exempted from quotas due to the PTAs or the GSP-scheme, whereas China was not yet a WTO-member and hence the EU was not forced to lift the quotas on Chinese products.[31]

Nonetheless, the textile and clothing sector in the EU saw its trade deficit increase sharply. This was due to a combination of almost a doubling of the trade deficit in the clothing sector between 1995 and 2001 and to the fact that the trade surplus in the textile industry grew much too slowly to compensate for this loss. In clothing, part of the trade deficit could be "blamed" on the PTAs and preferential treatment of least

---

29 Council Regulation (EEC) No. 88/656, OJ L 380 (31/12/1988).

30 OJ L 410 (31/12/1992).

31 Jaime Malaga & Samarendu Mohanty, 'The Agreement on Textiles and Clothing: Is It a WTO Failure?,' *Estey Centre Journal of International Law and Trade Policy*, Vol. 4, No. 1, 2003, pp. 75-85.

developed countries.[32] More importantly, imports from China kept on rising, despite the quota scheme. The logic behind this is as follows: there were still numerous Chinese products not subject to quotas, while, at the same time, almost all quotas put in place were filled completely. As a result, the total value of Chinese clothing imports into the EU rose by 61% in the 1995-2001 period (Table 1).

The EU's trade deficit, specifically on clothing products was also caused by the fact that its high-end exports did not grow as fast as European exporters had hoped. Ironically enough, this was, according to the exporters, partly caused by the restrictive trading regimes of a series of (potential) trading partners.[33] One of the most interesting of these potential, but relatively closed export-markets, was China. China had a fast growing high and middle-class, which was increasingly interested in European fashion, but because of Chinese import-restrictions, European exporters could not benefit from this increasing demand.[34]

Also in the textile segment of the market, European companies complained that their exports were subject to an increasing number of restrictions in many markets. Partly as a result of this, the trade surplus in the textile sector grew much more slowly than in the period between 1988 and 1995.[35] However, a more important reason for this declining growth seems to be the increase in imports from countries like Turkey, India, Pakistan, South Korea and most notably, China. The EU's deficit with China was the fastest growing and China climbed to the second place of Europe's most important suppliers in 2001 (see Table 2).

The aforementioned developments prompted the EU textile and clothing industry to rethink their corporate strategies again. Accordingly, the sector became subject to some far-reaching transformations.[36] First of all, companies in the EU tried to improve their competitiveness by further reducing or ceasing mass production and concentrating instead on a wider variety of more value-added products and niche-markets. Secondly, relocation and outsourcing of the low value-added segments of (especially) the clothing sector intensified. In contrast to the previous time-period, this replacement of production now took place mainly towards low-cost producing countries in Asia, especially China. The final

32 Stengg, *op. cit.*, p. 23.

33 *Ibid.*, p. 25.

34 Interviews conducted by the author.

35 Interviews conducted by the author.

36 Section based on: Gereffi, *op. cit.*, p. 45; Mick Dunford, 'The Changing Profile and Map of the EU Textile and Clothing Industry,' in M. Faust *et al.*, *European Industrial Restructuring in a Global Economy: Fragmentation and Relocation of Value Chains*, Göttingen, SOFI, 2004, pp. 295-318; and interviews conducted by the author.

transformation consisted of a move towards further market concentration. As a result of an unprecedented growth in acquisitions and mergers in the textile and clothing industry, a small number of large enterprises, especially in the retail sector, accounted for an increasingly large percentage of total turn-over during this period.

Trade Preferences towards China within the EU

Prompted by these transformations, trade preferences among European textile and clothing firms changed gradually.[37] Although the traditional production firms were still lobbying to prevent their markets from being flooded by Chinese products, their pro-protection coalition was weakened during the 1995-2001 period. After all, many traditional clothing and, to a lesser extent, textile firms had started to outsource (parts of) their production to China. Consequently, for many firms the quotas on Chinese imports became a burden rather than a blessing because of renewed imports from China were now such an important part of their production process.

In addition, firms which had moved towards the production of more high-end products became exporters. And exporters, as shown above, became very interested in exporting to China and hence started to lobby for Chinese market openings. At the same time, retailers and importers became better organised – they started to establish their own umbrella organisations on the EU level (i.e. FTA, Eurocommerce) – and, by doing so, increased their political clout. In other words, rather than having just a one-sided focus on the threats of China's economic rise, the opportunities became more visible in the political arena.

These changing preferences can also be seen among EU member states. Traditional textile and clothing producing countries such as Portugal, France and Italy fully supported trade restrictions on Chinese imports, but an anti-protection coalition started to take form. In the Netherlands, the UK, Germany and Scandinavia, the textile and clothing sector had almost disappeared or had specialised in niche markets. At the same time, retailers gained political and economic strength in these countries. This "Northern coalition" became increasingly wary of quotas on Chinese imports. I will now analyse several trade policy measures taken by the EU towards China between 1995 and 2001, and see whether they reflect the changing interests and preferences within the EU.

---

37 Section based on interviews conducted by the author.

EU Policy towards China

In 1995 the EU and China signed a new textile and clothing agreement,[38] in which the quotas on Chinese products were adjusted to take account of EU enlargement. In unison, a provision was made for the inclusion of several products that had not been covered by quotas before (i.e. silk, linen and ramie products), which came to be known as the Silk Agreement. At first sight, it appears as if this was just a continuation of the earlier protectionist agreements, but a closer look at the Silk Agreement, and the negotiations preceding it, reveals some interesting changes that took place in the EU's trade policy towards China.

One year before the Silk Agreement was signed the EU had unilaterally set a quota of 17.000 tonnes for Chinese silk, linen and ramie goods. This decision spurred heavy protest by the Chinese as well as by European importers (both retailers and import-users). The latter argued that "[…] the quotas are hurting consumers and financially damaging firms that had already contracted to import Chinese products but were suddenly cut from supplies."[39] At first, Brussels took the following stand: given that China was not a GATT/WTO member they had every right to fix unilateral limits on Chinese exports. However, importers kept on protesting and certain European exporters started to complain about restrictions on their exports to China. Prompted by this pressure, the EU agreed to start bilateral negotiations with Beijing. What followed were 10 months of meticulous negotiations, which eventually led to the signing of the Silk Agreement. Under this agreement, the EU, unexpectedly, agreed to more than double the quota for China's silk, linen and ramie exports, while China lifted restrictions on certain items of interest to European exporters.[40]

Around the same time as the Silk Agreement was signed, the EU announced the implementation of its new GSP scheme.[41] However, this time the decision taken by the EU was less beneficial for those in favour of lifting restrictions on Chinese imports. The new GSP scheme was, more so than its forerunner, oriented mainly towards the least developed countries (LDCs) and towards minimising the adverse effects on traditional and declining industries in the EU, such as the textile and clothing industry. The new scheme, which was partly the result of serious

---

38 Council of the European Union Decision 95/131, OJ L 94 (26/4/1995).

39 Shada Islam, 'A New Deal: European Union Increases Quotas for Asian Exporters,' *Far Eastern Economic Review*, 2 February 1995, p. 52.

40 Islam, *loc. cit.*

41 Commission of the European Communities, *The European Union's New Generalized System of Preferences (GSP) Scheme*, MEMO (1995) 1, Brussels, 19 January 1995, p. 3.

lobbying by European textile and clothing producers, had severe implications for textile and clothing imports from China.

One policy adjustments in particular had a restrictive effect on products entering the EU from China: the introduction of the so-called "graduation mechanism." This meant that the preferential tariffs were to be gradually abolished for countries whose GSP exports on a particular product exceeded 25% of the total GSP exports to the EU of that product.[42] China, who used to benefit from preferential treatment, was one of the few countries hurt by this "graduation mechanism." In fact, some Chinese textile and clothing products lost their tariff preference over night because they already exceeded the 25% margin when the new rules became effective in 1996. Many other Chinese textile and clothing products came to "graduate" in 1998 and hence preferential margins were abolished on these products too.[43] The inflow of Chinese textile and clothing products was clearly discouraged accordingly. It must be noted, however, that the new GSP scheme also, indirectly, facilitated some European exports. That is to say, those Chinese manufacturers who used component parts manufactured in the EU, could continually be granted the GSP.[44]

By the end of 2001, China has become a WTO member. During the 15-year negotiation process leading to Chinese accession, trade in textile and clothing products had played a prominent role, especially in the bilateral negotiations between the EU and China. This prominence became particularly apparent in the talks on "mutual market opening." The deal that was finally struck on market opening had two important dimensions and was a clear compromise between all parties involved (i.e. all European and Chinese firms).[45] First, China promised to abolish non-tariff barriers and to reduce tariffs on manufacturing exports (including textile and clothing products) from third countries. Secondly, the EU (and the US) agreed to abolish all quotas on textile and clothing imports from China. Accordingly, China, and in turn the European importers, could benefit from the ATC quota removals as of January 2002. The latter agreement was, however, qualified by a special Textile

---

42 *Ibid.*

43 Roger Strange, 'EU Trade Policy towards China,' in R. Strange *et al.*, *Trade and Investment in China: The European Experience*, London and New York, Routledge, 1998, pp. 65-66.

44 Xiyu Chen, *From Political Alliance in China's Conception to Comprehensive Partnership in Building: the Relations between China and the European Community/European Union*, PhD Dissertation, Eberhard-Karls Universität Tübingen, 14 April 2003.

45 World Trade Organization, *Working Party Report on the Accession of China*, Geneva, 1 October 2001. For the deal on textiles and clothing products, see pp. 45-46.

Specific Safeguard Clause (TSSC), which can be summarised by the following: until 2013 countries can apply safeguards on any Chinese products causing "material injury" (i.e. that creates or threatens to create market disruption) to domestic producers.[46] The safeguard clause was a concession to the European firms competing with Chinese imports. In fact, its has been suggested that without these special terms for the textile and clothing sector, the European Council might have refused to agree to China's WTO accession.[47]

2002-Present: Quota Elimination and Increasing Complexity

Just as during the first two stages of the ATC, the EU's overall quota elimination during the third ATC-stage (2002-2005) was limited. Especially the lifting of quotas on the most sensitive products and the products with the most value-added was postponed until the final stage (i.e. 2005). Despite this, calculations made by the European Commission figures showed that "[…] textile and clothing products, removed from quotas in the third stage, has seen a sharp increase of Chinese exports at the expense of other suppliers."[48] To be more precise, China's market share in EU imports of all categories that were liberalised during the third ATC-stage rose from 13.8% in 2001 to 31.8% in 2003.[49] Overall trade figures show (see Tables 1 and 2) that, after its WTO accession, China had overtaken Turkey as the EU's most important textile supplier, while strengthening its leading position as the EU's most important supplier of clothing products. At the same time, intra-EU trade dropped to a new low level and exports from the EU to third countries decreased.[50] The worst, however, was still to come.

On the 1st January 2005 the quota system came to an end and the EU had to remove all quotas on textile and clothing imports. China's growth figures during the first few months of 2005 were even more impressive than anybody had imagined beforehand. Almost all product categories experienced a large increase in Chinese imports, as high as 500% for

---

46 There are several limits to the use of safeguards: Chinese exports are allowed to rise by 7.5% a year – the control can only last for one year, although it can be renewed – and the safeguards must be abolished by the end of 2008.

47 Interviews conducted by the author.

48 Commission of the European Communities, *Evolution of Trade in Textile and Clothing Worldwide – Figures and Structural Data*, Commission Staff Working Paper SEC 1349, Brussels, 2003.

49 Jörg Mayer, *Not Totally Naked: Textiles And Clothing Trade In A Quota Free Environment*, Geneva, United Nations Conference on Trade and Development, 2004.

50 Commission of the European Communities' Directorate-General for Trade website, retrieved on 5 March, 2009, http://ec.europa.eu/trade/issues/sectoral/industry/textile/stats.htm.

some products. As a result, prices in the EU decreased considerably, up to almost 50% for certain products in just a few months.[51] And as Tables 1 and 2 reveal: the rest of 2005, as well as the years after, saw a continuation of these increasing growth figures. By the end of 2007, China had managed to capture 25.5% of market share of EU textile imports and more than 35% in its clothing imports. Regarding EU exports, the overall picture shows a continuation of the negative trend. Although global export volumes were fairly stable during the 2005-2008 period, European textile and, most notably, clothing producers saw a further drop in their intra-EU exports.[52]

Given the aforementioned developments, the restructuring efforts, as described earlier, continued in the post-ATC years. Thus, the textile and clothing sector in the EU witnessed a further move towards the production of more added-value products and niche markets. Moreover, subcontracting and relocation of production plants, predominantly to China intensified, and market concentration in all segments of the industry increased further as well. As a result, job losses also increased further during this period.[53]

Trade Preferences towards China within the EU

Because the developments during this period resemble those of the previous period (1995-2001), it is not surprising that the trade policy interests within the EU between these two periods are similar. However, the dividing lines between the pro-protection and anti-protection firms hardened considerably. After all, the quota elimination intensified China's competition for traditional European producers and, simultaneously, increased the opportunities for retailers, importers and exporters in the EU. Consequently, both sides lobbied intensively at the national and the European level in order to make sure that their interests were taken into consideration as much as possible. As a result, the division between the Northern Coalition (i.e. the Netherlands, the UK, Germany, and Scandinavia) and the Southern Coalition (i.e. Spain, Portugal, Italy, Greece, France, as well as new EU-members like Poland and Lithuania) became more apparent than ever. The consequences of all of this, for the EU textile and clothing trade policy towards China, will become clear when I analyse the 2005 "textile wars" in the next section.

---

51 EURATEX press conference, attended by the author, Brussels, 25 April 2005.

52 Commission of the European Communities, DG Trade website, retrieved on 5 March 2009, http://ec.europa.eu/trade/issues/sectoral/industry/textile/stats.htm.

53 Commission of the European Communities, Evolution of Trade in Textile and Clothing, *op. cit.*, p. 23.

EU Policy towards China

In the last week of April 2005 most EU member states made available import statistics for the first three months of the year, showing a sharp surge in textile and clothing imports from China. In some categories, import volumes had even risen above the "alert level" as defined by the European Commission.[54] After the release of these figures, several EU member states (Italy, France and Spain), pressured by European and national interest organisations, asked the Commission to impose emergency measures to protect their textile and clothing manufacturers.[55]

On 29 April the Commission opened investigations into imports from China in several textile and clothing categories and announced that it would "make a thorough assessment of market impact in the affected product categories [...] and if deemed necessary introduce safeguard measures."[56] The president of the European Textile and Apparel Organisation (Euratex), on behalf of the industry, as well as some member state officials cautiously welcomed the investigation.[57] Importers and the Northern EU countries were not amused and called the investigations "highly inappropriate,"[58] "politically motivated"[59] and "caused by the intense pressure exerted by some EU member states in conjunction with European [producers]."[60]

The anti-safeguard coalition convinced the Commission to at least start negotiations with China, instead of taking any unilateral action. Not much later, on 10 June 2005, the Commission announced that the EU and China had signed a Memorandum of Understanding (MoU) which ensured "a period [2005-2007] of adjustment for EU producers, provide greater predictability for importers and retailers, and preserve the price of market liberalisation and WTO membership for China."[61] Although many saw this agreement as a victory for import-competing firms, the fact that only 10 product categories became subject to safeguard measures and that the annual growth levels were higher than the 7.5% limit permitted under

54 Commission of the European Communities, Press Release, retrieved on 5 March 2009, http://europa.eu.int/comm/trade/issues/sectoral/industry/textile/pr240405.

55 'EU Warns China on Textile Imports,' *Financial Times*, 27 April 2005, p. 1.

56 Commission of the European Communities, Press Release, *loc. cit.*

57 Euratex, Press Release, retrieved on 5 March 2009, http://www.euratex.org/download/publications/pressreleases/china_safeguards_press_release25042005.doc.en.html.

58 Free Trade Association (FTA), Press Release, retrieved on 5 March 2009, http://www.fta-eu.org/ftapress101.pdf.

59 *Ibid.*

60 *Ibid.*

61 See http://europa.eu.int/comm/trade/issues/index_eu.htm.

the TSSC can be seen as a concession to the Chinese and the European importers.[62]

The Commission needed until the 12 July to get the MoU implemented. In the meantime, European retailers had placed very big orders with Chinese exporters on top of the goods already ordered. This created massive problems because the regulation included a footnote stating: "import authorisation for goods shipped between 11 June and 12 July shall be granted automatically and cannot be denied on the grounds that there are no quantities available within the 2005 quantitative limits. However, the imports of all products shipped from 11 June 2005 will be counted against the 2005 quantitative limits."[63] Consequently, quotas for the entire year were full within no-time and an additional 77 million items from China were blocked at European borders.[64]

European retailers were, accordingly, confronted with a big supply crisis and started to accuse former trade Commissioner Peter Mandelson of mismanagement and of disregarding their interests. This re-fuelled the debate between those in favour, and those against, undertaking free trade with China. The debate focused on whether or not to enlarge the quotas and, by doing so, releasing the blocked garments. In the end, the EU and China again managed to reach an agreement in which both sides agreed to share the quota burden "by letting half the amount of the blocked garments count towards the 2005 quotas, and the other half towards the 2006 quotas."[65] With this deal the Commission again had tried, and managed, to satisfy all sides.

When at the end of 2007 the safeguard quotas expired, the EU and China established a joint system in order to monitor EU imports from China. This double-checking surveillance system, which was put in place for one year, covered eight out of the ten previously restricted categories and was meant to maintain bilateral oversight, regarding the trade flows.[66] With the removal of the surveillance system, at the beginning of 2009, the days of restrictive measures against Chinese textile and clothing exports

62 Anna Comino, 'A Dragon in Cheap Clothing: What Lessons Can Be Learned from the EU-China Textile Dispute?,' *European Law Journal*, Vol. 13, No. 6, 2007, pp. 818-838.

63 Commission of the European Communities Regulation No. 1084/2005, OJ L 177/19, as cited in Comino, *op. cit.*, p. 832.

64 Tony Heron, 'European Trade Diplomacy and the Politics of Global Development: Reflections on the EU-China Bra Wars Dispute,' *Government and Opposition*, Vol. 42, No. 2, pp. 190-214.

65 Comino, *op. cit.*, p. 833.

66 Hong Kong Trade Development Council, retrieved on 25 May 2009, http//: www.hktdc.com/info/mi/a/baeu/en/1X005O8S/1/Business-Alert-%E2%80%93-EU/EU-textile-surveillance-system-established--with-a-view-to-smooth-transition.htm.

appeared to be over. It is, however, probably just a matter of time before the next conflict on textile and clothing trade between the EU and China erupts. After all, EU companies still have a variety of alternative defence measures at their disposal – most notably anti-dumping investigations – which they are very likely to use in the foreseeable future.

Conclusion

Until the mid-1990s EU textile and clothing trade policy towards China was rather straightforward: producers demanded protection against increasing Chinese imports and because they were backed by a majority in the Council and by the European Commission, ever tougher restrictions were imposed over time. Three reasons lay at the root of these developments. First, the political clout of traditional producers and the continuing importance of the textile and clothing sector persisted in several key EU member states. Second, the fact that no (serious) interest groups representing anti-protection interests were at this time able to organise an effective lobby in opposition; and third, European policy-makers did not see China yet as a fully equal negotiating partner.

In the course of the 1990s, changes started to occur. Spurred by increasing import competition, especially from China, the textile and clothing sector in the EU became subject to several far-reaching transformations. For one, many producers gave up mass production and started to produce more value-added products and/or started to focus on niche markets. Secondly, producers relocated (parts of their) production to low-cost countries, particularly China. Finally, a move to more market concentration, especially among retailers, took place. Consequently, some textile and clothing producers adhered to a more "free-trade oriented" mind-frame. In addition, retailers started to become better organised on a political level. This further strengthened the anti-protection coalition. At the same time, more member states started to reject the trade restrictions on Chinese textile and clothing imports. These developments were reflected in the EU's policy towards China, which became much more balanced. Although many of the trade policy measures taken were still aimed at restricting Chinese textile and clothing imports, the EU clearly took the trade preferences of anti-protection interests as well as the Chinese interest, much more seriously than before.

Due to the lifting of the quotas on Chinese textile and clothing products, the post-2002 period saw a very sharp surge in Chinese imports. This led to another harsh confrontation between protectionist interests, backed by the Southern European member states, and exporters and importers, supported by Northern member states. Especially during the 2005 "textile war" between the EU and China these two camps fought a grim political battle. It is hard to say which side has won this battle, because the European Commission performed a relatively good balancing act and managed to construct a compromise that was acceptable for all parties involved. Although it seems fair to say that the days of fully-blown protectionism are definitely over, it would be overstating to claim that the anti-protectionist forces are the glorious winners. Nevertheless, the quota system is history, but there are many other trade defence instruments left, and the textile and clothing producers are well aware of this. Therefore, it is very likely that the 2005 textile wars will be set-in-stone as the last political and legal battle fought over EU-China trade in textile and clothing products.

CHAPTER 7

The EU-China Partnership

Forging a New Space on Global Climate Change

Edward CAMERON & Hilary MCMAHON[1]

This chapter looks at how the pivotal partnership between the EU and China can forge a new space for climate change policy and other innovations leading to a post-2012 global climate change consensus.

In January 2007, when launching the EU's integrated energy and climate change strategy, European Commission President José Manuel Barroso said "we must act now to shape tomorrow's world."[2] To this sentiment he might have added "and we must act together."

While recognising the primacy of the United Nations Framework Convention on Climate Change (UNFCCC) process, the ongoing international negotiations on climate change, our founding assumption is that an enhanced partnership between the EU and China is essential to securing the large-scale political, economic and technological transformation needed to ensure "the stabilisation of greenhouse gas concentrations in the atmosphere at a level that would prevent dangerous anthropogenic interference with the climate system."[3]

Forging the space for this transformation will be difficult. From a political standpoint, agreement within the UNFCCC process will remain out of reach in the absence of buy-in and active support from the EU and China. Long-term implementation of the agreement will be difficult unless both parties feel they are properly equipped and resourced to deliver on their commitments while also safeguarding their respective agendas for sustained economic growth. For the EU, this means

---

1 The opinions and analysis expressed in this paper are strictly those of the authors and should not be interpreted as being reflective of the views of any organisation or institution. All statements, judgments, and errors are our own.

2 Commission of the European Communities, *Working with Developing Countries to Tackle Climate Change*, Report, Brussels, 2007.

3 United Nations, *Framework Convention on Climate Change*. UNFCCC, Bonn, 1992. The Framework Convention on Climate Change, which entered into force on 21 March 1994, is the principle international instrument for addressing climate change. The Convention currently has 192 signatories including China and the EU.

delivering on the goals of the March 2000 Lisbon Agenda to turn the Union into "the most dynamic and competitive knowledge-based economy in the world."[4] For China, the goals are presented in the 11th Five Year Development Guideline Plan. Among the listed objectives for 2006-2010 are annual Gross Domestic Product (GDP) growth of 7.5% and annual per capita GDP growth of 6.6%.[5]

It should be noted that the EU and China face significant governance challenges, particularly with regard to implementation of climate policy on the ground. Furthermore, China is also known to be somewhat risk adverse in setting national targets that are ambitious in nature, preferring to ensure that all set-targets are achievable. Despite this, there is room for optimism and the potential that could be unlocked by a strengthened EU-China partnership is enormous. An alliance between the world's fastest growing economy and the world's biggest single market is critical to the global economy, as well as the global effort to reduce Greenhouse Gas Emissions, the principle cause of climate change.

This chapter examines the principles and practical components that can help to shape this alliance. Section one outlines why climate change represents an unparalleled and unprecedented global challenge and how its diverse impacts will affect Europe and China. Section two presents the policy responses being prepared by the EU and China to meet this challenge. Section three assesses the current context for building climate policy architecture, explores the political dynamics of the negotiations and contains our recommendations for unlocking the full potential of the EU-China partnership.

We suggest that a strengthened EU-China climate partnership ought to focus on the following:

- Developing a common understanding of each others' needs and capacities;
- Developing a common vision for new commitments;
- Promoting equity and enhance financing;
- Building better governance into the global climate regime and individual policy architecture;
- Creating mutual recognition and trust;

---

4 Council of the European Union, *Lisbon European Council Presidency Conclusions*, Lisbon, 2000. Specific targets contained within the Lisbon Agenda include 3% annual economic growth across the Union; the creation of 20 million new jobs by 2010; raising the employment rate to 70% of the population; and reducing red tape to promote entrepreneurship.

5 People's Republic of China, *11th Five-Year Guidelines (2006-2010)*, Beijing, 2006.

- Expanding practical collaboration, particularly in the area of technology, leading to effective and efficient investment in low carbon technologies.

Climate Change – the Human Imperative of the 21st Century

In recent years our understanding of climate change has evolved considerably as a result of a number of landmark publications.

In 2006, the *Economics of Climate Change* by Lord Nicholas Stern stated that unchecked climate change could create risks of major disruption to economic and social activity on a scale similar to those associated with the great wars and the economic depression of the first half of the 20th century, and precipitate the largest migration in modern history.[6] In 2007, the United Nations Development Program (UNDP)'s *Human Development Report* established climate change as the "defining human development issue of our generation" which "threatens to erode human freedoms" and "calls into question the Enlightenment principle that human progress will make the future look better than the past."[7]

Perhaps most notable of all was the *Fourth Assessment Reports of the Intergovernmental Panel on Climate Change*, published in December 2007. This seminal text concluded that climate change is unequivocal, very likely human-induced, and accelerating.[8] The emerging scientific consensus has helped to galvanise public opinion and generate political momentum which should have lead towards a global agreement in Copenhagen.

As a result of these and other efforts, climate change is today recognised as being the pivotal environmental, social and economic challenge of the 21st century. Although the long-term implications are likely to resonate in every nation, community and neighbourhood, the immediate and far reaching effects will disproportionately impact the poor and marginalised, as they are heavily dependent on the natural systems that are most susceptible to, and least able to cope with, adverse climate impacts.

Efforts to eradicate extreme poverty and hunger will be affected by changing patterns of food production, shifting access to natural resources and the undermining of livelihoods. Extreme weather events that will

---

6 Nicholas Stern, *The Economics of Climate Change: The Stern Review*, London, Cambridge University Press, 2006.

7 United Nations Development Program, *Fighting Climate Change: Human Solidarity in a Divided World*, Human Development Report, New York, 2007.

8 Intergovernmental Panel on Climate Change, *Climate Change 2007: The Fourth Assessment Reports*, Valencia, IPCC, 2007.

increase in frequency and magnitude will destroy homes and infrastructure; threaten social assets and governance systems; and impede public service delivery in areas such as education and health care.[9] Increased incidence of water-borne, vector-borne, and diarrhoeal diseases, combined with variations in the available levels of safe drinking-water, will have devastating consequences for individual health and the prosperity of whole communities.[10]

Finally, the capacity to adapt to inevitable climate impacts is seriously impeded as poor communities lack the financial, technological knowledge, governance, human and other resources that can be mobilised to build resilience.

Together, exposure to risks, sensitivity to those risks and lack of adaptive capacity combine to create a recipe for enhanced vulnerability that will push many on the margins over the edge.

Although climate change can often seem like someone else's complex crisis, neither China nor the EU is immune from the diverse natural, social, economic and political impacts.

According to the New Economics Foundation (NEF), "the human drama of climate change will largely be played out in Asia, where 60% of the world's population lives (over half near the coast) making them directly vulnerable to sea level rise."[11] A one meter rise in sea level would inundate coastal cities and communities in South, East and South-East Asia.[12]

Environmental change associated with global warming has already affected China. A large number of floods have occurred in China in the last few years, mainly over the middle and lower basins of the Yangtze (Changjiang), Huaihe and Haihe.[13] In 2006, saline water intrusion and coastal erosion intensified in the Yangtze Delta region leading to substantial financial and livelihood losses, as well as significant fatalities. Shanghai's water supply was affected, reducing the quality of groundwater supplies and soils, with even broader impacts on local ecosystems.

---

9 United Nations Development Report 2007, *op. cit.* and Intergovernmental Panel on Climate Change, 2007, *op. cit.*

10 World Health Organization, *Protecting Health from Climate Change: World Health Day 2008*, Geneva, WHO, 2008.

11 New Economics Foundation, *Up in Smoke: Asia and the Pacific – The Threat from Climate Change to Human Development and the Environment*, London, NEF, 2007, p. 3.

12 Intergovernmental Panel on Climate Change, 2007, *op. cit.*

13 New Economics Foundation 2007, *op. cit.*, p. 4.

Coastal areas provide an important habitat for many species and support countless livelihoods. Both will suffer from high tides, coastal erosion and saline water intrusion with the global rising of the sea levels. Impacts will also stretch inland, with the most adverse effects likely to occur in agriculture, livestock breeding, forestry, natural ecosystems, and water resources. The latest climate National Assessment Report published by the Chinese Government estimates that climate change is already having a negative impact on Chinese agricultural production. If no action is taken, it warns that Chinese agricultural productivity will fall by 5 to 10%.

According to the Intergovernmental Panel on Climate Change (IPCC), Europe is also braced for multiple climate impacts. Access to resources and assets are also likely to be affected as a result of the increased risk of flooding, both inland and in coastal regions; glacier retreat; reduced snow cover; reduced revenue from winter tourism; and extensive species losses (in some areas up to 60%) in mountain regions. In Southern Europe, climate change is projected to worsen conditions due to increasing temperatures and drought, and to reduce water availability, hydropower potential, summer tourism and, in general, crop productivity.[14]

Europe will also need to contend with impacts to human health such as excess heat-related mortality, and changes in infectious disease vectors.[15] Stephan Faris has detailed such an occurrence in an Italian village called Castiglione di Cerva, which was the setting of an unusual occurrence in summer 2007. More than one hundred of the town's two thousand residents were afflicted with a high fever, rashes and crushing pain in their bones and joints. According to Faris "an unusually mild winter had allowed Asian tiger mosquitoes to start breeding early and their population had soared. When a tourist returned from India with cjikungunya, a relative of dengue, the insects provided the perfect vector. It was the first time in recorded history that the disease had broken out on the continent." The World Health Organization (WHO) has described this epidemic "as the first European outbreak of a tropical disease caused by climate change."[16] It is not likely to be the last.

These cumulative impacts across the globe, in China, and throughout the EU provide clear evidence that we are in the process of crossing a threshold beyond which we will reduce the ability of human, environmental and social systems to cope with climate change, and associated

14 New Economics Foundation 2007, *op. cit.*, p. 50.

15 IPCC, 2007, *op. cit.*, p. 33.

16 Stephan Faris, *Forecast: the Consequences of Climate Change, from the Amazon to the Arctic, from Darfur to Napa Valley*, New York, Henry Holt, 2009, p. 110.

with the threat to these physical systems, will be a very high cost to the economy.

Rising to the Challenge of Global Climate Change – Policy Responses from the EU and China

According to the European Council Presidency "an effective, efficient and equitable response to the scale required to face climate change challenges" is necessary.[17] The EU has rightly earned credit for being a strong supporter of the international climate regime and the international climate treaty, the Kyoto Protocol (KP), which is central to this regime. Pallemaerts and his colleagues stated that "standing by the KP and seeing it enter into force, was one of the central successes one can fairly link directly to the EU's strong support of international climate policy."[18] Most analysts agree that the EU's green diplomacy was instrumental in convincing other parties to ratifying the KP, notably Russia, to proceed with ratification of the Protocol, thus paving the way for its entry into force on 16 February 2005.

Today the EU's position remains progressive and engaged, particularly when compared with other OECD members. Despite this, there exist significant failings, which undermine the Union's ability to meet its own ambitious targets and erode its credibility with the rest of the world. This section of the chapter will look at the policies, their strengths, and their shortcomings.

The European Climate Change Programme (ECCP) consists of more than forty European-level policies and measures to reduce Greenhouse Gas Emissions. These are designed to complement actions taken by stakeholders at national and sub-national levels throughout the Union.

Adopted by the Council of the European Union in November 2004, the EU Climate Change Action Plan has five strategic objectives: raising the policy profile of climate change; promoting exchange programmes between the EU and partner countries to foster mutual understanding; supporting adaptation; developing guidelines for integrating climate change into development programmes; supporting capacity-building in developing country institutions to prepare for and reduce the impact of climate change related disasters; and supporting mitigation and low Green House Gas (GHG) development paths.

---

17 Council of the European Union, *Presidency Conclusions*, Brussels, 2007.

18 Marc Pallemaerts *et al.*, *Drowning in Process? The Implementation of the European Union's 6th Environmental Action Programme*, London, European Environment Bureau, 2006, p. 6.

The EU's stated objective on climate change is to limit the average global temperature increase to less than 2°C[19] compared to pre-industrial levels. In addition to the goal of combating climate change, European climate policy is also driven by the goals of reducing energy costs; improving environmental and social conditions; contributing to the Lisbon Agenda by encouraging innovation in the energy sector; and creating jobs. The European Commission has calculated savings in the region of €50 bn and the creation of approximately one million new jobs by 2020.[20] Moreover, the EU hopes to enhance its position as a leading player in eco-innovation and sustainable energy and hopes that this in turn will spur economic growth. Renewable energy technologies already account for a turnover of €20 bn and have created 300,000 jobs. A 20% share for renewables is estimated to represent almost a million jobs in the industry by 2020 – more if Europe exploits its full potential to become a world leader in this field. In addition, the renewable energy sector is labour-intensive and reliant on many small and medium sized enterprises (SMEs), spreading jobs and development to every corner of Europe.[21]

The active ingredients of achieving this goal begin with internal EU targets, the heart of which is the "20 20 by 2020" plan. This commits the EU to reducing overall emissions by at least 20% below the 1990 levels and increasing the share of renewable energy use by 20% by the year 2020.

19 "Dangerous anthropogenic interference with the climate system" is expected to occur around a 2°C rise above pre-industrial temperatures. Much of the policy response to the climate challenge is centred around this 2°C target.

20 Commission of the European Communities, *20 20 by 2020: Europe's Climate Change Opportunity*, COM(2008) 30 final, Brussels, 32 January 2008.

21 *Ibid.*

Figure 1. Aggregate GHG Emissions

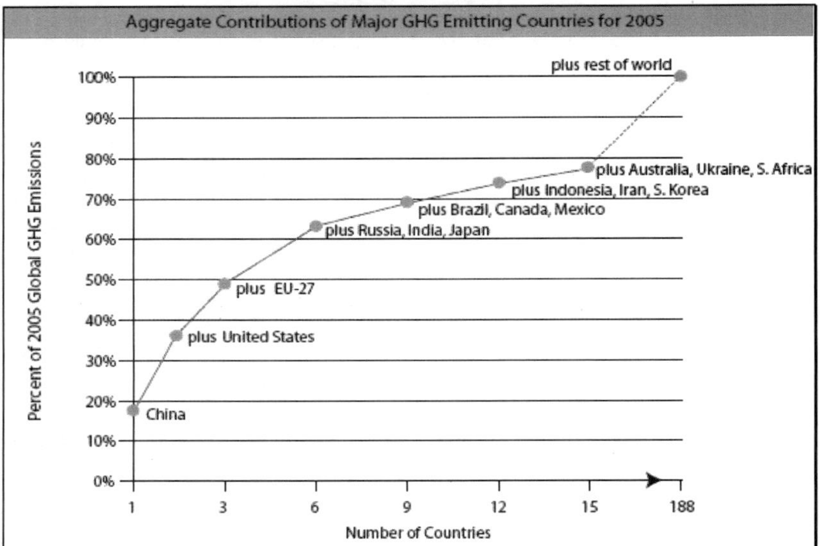

Sources & Notes: WRI, CAIT. Percent contributions are for year 2005 GHG emissions only. Moving from left to right, countries are added in order of their absolute emissions, with the largest being added first. Figures exclude emissions from land-use change and forestry and bunker fuels. Adapted from Figure 2.3 in Baumert et al. (2005).

In addition to its own targets, the EU hopes to persuade other developed countries to join a joint target of reducing emissions by 30% from the 1990 levels by 2020. The goal would be to use this as a first step to larger reductions in the regions of 60% to 80% by 2050 compared to 1990.[22] Additional aspects of the strategy include engaging with developing countries with a view to persuading them to commit to deviate 15-30% below "business as usual trends," by 2020. This particular target has proved controversial and perhaps unhelpful in the context of the international climate negotiations, as developing countries are reluctant to take on targets that may be beyond their reach and are difficult to measure with certainty. A more useful component of the EU's position has been to consider providing large-scale financial contributions in support of developing countries mitigation and adaptation efforts.[23] Another aspect is the design of an OECD carbon market by 2015, with

[22] Council of the European Union, 2007, *op. cit.*

[23] The European Council Conclusions (19-20 March 2009) announced €1.2 bn from the EU's budget will be spent on CCS projects and €505 mn for wind-farm projects, some of which could be channeled to developing countries.

room to extend the market to more advanced developing countries by 2020.[24]

These efforts to engage with developing countries, such as China, will be key to meeting these goals. As Figure 1 demonstrates, developing country emissions are expected to overtake those of developed countries shortly after 2020.

With this in mind, the Commission is encouraging developing countries to commit to adopting low-carbon development strategies, or low carbon growth plans, by the end of 2011. These national plans would cover sectors such as power, transport, major energy-intensive industries and, where significant, forests and agriculture.[25] A number of mechanisms have been designed to this end:

- The SNAPP (Supporting National Assessments of Post-2012 Proposals for Climate Protection and Sustainable Development) project is helping Brazil, South Africa, India and China to examine various options for the post-2012 international climate change regime.
- The Commission has also launched a Global Climate Change Alliance with Least Developed Countries (LDCs), which aims to establish a dialogue, provide technical and financial support for adaptation and mitigation measures, and integrate climate change into development strategies.
- The EU-China partnership on climate change, launched in 2005, is principally focused on promoting clean technology, energy efficiency and conservation and providing support for renewable energy. The Partnership contains two concrete cooperation goals – the first is to develop and demonstrate advanced "zero-emissions coal technology" – the second is to reduce the cost of key energy technologies and promote their deployment and dissemination.[26] The Partnership will also support efforts to reduce the energy intensity of economies.

Through these and other programs, the EU is making substantial investments in order to reduce global emissions, but these will need to increase substantially – somewhere in the order of €175 bn by 2020 according to the European Commission.[27] Some of that financing is now being made available through the 7th Research and Technology Development (RTD) framework programme. The programme, covering

---

24 Commission of the European Communities, *Towards a Comprehensive Climate Change Agreement in Copenhagen*, COM(2009) 39 final, Brussels, European Commission, 2009, pp. 12-13.

25 *Ibid.*, p. 3.

26 Commission of the European Communities, *EU and China Partnership on Climate Change*, MEMO(2005) 298, Brussels, 2 September 2005, p. 1.

27 Commission of the European Communities, 2009, *op. cit.*, p. 9.

2007-2013, allocates some €9 bn to research projects directly or indirectly addressing climate change, plus a further €2.7 bn for nuclear research between 2007 and 2011. This represents a substantial increase from previous programmes. The funding through the framework programmes is additional to the financial resources the 27 EU member states commit to their own climate change-related research and development activities at the national level.[28] The EU has also proposed a strategic European Energy Technology Plan and will increase by at least 50% its annual research on energy for the next seven years.[29]

The European Emissions Trading Scheme

The European Emissions Trading Scheme (ETS) is perhaps the most visible component of the ECCP. Launched in January 2005, the ETS covered around 13,000 factories and power stations across Europe. Under the scheme, these installations are allowed to emit carbon dioxide only if they possess a permit. Companies exceeding individual carbon dioxide (CO2) emissions targets are able to buy allowances from "greener" ones. Carbon permits[30] are intended to be a financial incentive to invest in clean technology and cut emissions. The price of tradable permits tripled between January 2005 and March 2006. *The Economist* highlights that when the Scheme was originally established the politicians expected the permit price to hover around €10 per tonne. Instead, it rose to a peak of €30 per tonne.[31] However, the system soon showed it limits: as soon as the Commission had declared victory, the actual results pointed to surpluses in emissions, caused by member states granting more permits than needed. What ensued was a drastic and sudden collapse in the permit price, but more importantly a reality-check to the Commission's ambitions.

At first glance, a large surplus of permits may indicate success in reducing carbon emissions as cleaner industries would have less demand for tradable permits. Unfortunately, the surplus had little to do with reduced emissions – indeed emission levels have remained reasonably stable. Instead, the surplus has been caused by companies' ability to persuade national governments to issue more permits than actual emissions warranted. To date, the ETS has been a great source of

28 Commission of the European Communities, 2007a, *op. cit.*, p. 24.

29 Commission of the European Communities, Press Release, *Commission Proposes an Integrated Energy and Climate Change Package to Cut Emissions for the 21st century*, IP/07/29, Brussels, 10 January 2007(c), p. 3.

30 Permits effectively transform the right to pollute into a tradable commodity – giving companies the ability to buy and sell permission to emit extra carbon dioxide.

31 'Cleaning Up,' *The Economist*, 6 May 2006, p. 75.

additional revenue for power-generating companies but has had little effect on emissions. With carbon rights being allocated at no cost, the subsequent rise in the value of those permits led to large profits. Some power generators have gained by as much as €1 bn per year.[32]

Initially the system earned plaudits worldwide but regrettably the early promise of the ETS has suffered greatly as a result of familiar failings in EU governance. The first mistake was the failure to identify the number of permits that should be allocated, the number of sectors that should be covered, and the price at which permits should be sold. This demonstrated large deficiencies in the Commission's participatory and consultative approach, as many stakeholders had advised that these issues would be crucial in determining the success of the programme.

There was a complete break down of transparency and co-ordination in managing how member states allocated the permits. As a result, too many member states issued too many trading rights and this has already led to distortions in terms of competition and the internal market.[33] There was also, until recently, a failure to communicate how the EU plans to develop the ETS in the future. As a result, companies were unsure as to where the ETS would go beyond its pilot phase and so they were reluctant to invest large sums of money in cleaner technologies. Moreover, by concentrating solely on five sectors, the Commission failed to integrate other polluting sectors such as transport into the trading scheme.

While implementation of the first phase of the ETS has been mishandled, there are some grounds for optimism. The reform of the ETS, which formed part of a climate package adopted in December 2008, has sought to overcome some of the problems outlined above. Firstly, the scope has been extended to include GHG, other than CO2 and all major industrial emitters. The Commission has proposed replacing national allocation plans with auctioning or free allocation through single EU-wide rules but this has been met with stiff resistance from the member states. The aim is to reduce allocations annually to facilitate a general emission reduction, in the range of 21%, from the 2005 levels, by 2020.

While providing assistance to developing countries, member states should use the auctioning process to generate investments in research and innovation on low-carbon technologies, renewables and carbon capture and storage. Member states are being encouraged to use as much as 20% of the revenue generated from the sale of the permits, for these aforementioned purposes.[34]

---

32 The Economist, *op. cit.*

33 Commission of the European Communities, 2008a, *op. cit.*, p. 5.

34 *Ibid.*, p. 6.

A number of challenges remain. The power sector will only be subject to full inclusion from 2013 onwards, whereas aviation may only participate in 2020. For the sectors not covered by the ETS, emissions will be cut to 10% below the 2005 levels by 2020 through binding national targets (with higher reductions for richer countries and limited increases for the poorest ones).

While many inside the EU have claimed that the paradigm between keeping economic growth high and emission levels low, the picture is more complex. The EU's economy grew in the period from 1990 to 2006, while reducing overall emissions by 10.8%. However, most of the credit for this goes to the absorption of central and eastern European states into the Union and the industrial decline they experienced throughout the 1990s. The fifteen "older" member states (EU-15) had more limited success, reducing their emissions by a total of 2.7% between 1990 and 2006. Even this modest success, far below the Kyoto target of 8% reductions by 2012, is actually less than it first appears, as it is largely the result of German reunification (merging East Germany into the EU-15) and the larger exploitation of British natural gas reserves.

Writing in 2005, Meadowcroft and his colleagues had suggested that EU leadership required a more structured approach with greater emphasis on action rather than rhetoric. This, they argued, involved governance reform to ensure that sustainable development has a chance of becoming "a reality rather than a slogan."[35] In practice this means improving the conception and design of policy through enhanced consultation, participation, transparency and accountability; ensuring coherence and integration of policies across sectors and spheres; and substantially improving the record on financing, capacity building and implementation.

The EU aims to make the European economy a model for sustainable development in the 21st century.[36] To do so, the EU will need to make European governance a model as well.

Reconciling Climate Policy with Economic Development: A Sustainable Climate Policy for China

In the past 25 years, China has become one of the fastest developing economies in the world. As a result of this growth and a tripling in demand for energy to sustain this growth, GHG emissions in China have grown significantly. This is due to China's dependence on coal based

35 James Meadowcroft *et al.*, 'Developing a Framework for Sustainability Governance in the European Union,' *International Journal of Sustainable Development*, Vol. 8, No. 1-2, 2005, pp. 3-11.

36 Commission of the European Communities, 2008a, *op. cit.*, p. 2.

fuels. In 2006, the International Energy Agency (IEA) reported that over 100 GW of new electric generation capacity was added to meet growing demand for supplies, of which at least 80 GW was coal-fired.[37] The major obstacle remains out-growing this dependency on coal, and halting the distribution of subsidies which China continues to delve out to many sectors,[38] in particular to the steel industry. However, everything is not as bleak as it may seem. China has undertaken some very aggressive climate policies to diversify its energy portfolio and has acknowledged its contribution to the global challenge of climate change. China is also increasingly aware of the challenges that the future will hold if it does not choose a low carbon pathway that promotes sustainable development, in particular the threat to Chinese prosperity and continued growth. This threat to prosperity highlights a real dilemma for China. As a report by the Brookings Institute highlights, China sees itself as having "the problems of developing countries and many of the attributes of an industrialised nation."[39]

Concerns about the relation between prosperity, growth and climate change, have begun to manifest themselves in some domestic policy commitments. At the September 2007 Asia Pacific Economic Cooperation (APEC) gathering, Chinese President Hu Jintao informed his fellow Heads of State that: "we should optimise the energy structure, promote industrial upgrading, develop low-carbon economy, build a resources-conserving and environment-friendly society and thus address the root cause of climate change."[40] China's White Paper on climate change further states that "China strives to control and mitigate the emission of GHG and continuously enhance the capability of adapting itself to climate change."[41]

Furthermore, as is the case for the EU, China sees an opportunity in the emerging energy technology landscape. China is keen to position itself as a leader in the clean energy revolution, for example, Chinese renewable-energy manufacturers are already among the world's leaders in the solar-panel sector.

---

37 International Energy Agency, *World Energy Outlook 2007*, IEA, Paris, 2007.

38 Usha C.V. Haley and George T. Haley, 'Subsidies and the China Price,' *Harvard Business Review*, Cambridge, June 2008.

39 Kenneth Lieberthal & David Sandalow, *Overcoming Obstacles to US – China Cooperation on Climate Change*, The Brookings Institution, 2009.

40 'Hu Jintao Expounds China's Stance On Climate Change at APEC Meeting,' *Xinhua News Agency*, September 2007, retrieved at http://news.xinhuanet.com/english/2007-09/08/content_6687377.htm.

41 People's Republic of China, *White Paper: China's Policies and Actions on Climate Change*, Beijing, 2008.

However, despite a significant commitment to reduce GHG emissions and explore low carbon pathways to secure prosperity, China has garnered only limited success. Most of the solar industry products are exported to overseas markets – China lacks significant "demand-side incentives" in important sectors and many of their climate policies are in direct competition with China's economic development policies, with the latter often taking precedent.

To address these and other shortcomings, China embarked on a programme for sustainable development which aimed to reconcile growth with a more diversified energy portfolio and a lower emission pathway. China adopted a national climate change programme in June 2007. The National Development and Reform Commission had before this established climate-related targets five years ago.[42] While implementation of the policies to support the national climate programme and the climate targets remain at an embryonic stage, analyses of achievements to date, as well as some insights into what future supportive initiatives will be necessary, are beginning to emerge.

Adoption of a 20% Reduction in National Energy Intensity by 2010

China reduced national energy intensity (energy use per unit Gross Domestic Product) by 4.2% in 2008.[43] However, if energy consumption and the GDP continues to grow (albeit at a somewhat slower rate than previous years), these figures are likely to remain unpredictable. China will have to compliment energy intensity reductions with incentives for the diversification of China's energy portfolio towards renewable sources, given the growing demand for energy. As the European Commission notes "the key policy shift which is largely missing from the above mix [National Energy Intensity Target] is energy pricing: energy consumption remains heavily subsidised, for both economic and social reasons. Pricing China's energy in line with world prices would be the biggest step it could take to help curb demand."[44]

China's Top 1000 Enterprises programme – which includes businesses accounting for 33% of China's total energy consumption – is on track to meet its 2010 target to reduce energy intensity by 20%. This represents a key contribution to the overall national goal and an encouraging trend in

---

42 China's greenhouse gas mitigation efforts are reflected in its National Assessment Report on Climate Change, National Climate Change Action Plan, and a Climate Change White Paper.

43 Adapted from *Earthtrends*, 2008.

44 Commission of the European Communities, *Climate Change: EU Heads of Mission Report*, Brussels, 2008.

industrial efficiency. However, although this policy targets large enterprises, it has yet to filter down to companies and Small and Medium-sized Enterprises (SMEs) at the provincial and local levels. Nevertheless, even if a relatively strong system of verification exists, the Top 1000 Enterprises programme is mainly administered by local authorities who are already stretched in terms of staff and resources – this could prove problematic if the Programme continues to grow.

China's new Energy Conservation Law also contributes to the National Energy Intensity Target. This law went into effect on 1 April 2008. This law requires that all local governments submit their plans for increased urban energy efficiency, including buildings and public transportation, to the central government for review. The addition of more sectors to be covered by this law is an important step to ensure that energy conservation happens across all industries, in particular in the area of construction, transportation, and government buildings, which represent major sources of GHG emissions. Furthermore, much will depend on how these plans are reviewed and enforced over time.

A National Renewable Energy Standard of 15% by 2020

As noted above, total energy capacity in China is growing on an annual basis. Some of this increased supply is generated through renewable energy sources. For example, in the wind energy sector investment, wind power production increased by 88% on a yearly basis, with 4.66GW of installed wind power capacity added between 2005 and 2007. As a result of these successes, China revised its goal of 5GW by 2010 to 100GW by 2020. Any increase in renewables, however, will have to be met with a decline in China's dependence on coal, as aforementioned, if China is to attain overall GHG emission reductions.

Funding for Green Initiatives in China's Stimulus Package

Similarly, it is interesting to note that China's 4 tn RMB (€430 bn) economic stimulus package includes 600 bn RMB (€65 bn) for building intercity rail lines, in order to reduce emissions from road transport, 476 bn RMB (€51 bn) for new electricity grid infrastructure, which should result in important efficiency gains, and €22 bn for energy efficiency and environmental protection projects.[45] This is, by far, the largest amount of money provided for green projects, in comparison to any other countries' stimulus package. However, some critiques point out that a portion of the total sum for projects represents an umbrella for

[45] D. Seligsohn, 'A "Green Lining" in China's Economic Stimulus Plan,' *World Resources Institute*, November 2008, retrieved at http://www.wri.org/stories/2008/11/green-lining-chinas-economic-stimulus-plan.

projects which were already approved or begun.[46] Furthermore, some of the 4 tn RMB is supposed to come not from the central government but from local and provincial authorities, who have no obvious way to raise these funds during a recession.[47] If these funds are raised, however, this could help support China's ambitious plans to move towards a low carbon pathway and should provide important incentives for the implementation of the aforementioned targets.

How successful China's climate-related policies and plans will be, however, depends very much on China's ability to overcome the various obstacles towards progress and to integrate these climate change ambitions, into Chinese policy choices. The next section outlines how this might be made possible.

It is important that any approach to climate change draws on the strength of China's institutions and political tradition. According to one commentator, "bureaucratic approaches will be increasingly effective in cleaning up the environment."[48] The central role of the bureaucracy is a long one in Chinese history – that signifies that "sovereign power is mediated through a meritocratic bureaucracy that is obliged to take a paternalistic interest in the people's welfare."[49] Meanwhile, the distance between the bureaucracies' perception from theoretical to practical issues on the ground will need to be considered and is one of the many governance issues hindering the implementation of Chinese climate policies. This is a challenge equally shared by the EU. The European Commission has commented on this fact, stating that: "the [Chinese] government is well aware that institutional capacity to deliver the various targets is weak and its priority is now to build capacity at provincial level. UNDP and the EC are supporting the development of provincial level plans to implement the National Climate Change Programme."[50] In a recent report submitted to the UNFCCC, China itself calls for support from developed countries in capacity-building.

The lack of capacity across key matters of governance is reflected in the inability of the central government to ensure implementation of policies and measures at the provincial and local levels, and within certain sectors. Lessons on how to better achieve effective implementation can be drawn from other sectors. China, for example, has been

46 James Fallows, *China's Way Forward*, The Atlantic Asia, April 2009.

47 *Ibid.*

48 Joseph W. Dellapenna, 'A Few Words on Law and the Environment in China,' *Temple Journal of Science, Technology & Environmental Law*, Vol. 24, 2005, pp. 367-374.

49 Arthur Kroeber, 'Rising China and the Liberal West,' *China Economic Quarterly*, No. 193, March 2008.

50 Kroeber, *op. cit*, p. 44.

making significant improvements in the tracking of infectious disease cases over the past six years, as the government learnt its lessons from the 2003 Severe Acute Respiratory Syndrome (SARS) crisis.[51]

For any of these initiatives to work, the government needs to be equipped with robust measuring, reporting and verifying (MRV) structures. Table 1, illustrates MRV structures for climate related policies in China, and highlights areas where these structures exist and are currently being implemented with some success.[52]

Table 1. Summary of MRV approaches in China[53]

Name	Scope	Metric	Reporting Mechanism	Verification Mechanism	Time Frame
Technology Development	National	Share of R&D spending in GDP	NBS, MOST and MOF jointly publish a yearly statistics bulletin	NBS and MOS collect enterprise level data separately	5 year goal, annual progress reported
Renewable Energy	National with targets given to provinces and power generation companies	Renewable energy portfolio standard (percentage renewable in total output)	Energy Bureau aggregate data from NBS, various ministries and industrial associations	Internal data quality assurance system within various ministries and cross checking	Goals to year 2010 and 2020, calculated annually
Forest Cover	National	Percentage of total landmass planted in trees	State Forestry Administration conducts national forest resource inventory	Remote sensing and ground-truthing	Five year and longer-term goals

The challenge of MRV in China is worsened by the lack of robust data and the strict limitations on transparency and accountability. These shortcomings have been recognised by the Chinese government and steps are being taken to provide more robust and regular data. In particular, China's National Bureau of Statistics (NBS) announced recently that it

51 For a description of how the Chinese public health system has developed over the past 5 years, please see Longde Wang *et al.*, 'Emergence and Control of Infectious Diseases in China,' *The Lancet*, Vol. 372, Issue 9649, 2008, retrieved on 20 February 2009, http://www.thelancet.com/journals/lancet/article/PIIS0140-6736(08)61365-3/abstract., pp. 1598-1605.

52 Teng Fei *et al.*, *Mitigation Actions in China*, E3G, London, June 2009.

53 *Ibid.*

would hold monthly press conferences to publicise economic data,[54] a huge improvement on the *ad hoc* and often confusing manner in which data was previously made public. At the same time, China has revised existing legislation which will clamp down on the falsification of data. The Bureau has also shown an appetite for technical exchanges with developed countries that will help inform their data collection. The EU could be an obvious partner on this as much room for improvement still exists.

Given these numerous challenges, China will have to draw upon its own strengths to choose which approach to "climate-change mitigation," might produce the best results on the ground – in most cases China will have to provide itself with a large portfolio of different instruments so as to obtain success, including international engagement under the UNFCCC. The US is currently considering a cap and trade system, as described in Section 2, whereas the EU already has a functioning cap and trade system. Part of the discussions around these systems is how to foster similar systems around the globe, and how to link these systems. It is not obvious, however, that a cap and trade system is the best way for China in the short-term. Some new research suggests that a variety of regulatory structures such as: targets and quotas, taxes and financial incentives and penalties might suit the Chinese approach better in the short-term.[55] The reasoning behind this hypothesis is that there are certain constraints which exist in China that are particular to China, including technical capacity limitations (that is the capacity to measure and verify GHG emissions – something which the EU also struggled with at the inception of the ETS), and market maturity (Chinese financial markets are much less developed than those of the EU and the US).

Whichever approach China chooses, it is a country with significant potential that can play a large part in solving the problem of climate change.

---

54 Andrew Batson, 'China's Stats Bureau Boosts Transparency,' *China Journal*, 10 August 2009, retrieved on 20 August 2009, http://blogs.wsj.com/chinajournal/2009/ 08/10/chinas-stats-bureau-boosts-transparency/.

55 Fei *et al.*, *op. cit.*, 2009.

To Copenhagen and Beyond: Key Components of an EU-China Climate Partnership

The KP, agreed under the auspices of the UNFCCC, sets GHG targets until the year 2012 for developed (Annex 1 countries)[56] countries. The UNFCCC's 193 members, which include China and the EU, have agreed to a timetable to set new targets as part of a wider negotiation on the post-2012 climate regime. The deadline for the conclusion of negotiations is December 2009, or more specifically, the fifteenth Conference of Parties (CoP15) meeting to be held in Copenhagen, Denmark. This deadline was agreed in December 2007 in Bali, Indonesia (at CoP 13), which laid down a roadmap for the negotiations, referred to as the Bali Action Plan (BAP).[57]

Figure 2. International Climate Change Processes[58]

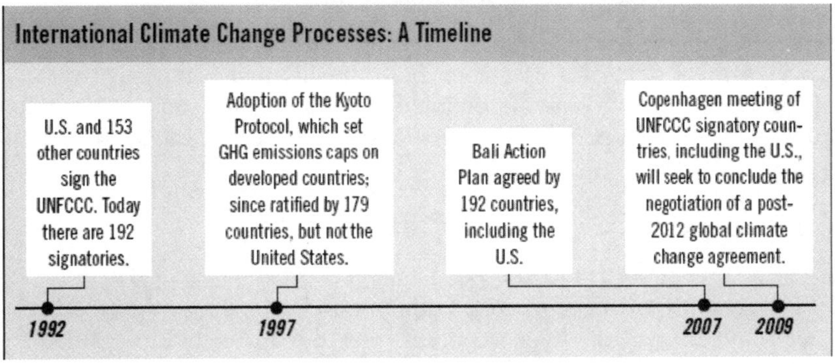

The negotiating mandate provided by the BAP aims for a radically different agreement than the KP. In particular, it provides for mitigation actions from both developed and developing countries. This is a major departure from earlier models of international climate change action, and it reflects changes in our understanding of climate change, as well as the shifting political dynamics that have occurred during the past 12 years.

---

56 Annex I refers to the group of countries listed under the UNFCCC, including industrialised countries that were members of the OECD (Organisation for Economic Co-operation and Development) in 1992, plus economies in transition (the EIT Parties), including the Russian Federation, the Baltic States, and several Central and Eastern European States (see http://unfccc.int/parties_ and_observers/parties/annex_i/items/2774.php).

57 United Nations, Framework Convention on Climate Change, *op. cit.*

58 Rob Bradley, *Testimony to the US House of Representatives Select Committee On Energy Independence and Global Warming*, Washington, World Resources Institute, 1992, pp. 1-13.

The BAP further stipulates that developed countries will provide technology, finance, and capacity to support mitigation actions. Determining how these actions and support will be measured, reported and verified, is a key part of the current negotiations. The phrase "measurable, reportable, and verifiable" is critical to the agreement of the BAP, as a trust-building exercise. The manner in which MRV is reflected in the post-2012 agreement, will have significant implications for the effectiveness of that agreement for stakeholders in both developing and developed countries.

Reaching agreement in Copenhagen will, however, be extremely difficult. There are already more than 90 items on the agenda, each as contentious and complex as the next. The negotiation process is dependent on consensus among almost 200 sovereign states. Moreover, the convention to date has been that "nothing is agreed until everything is agreed."[59] This means that the larger players in the process assume a greater responsibility in leading the rest towards consensus. This dynamic places a great deal of pressure on both the EU and China, as two key players in the arena. With our concluding recommendations we examine how the EU-China partnership can work to build the capacity of both to meet this burden.

Conclusion

First, it is important to *develop a common understanding*. The EU and China need to start developing a common understanding of each other's needs and capacities. It is important that the EU should continue to recognise the principles of historic responsibility for GHG emissions and acknowledge its respective capabilities, and exert leadership by sharing its respective capabilities. China should continue to explore the new space created by the BAP to bring forward new and innovative mitigation actions domestically, and also recognise its necessary role as a leader within the G77. These priorities should guide their participation in a variety of international fora including the WTO, the G20 and the UNFCCC. Bilateral initiatives in capacity-building and technology collaboration would also be essential to act as models for other countries and partnerships.

Second, *develop a common vision for new commitments*. There is no doubt that the current round of negotiations needs to conclude with new targets and commitments for developed countries. The scope and scale of those commitments will be subject to intense debate but they may come to resemble the terms laid out by the EU (20% reductions by 2020 with a

59 This refrain is frequently heard at international conferences as well as at meetings of EU heads of government.

view to moving towards 60% to 80% reductions by 2050). Securing the buy-in of other OECD countries, particularly the US, Australia and Canada, who have been reluctant partners to date, will be essential. Developing countries must also be part of the solution. Rapid economic growth and the volume of fossil fuel consumption in China and India have made these countries significant contributors to climate change. There cannot be a global solution without plans to ensure that these economies also become low-carbon emitters. The meeting of the Major Economies Forum (MEF) in July 2009 committed the World's major economies, including the EU and China, to developing such plans. Embarking on this process in a serious and transparent manner would go a long way in showing the rest of the UNFCCC Parties that both are looking for real and long-term solutions. Furthermore, the EU can and should lead efforts to get developed country buy-ins to urgent and ambitious commitments. For its part, China can demonstrate that being serious about mitigating GHG emissions is compatible with economic growth and development.

Third, *promote equity and enhance financing*. The UNFCCC is looking for ways to provide a basis for developing countries to seek support for mitigation and adaptation actions from developed countries, in line with Convention principles of historic responsibility and respective capabilities. This approach will help to support an equitable outcome, which will be essential to getting any global deal on climate change. Thus far, neither the US nor the EU has raised substantial capital to support mitigation and adaptation in developing countries, outside of the carbon market. And although the Clean Development Mechanism (CDM) has been particularly helpful in generating funding for projects in China, this is nowhere near the monies required for mitigation and adaptation at the scale required. The G20 could prove an important forum to discuss possible financing commitments and could help engage finance ministers in the climate negotiations – a necessary step if Parties to the UNFCCC are going to see any real movement towards financing climate change. Furthermore, new mechanisms, and revisions of existing ones, will be required at the international level to ensure that principles of good governance and equity apply to all climate related funding.

Building Better Governance: Globally and Nationally

First, there is a need to exert *governance reforms*. Writing recently in the *Business Standard*, Sunita Narain commented that the developing world needs experience and not lessons from their partners. As our analysis of climate policies in the EU and China highlight, both countries have been progressive in terms of political direction but less successful with regard to implementation. This disconnection between rhetoric and reality undermines good policies, but more so, it further undermines the credibility of both the EU and China to engage with international partners. A detailed study of governance is beyond the scope of this paper but it is clear that both these partners will need to significantly improve their approaches to consultation, participation, transparency and accountability in the preparation of policy; coherence and integration across policies; capacity-building through the different spheres of governance (regional, European, national, and sub-national); proper enforcement and implementation of policy; and enhanced monitoring, review, and re-design of instruments. This is the most important component in terms of developing the types of lessons that other partners are now demanding.

Second, *create mutual recognition and trust.* Providing information about the progressive actions that various countries are taking – and how these actions are being implemented through, for example, new MRV structures – is essential for a positive mitigation outcome. However, it is not just about data or information collection, but how one uses the data for measuring, accounting and verifying the mitigation outcomes. Better MRV systems could help inform policy choices, garner support for these policies and allow for the comparability of actions across sectors, provinces and countries. Some examples would be to develop better methodologies for energy and emissions modelling, creating reporting structures such as registries of actions and expert review verification systems.

Third, *expand practical collaboration.* Collaboration, particularly in the area of technology, will allow for the sharing of best practice and for effective and efficient investment in low carbon technologies. Collaboration will also support achieving large scale deployment and the reduction of barriers to the dissemination of green technologies. It should be noted, however, that the UNFCCC forum will not prove as important for technology development and deployment, as provisions for some technology support (that will prove essential in order to garner an agreement). Finding ways to better leverage private investment and achieve economies of scale, in the context of the fight against climate change, should happen within other fora.

The EU and China have begun to make the transition into a "climate-constrained" world. Both have recognised the importance of finding an agreement to an urgent and ambitious global framework on mitigation, adaptation, technology and finance. Both will be key players in shaping this framework, by persuading others to actively engage.

The UNFCCC process is not taking place in an isolated fashion. Other related and linked processes include the G20, G8, Major Economies

Forum (MEF) and the WTO discussions. The EU, and increasingly China, both play a leading role in these fora. As we look to Copenhagen, we must also be mindful of the implications stemming from the global financial crisis and the need to support sustainable development.

In this paper we have argued that the EU-China partnership has the potential to steer the global community from principles to practice. We have further argued that both partners need to enhance their own governance capacity to ensure that when the final round of applause in Copenhagen dies down, and the real work of implementation begins, that political rhetoric is matched by real groundwork.

When the international community meets in Copenhagen in December, both the EU and China will have a lot to do and a lot to prove. The world will be watching. It is time for both to rise to the challenge.[60]

[60] The authors would like to thank the following colleagues for their important contributions to this text: Patrick McMullan of the Permanent Mission of the Republic of Maldives to the European Union; Rob Bradley, Seth Ort, and Deborah Seligsohn of the World Resources Institute (WRI).

CHAPTER 8

The EU, China and Human Rights

Normative Partnership or Antagonism in Disguise?

Katrin KINZELBACH[1]

Prior to the agreement reached at the 2006 EU-China Helsinki Summit, it was decided to start negotiations on the PCA – the EU's policy papers on China were already full of references to the concept of partnership, such as the 1998 Communication *Building a Comprehensive Partnership*, the 2003 Paper *A Maturing Partnership* and, issued shortly after the Helsinki Summit, the 2006 Communication *Closer Partners, Growing Responsibilities*. None of these papers define the term partnership or mention conditions for the partnership. The 2003 European Security Strategy (ESS) *A Secure Europe in a Better World*, on the other hand, specifies a normative condition for the EU's partnerships. It is consistent with the China policy papers in that it mentions China among the EU's key strategic partners, but the ESS also clarifies that this category is reserved for countries that "share our goals and values, and are prepared to act in their support."[2] The security policy leaves no doubt that democracy and human rights form a prominent part of the EU's goals and values. For example, it states that: "the best protection for our security is a world of well-governed democratic states. Spreading good governance, dealing with corruption and abuse of power, establishing the rule of law and protecting human rights are the best means of strengthening the international order."[3] The security policy recognises that the promotion of democracy and human rights was identified as a general objective of the Common Foreign and Security Policy (CFSP) in the Treaty of the European Union (TEU).[4]

---

1 The author gratefully acknowledges a research grant from the Volkswagen Foundation.

2 Council of the European Union, *A Secure Europe in a Better World*, 10881/03, Brussels, 25 June 2003, p. 13.

3 *Ibid.*, p. 8.

4 Council of the European Union, *Consolidated Version of the Treaty on the European Union: TEU*, OJ C 325, 2002, Title V, Article 11.1., pp. 5-181.

The China policy papers are more nuanced than the security strategy in that they do not state, or imply, that the EU and China share fundamental goals and values. Rather, they state that one of the EU's key policy goals is "supporting China's transition to an open society based upon the rule of law and the respect for human rights,"[5] or in the more subtle formulation of 2006, "supporting China's transition towards a more open and plural society."[6] Notwithstanding this more nuanced treatment, the language still suggests a consensus with China on the need to do so. It can thus be said that the EU's policy statements imply the absence of a normative conflict between Europe and China. The December 2008 report on the security strategy, entitled *Providing Security in a Changing World* does not retreat from this consensual position. It praises China for having led poverty eradication in the developing world, being a partner in energy security and in dual-track diplomacy *vis-à-vis* Iran – it concludes: "we have substantially expanded our relationship with China."[7] Reading this report one would not guess that the EU-China relationship just underwent a rather dramatic crisis over the human rights issue, ending in an unprecedented cancellation by China of the annual EU-China Summit.

This paper discusses the normative dimension of the EU-China relationship and its implications for the ongoing negotiations on the PCA. The normative framework adopted for this purpose is that of international human rights law, by which both the EU and China are bound (although there exist, of course, differences in the ratification status of specific treaties). The paper first introduces the concept of partnership and identifies the elements necessary for a genuine partnership. It then establishes the links between the concept of partnership and universal human rights and asks whether the EU's human rights policy, and human rights' clauses are based on a spirit of partnership, and how the concept of partnership relates to bilateral human rights dialogue. In the second part, the paper reviews the normative interaction between the EU and China since 1995, focusing on the EU-China human rights dialogue. All documents produced on the dialogue are confidential. Information contained

5 Commission of the European Communities, *Commission Policy Paper for the Transmission to the Council and the European Parliament: A Maturing Partnership – Shared Interests and Challenges in EU-China Relations*, COM(2003) 533 final, Brussels, 10 September 2003, p. 12.

6 Commission of the European Communities, *Communication from the Commission to the Council and the European Parliament: EU-China: Closer Partners, Growing Responsibilities*, COM(2006) 631 final, Brussels, 24 October 2006, p. 4.

7 Council of the European Union, *Report on the Implementation of the European Security Strategy: Providing Security in a Changing World*, 17104/08, Brussels, 10 December 2008, p. 17.

in this paper, that is not referenced otherwise, is based on a series of interviews, conducted by the author in Brussels, European capitals and in Beijing over several months in 2008. In particular, the paper discusses whether the human rights dialogue is guided by a spirit of partnership or whether the relationship between the EU and China on human rights is in fact best described as antagonism in disguise.

It is concluded that the dialogue process does not successfully contribute to building a genuine partnership in the normative dimension. Firstly, it does not meet the necessary criteria identified in the first part of the paper. Secondly, it has failed to practically promote human rights norms. Thirdly, it did not prevent the recent clash between China and the EU over human rights issues. The EU's celebration of partnership in its China policy papers obscures an ongoing normative struggle. Therefore, if the two actors are genuinely guided by the doctrine of partnership, the human rights clause that the EU intends to incorporate into the PCA with China, would not merely formalise an existing normative consensus. Rather, the task of the PCA negotiators is to substantially change the current relationship on normative matters.

Partnership and Human Rights

By emphasising the concept of partnership, the EU's China policy papers fall in line with a prevalent trend that has characterised a significant portion of the West's international relations since the Cold War and, indeed, dominates the mainstream discourse on technical cooperation between states. Partnership is understood here as a "working relationship that is characterised by a shared sense of purpose, mutual respect and willingness to negotiate. This implies a sharing of information, responsibility, skills, decision-making and accountability."[8] The ubiquitous use of this consensus-oriented concept to characterise relations between states, especially in relation to issues of democratic governance, the rule of law and human rights protection, calls for careful reflection. Have all conflicts in this field been resolved? Do all states genuinely try to advance the same normative goals? Any session of the UN's Human Rights Council demonstrates that this is not the case. Why then claim this ubiquitous doctrine of partnership in this field? Focusing on development cooperation, Fowler has presented a very critical assessment, highlighting that the reference to partnership may appear innocuous but that it can also be considered as "a terminological Trojan Horse:"

---

8 Gilian Pugh *et al.*, *Partnership in Action*, London, NCB, 1987, p. 5.

> By appearing to be benign, inclusive, open, all embracing and harmonious, partnership intrinsically precludes other interpretations of reality, options and choices without overtly doing so. [Thus, it serves to] co-opt and sideline potentially opposing ideas and forces that express and propagate alternative views.[9]

According to Fowler, then, one reason for the mobilisation of a partnership myth is to hide differences, but also to seek to influence a country's development path in a direction that is not envisaged by the country's government. This objective is not pursued openly but couched in non-confrontational language and decision-making procedures that pretend to be inclusive without effectively allowing the partner to influence important decisions, for example, on resource flows. Indeed, this probably applies to many international relationships (including certain of the EU's external relations),[10] but it is not likely to be applicable in the EU-China case because the relationship is not characterised by a clear power-asymmetry. In other words, China would never allow the EU to act in this way.

Another critical thinker on the currently fashionable "post-political" trend is Chantal Mouffe who, in her book *On the Political*, identifies and challenges the prevailing "post-political Zeitgeist" which, in her opinion, fails to think in a political way and, more specifically, fails to understand "the Political" as inherently antagonistic. By focusing on consensual modes of decision-making, and by misunderstanding political questions as mere technical issues to be solved by experts, prevalent policy-making by liberal democracies (both in internal and foreign policy matters), ignores or even denies "the Political" and thus fails to devise institutions that allow political antagonism to be played out in an agonistic way. To tame the persistent antagonistic potential of any conflict, or relationship, she calls for "abandoning the dream of a reconciled world that would have overcome power, sovereignty and hegemony." [11] Indeed, this appears more applicable to the EU's approach to China. For both economic and geopolitical reasons, the EU is set on cooperating with China. The fact remains ignored that this cooperation is overshadowed by serious political differences. After a controversial policy-iteration process in the mid 1990s, the EU came to the conclusion that the so-called

9 Alan Fowler, 'Introduction – Beyond Partnership,' *IDS Bulletin*, Vol. 31, No. 3, 2000, p. 7.

10 See for example a study on the EU Partnership for Governance Reform in Indonesia: Gordon Crawford, 'Partnership or Power? Deconstructing the "Partnership for Governance Reform" in Indonesia,' *Third World Quarterly*, Vol. 24, No. 1, 2003, pp. 139-159.

11 Chantal Mouffe, *On the Political*, London, Routledge, 2006, p. 130.

constructive engagement was the most appropriate answer to China's Open-Door Policy.[12] This conclusion is fundamentally rooted in the neo-functionalist assumption that increased economic interdependence will have a spill-over effect and will eventually also lead to a liberalisation of the Chinese political system. More than a decade later, there are few signs that confirm this assumption. Nevertheless, the EU appears unshaken in the belief that a partnership with China is not only possible but also desirable, even in the normative field.

In specific reference to the idea of human rights, Mouffe writes: "it is a terrain shaped by power relations where a hegemonic struggle takes place, hence the importance of making room for a plurality of legitimate understandings."[13] She sees the persistent antagonism on human rights between the Western and non-Western understandings of human dignity, with human rights being only one way of conceptualising human dignity. China has argued at length in a similar vein but since the Vienna World Conference on Human Rights in 1993, has eventually accepted the universality of human rights (which in then constitutionalised via legislation in 2004). In her discussion on "the Political" in human rights, Mouffe falls not only into the trap of cultural relativism but also misconceives states and societies as monolithic actors. Contrary to this conception, the Political in human rights must be understood not as antagonism between cultures or states but as a potentially antagonistic relationship between the rulers and the ruled in a given society. Human rights make citizens become claim-holders and the state a duty-bearer, rather than a distributor of benevolence. This empowerment of citizens is often resisted by those in power and that is what characterises "the Political" in human rights.

Whilst recognising the political dimension in the discourses on partnership and in the doctrine of human rights, how can the two be reconciled? In fact, a genuine commitment to human rights and a genuine partnership have much in common. As stated above, partnership entails a shared sense of purpose, mutual respect and a willingness to negotiate. Matching these criteria, human rights entail the recognition of universal standards, inclusive participation/non-discrimination and the concept of progressive realisation. But to what extent does it make sense to speak of a normative partnership between state actors who are both guarantors and

12 Key points raised in the discussion on this strategy are captured in the so-called Reymond Report: European Parliament Committee on Foreign Affairs, *Report on the Communication from the Commission – Building a Comprehensive Partnership with China. Rapporteur: Mr Pierre Bernard-Reymond*, PE 228.395/fin, Strasbourg, 4 December 1998.

13 Mouffe, *op. cit.*, p. 126.

also always (potential) violators of human rights? The litmus test for a governmental partnership on human rights is participation. Participation is not only required as a matter of transparency, recognising the role of "the Political" in human rights, it is also evident that a genuine partnership in the field of human rights must provide space for collaboration among non-governmental actors in addition to collaboration among governments. In the end, the human rights doctrine commits states as duty-bearers to be judged by their citizens (the claim-holders). Therefore, any partnership struck by governments on human rights must permit for the claim-holders to oversee procedures.

It is unthinkable that China would accept an interaction between independent European and Chinese non-governmental actors with the aim of monitoring and critically reviewing state action in Europe and in China, from a human rights perspective. Whether this is specific to China or to the nature of relations between governmental actors, becomes clearer when one puts into perspective the normative dimension of the relationship between Europe and the United States (US). One of the most noteworthy normative conflicts between the EU and the US in the past years was the use of extraordinary renditions by the Bush administration in the so-called "War on Terror." Surely, there was not a clear-cut confrontation between Europe and the US, not least because some EU member states were accomplices in that they allowed secret places of detention to be set up on their territories. The EU as a whole, however, promoted the absolute prohibition of torture and stated publicly that the use of torture and the detention of persons was not in conformity with international human rights law.[14] The crucial point of this example is that these violations were brought to light by non-governmental actors, namely by human rights activists in Europe, the US and in third countries as well as by the Parliamentary Assembly of the Council of Europe and the European Parliament (EP). Although the EU and the US were in the middle of a normative conflict on the use of extraordinary renditions, secret places of detention and torture in the fight against terrorism, this did not put on hold the collaboration of non-governmental actors on both sides of the Atlantic, that were working towards holding their governments accountable to their human rights commitments. Any bilateral partnership on human rights that does not allow for such a process is not only incomplete but seriously deficient.

14 Council of the European Union, *Council Conclusions on the Implementation of the EU Policy on Human Rights and Democratisation in Third Countries*, 16719/06, Brussels, 13 December 2006, p. 3.

The EU as a Partner on Human Rights

In its official proclamations, the EU portrays human rights to be constitutive not only for its internal policies but also for its external policies. For example, the Lisbon Treaty states that the Union's external action:

> shall be guided by the principles which have inspired its own creation, development and enlargement, and which it seeks to advance in the wider world: democracy, the rule of law, the universality and indivisibility of human rights and fundamental freedoms, respect for human dignity, the principles of equality and solidarity, and respect for the principles of the United Nations Charter and international law.[15]

As aforementioned, human rights promotion has also been enshrined as a general objective of the CFSP in the TEU. To advance this goal, the EU has a number of mechanisms at its disposal, including:

- Technical cooperation projects;
- Human rights dialogue;
- Joint demarches;
- Joint statements;
- Joint positions at the United Nations or in other international fora;
- Accession conditionality (Copenhagen criteria);
- Essential elements and non-execution clauses in bilateral agreements;
- Sanctions.

In addition, the European Parliament can conduct hearings, adopt resolutions on human rights issues and approve or reject funding for the Commission's technical cooperation programmes; it also awards the Sakharov Prize for human rights defenders. While sanctions are the most coercive of the EU's mechanisms, technical cooperation and human rights dialogue can be conceived as the least coercive ones. In 2005, the EU also lobbied for the UN World Summit to endorse the idea of "the responsibility to protect." That is, the EU does not rule out the use of force to protect populations in third countries from genocide, ethnic cleansing, war crimes and crimes against humanity. Generally, however, the EU avoids punitive measures. Already in 1991, and in the context of agreements with third countries, the EU highlighted that it pursued a

15 Council of the European Union, *Treaty of Lisbon Amending the Treaty on the European Union and the Treaty Establishing the European Community: Lisbon Treaty*, OJ C 306, 2007, Chapter 1, Article 10 A.1., pp. 1-271.

positive approach to human rights and only considered punitive measures as a last resort.[16]

Just like other clauses, the essential elements clause of a PCA, are in theory, mutually agreed. In reality, the negotiations are in many cases shaped by an asymmetry of power which puts the EU in a position to simply demand the inclusion of the clause. That is also demonstrated by the fact that there is a standard formulation for the clause, drafted by the EU.[17] A decade later, in a 2001 Communication on the EU's human rights policy, the Commission elaborated once again on the intention behind the EU's insistence on the essential elements clause in agreements with third countries:

> However the EU's insistence on including essential elements clauses is not intended to signify a negative or punitive approach. They are meant to promote dialogue and positive measures, such as joint support for democracy and human rights, the accession, ratification and implementation of international human rights instruments where this is lacking, as well as the prevention of crises through the establishment of a consistent and long-term relationship. The dialogue on human rights that they enable should be reciprocal, with the EU also agreeing to discuss human rights and democratisation issues within its own borders.[18]

The EU wants to be perceived as a partner on human rights, equally subject to human rights scrutiny as other states, and not a hegemonic

16 Commission of the European Communities, *Commission Communication to the Council and Parliament Human Rights: Democracy and Development Cooperation Policy*, SEC(91) 61 final, Brussels, 25 March 1991, pp. 6-7.

17 It reads: "respect for the democratic principles and fundamental human rights established by (the Universal Declaration of Human Rights)/(the Helsinki Final Act and Charter of Paris for a New Europe) inspires the domestic and external policies of the Community and of (the country or group of countries concerned) and constitutes an essential element of this agreement." The non-execution clause reads as follows: "if either Party considers that the other Party has failed to fulfil an obligation under this Agreement, it may take appropriate measures. Before doing so, except in cases of special urgency, it shall supply the Association Council with all relevant information required for a thorough examination of the situation with a view to seeking a solution acceptable to the Parties. In the selection of measures, priority must be given to those which least disturb the functioning of this agreement. These measures shall be notified immediately to the Association Council and shall be the subject of consultations within the Association Council if the other Party so requests." Commission of the European Communities, *Communication from the Commission on the Inclusion of Respect for Democratic Principles and Human Rights in Agreements between the Community and Third Countries*, COM(95) 216 final, Brussels, 23 May 1995, p. 13.

18 Commission of the European Communities, *Communication from the Commission to the Council and the European Parliament: The European Union's Role in Promoting Human Rights and Democratisation in Third Countries*, COM(2001) 252 final, Brussels, 08 May 2001, p. 9.

force that uses power asymmetry to demand respect for human rights. Consequently, human rights dialogue is singled out in the Communication as a key component of the EU's policy. Indeed, the EU conducts a great number of such dialogue, ranging from human rights dialogue under the CFSP, like the one with China, to agreement-based dialogue (for example under the Cotonou Agreement with the ACP states, the Trade, Development and Cooperation Agreement with South Africa or in the framework of association and cooperation agreements), *ad hoc* dialogue, and human rights dialogue with like-minded states.[19]

Is official human rights dialogue always conducive to partnership, or are there specific conditions that have to be met? In its own *Guidelines on Human Rights Dialogues*, the EU states that the decision to initiate a human rights dialogue is taken "in accordance with certain criteria, while maintaining the degree of pragmatism and flexibility required for such a task."[20] The guidelines do not give any details on these "certain criteria" – they are also not specified in a classified paper on human rights dialogue, submitted by the Working Party on Human Rights (COHOM) to the Peace and Security Committee (PSC) on 15 February 2008. A public Update of the Guidelines endorsed by the Council in December 2008 sets out a multi-step process for the initiation of human rights dialogue but, procedural milestones aside, falls short of defining substantive criteria. On the other hand, the Update of the Guidelines implicitly acknowledges an ongoing debate about the impact of human rights dialogue: "the decision to create new dialogues must therefore be taken with due regard for the anticipated added-value and the resources available for their implementation."[21] Ultimately, the decision to initiate, suspend or terminate a human rights dialogue remains a political one and is not backed up by a standardised review of the counterpart's willingness to engage in meaningful dialogue or of the dialogue's impact potential. Accordingly, the Update of the Guidelines emphasises that: "the final decision to initiate a human rights dialogue and to define the practical arrangements for such a dialogue [...] lies with the Council of the EU."[22]

The EU's human rights dialogue have often been criticised as political window-dressing, for example, in the case of the EU-Uzbekistan human

19 Commission of the European Communities, *European Union Guidelines on Human Rights Dialogues*, Brussels, 13 December 2001, retrieved on 12 January 2009, http://www.consilium.europa.eu/uedocs/cmsUpload/14469EN_HR.pdf., p. 2.

20 *Ibid.*, p. 3.

21 Council of the European Union, *EU Guidelines on Human Rights Dialogues with Third Countries: Update*, 16526/08, Brussels, 22 December 2008, p. 2.

22 Council of the European Union, EU Guidelines on Human Rights Dialogues with Third Countries: Update, *op. cit.*, p. 8.

rights dialogue that led to the suspension and later cancellation of sanctions raised in response to the Andijan massacre in 2005, or the EU-China human rights dialogue that initially complemented and soon replaced the EU's efforts towards a resolution about the human rights situation in China at the UN Commission on Human Rights (the predecessor of the Human Rights Council). What, then, are the potential merits and pitfalls of a dialogue approach to human rights promotion? Viewed from the perspective of realist political theory, the dialogue approach to human rights promotion is doomed to fail. In the absence of economic or military constraints, realist theory predicts that states do not respect any restrictions on their decision-making. Adopting a constructivist approach, however, the conclusion is less straight-forward. Risse, Ropp and Sikkink, inspired by Habermas' theory of communicative action, have analysed how human rights socialisation may be advanced through moral discourse – including processes of communication, argumentation, and persuasion. Their spiral model (that is composed of five different phases) of human rights norms transfer categorises the response of norm-violating states to human rights criticism into five phases, namely: repression and activation of network, denial, tactical concessions, prescriptive status, and rule-consistent behaviour. Based on data from various countries, they conclude that constructive engagement works only at the later stages of the spiral model, when argumentative processes constitute the main dynamic. In the early stages, when a norm-violating government still adopts a strategic, instrumental mode of response, engagement strategies are very likely to be taken for weakness and indecisiveness. Crucially, this model views the collaboration between domestic change-agents and international human rights actors as essential for progress, as this collaboration induces self-entrapment by governments that start to make tactical concessions.[23] Consequently, it can be said that a dialogue in the spirit of partnership is only possible among like-minded states and between states that have not only endorsed but also internalised human rights and which are at a different stage of progressive realisation. The model also confirms the assumption that interaction between dialogue partners and the interested public is a key variable determining the impact of human rights dialogue.

The EU, in contrast, uses the tool of human rights dialogue in a relatively indiscriminate fashion, engaging countries with very diverse human rights policies and practices, ranging from Australia to Haiti, Moldova, South Africa, Uzbekistan and Vietnam. It has not set clear

23 Thomas Risse and Stephen C. Ropp, 'International Human Rights Norms and Domestic Change: Conclusions,' in Thomas Risse *et al.*, *The Power of Human Rights: International Norms and Domestic Change*, Cambridge, Cambridge University Press, 1999, p. 278.

criteria for conducting dialogue on human rights and very rarely rejects requests for human rights dialogue.[24] These various dialogues are conducted on a confidential basis and only very little information is made public, typically consisting only of very general statements praising a constructive atmosphere and lacking specific details. Therefore, it is very unlikely that all of the EU's human rights dialogues are an expression of normative partnership. The key points that are worth considering when making this categorisation are: equality of partners, good faith, and agreement on goals.

EU-China Human Rights Dialogue

In 1994, the Chinese government approached the EU with a proposal to start a regular human rights dialogue. The first meeting of this dialogue took place between the Troika and the Chinese government in January 1995 in Brussels. Although there had been some human rights-related visits and discussions between Europe and China before 1995, the new dialogue was meant to be less *ad hoc*. There are two dominant schools of thought on the origin of the EU-China human rights dialogue. The first school of thought holds that the dialogue was initiated by China to silence public human rights criticism. According to this interpretation, economic cooperation was used by China, as an instrument, to impress upon individual EU member states in the mid 1990s and after a short period of indecision, the EU settled on intensifying its economic relations while only paying lip service to its normative foreign policy goals – in a dialogue behind closed doors. This argument was mostly used by human rights NGOs and by pertinent academic experts on human rights.[25] The fact that China saw the bilateral dialogue as a substitute for the multilateral monitoring of her human rights record, became clear when she suspended the dialogue in 1996 in response to the EU's refusal to drop its annual co-sponsorship of a China resolution in the UN Commission on Human Rights in Geneva.

---

24 In fact, it only did so once, namely in the case of North Korea.

25 See Human Rights in China, *From Principle to Pragmatism: Can 'Dialogue' Improve China's Human Rights Situation?*, New York, 1998; Human Rights Watch, *Chinese Diplomacy, Western Hypocrisy and the UN Human Rights Commission*, 1997, retrieved 12 January 2009, http://www.hrw.org/legacy/reports/1997/china2/; Philip Baker, 'Human Rights, Europe and the People's Republic of China,' *The China Quarterly*, Vol. 169, 2002, pp. 45-63; Rosemary Foot, *Rights Beyond Borders: The Global Community and the Struggle over Human Rights in China*, Oxford, Oxford University Press, 2000; Ann Kent, *China, the United Nations, and Human Rights: The Limits of Compliance*, Philadelphia, University of Pennsylvania Press, 1999; Ming Wan, *Human Rights in Chinese Foreign Relations: Defining and Defending National Interests*, Philadelphia, University of Pennsylvania Press, 2001.

The second school of thought is that, due to the lack of success in the Commission on Human Rights, where the annual vote on the EU co-sponsored resolution had, with one exception in 1995, successfully been prevented by China with a "no action motion," the EU grew increasingly frustrated with the Commission process. Furthermore, even when the "no action motion" was overturned in 1995, the actual resolution failed to be adopted. According to EU officials, the lack of success in the Commission on Human Rights significantly shaped the EU's decision to enter into the human rights dialogue with China. As previously cited, the EU, after a contentious policy-iteration process, came to the conclusion that "constructive engagement" was the most appropriate answer to China's own Open-Door Policy. Several years prior to this decision, in 1991, the EU had already stressed the importance it attached to human rights dialogue:

> The Community will also seek to promote frank and trusting dialogue on human rights with developing countries, and to keep the channels for that dialogue open as far as possible, even in difficult situations, notably where the aim is to protect specific rights.[26]

Rather than being bullied into a decision that ran against its own normative principles, this above-cited line holds that the dialogue approach represents one of the EU's genuine and self-defined interests – namely to promote human rights through economic cooperation and normative persuasion – rather than through confrontation. Secondly, the normative interests were only one component of EU policy goals *vis-à-vis* China, with the EU also calling for closer cooperation in the area of economic and geopolitical interests. A more detailed reconstruction of the dialogue's beginning is beyond the scope of this paper. But what already appears from this rough sketch is that from the beginning of the EU-China human rights dialogue, there were doubts about China's good faith and whether the EU was "window-dressing" or conducting impact-oriented engagement.

According to official statements, the EU and China pursue quite different objectives within the human rights dialogue. The EU published a list of benchmarks which specify not only the issues that the EU wishes to discuss with China but, more accurately, what the EU wants China to do. In the dialogue, the EU tries to persuade China to take action on:

- Ratification and implementation of the Covenants on Civil and Political Rights and on Economic, Social and Cultural Rights;

---

[26] Commission of the European Communities, Communication, SEC(91) 61 final, *op. cit.*, p. 6.

- Cooperation with human rights mechanisms (visit by the *Rapporteur* on Torture, invitation to other *Rapporteurs*, follow-up to recommendations from conventional mechanisms and recommendations by *Rapporteurs*, implementation of the agreement with the Office of the High Commissioner for Human Rights);
- Compliance with ECOSOC (UN Economic and Social Committee) guarantees for the protection of those sentenced to death and restriction of the cases in which the death penalty can be imposed, in keeping with Article 6 of the Covenant on Civil and Political Rights; provision of statistics on use of the death penalty;
- Reform of administrative detention; introduction of judicial supervision of procedures; respect for the right to a fair and impartial trial and for the rights of the defence;
- Respect for the fundamental rights of all prisoners, including those arrested for membership of the political opposition, unofficial religious movements or other movements, such as the Falun Gong; progress on access to prisoners in Chinese prisons, including in the autonomous regions; constructive response to individual cases raised by the EU;
- Untrammelled exercise of freedom of religion and belief, both public and private;
- Respect for the right to organise;
- Respect for cultural rights and religious freedoms in Tibet and Xinjiang, taking account the recommendations of the UN Convenants' committees; halt to the "patriotic education" campaign in Tibet; access for an independent delegation to the young Panchen Lama, Gedhun Chohekyi Nyima, who has been recognised by the Dalai Lama.[27]

These benchmarks are in fact a list of demands directed towards China. In terms of the set goals, there is no agreement between the dialogue partners, otherwise there would be a jointly-endorsed list of common objectives. However, China's EU policy paper includes a rather different statement on the human rights dialogue, namely:

> There are both consensus and disagreements between China and the EU on the question of human rights. The Chinese side appreciates the EU's persistent position for dialogue and opposition to confrontation and stands ready to continue dialogue, exchange and cooperation on human rights with the EU on the basis of equality and mutual respect so as to share information,

27 Council of the European Union, Press Release, Point 6, *2327th Council Meeting – General Affairs: EU-China Dialogue on Human Rights – Council Conclusions*, 5279/01 (Presse 19), Brussels, 23 January 2001.

enhance mutual understanding and deepen cooperation in protecting, *inter alia*, citizens' social and cultural rights and the rights of the disadvantaged.[28]

This paragraph not only highlights that the Chinese Ministry for Foreign Affairs (MFA) views the exchange of information and the promotion of mutual understanding as primary goals of the dialogue – it also suggests that cooperation focuses on social and cultural rights rather than on civil and political rights which constitute a key areas of focus for the EU. There is of course a marked difference between exchanging information and better understanding each others' views on the one hand and forging agreement on contentious issues on the other. But without a consensus on the purpose of the dialogue, it is very unlikely that the process will lead to a consensus on these controversial issues.

After its interruption in 1996, the dialogue was resumed in the autumn of 1997 and has since then taken place twice a year, complemented since February 1998 by a legal seminar. In the political dialogue, the EU is represented by the Troika (the Presidency, the incoming Presidency, the Commission and Council Secretariat). The Chinese delegation includes the MFA and other ministries which typically include the Ministry of Justice, the Ministry of Public Security, the Supreme People's Procuratorate and the Supreme Peoples' Court, as well as other official bodies, depending on the topic. The head of the Chinese delegation is the Director General of the MFA Department of International Organisations and Conferences. This is matched by the respective EU Presidency, represented either by an Ambassador or a Director General. In recent years, the political dialogue has been complemented with a "courtesy call" at vice-ministerial level. Furthermore, the EP is now invited to send a representative to the expert seminar. The EP also requested the right to participate in the actual dialogue sessions, mirroring the (irregular) participation of the Standing Committee of the National People's Congress, but this was declined by the Council in May 2008.[29]

Although there is no evident power asymmetry between Europe and China, it would be wrong to say that the dialogue setup ensures equality between the partners. First of all, due to the EU's rotating presidency, the EU is always represented by someone new. Although the Commission, the Council Secretariat and the Troika arrangement can ensure a minimum level of continuity, there have been occasions where the Chinese delegation reportedly recycled speaking notes from previous

---

28 Ministry of Foreign Affairs of the People's Republic of China, *China's EU Policy Paper*, Beijing, 13 October 2003, Point I.5, retrieved on 19 February 2009, http://www.fmprc.gov.cn/eng/topics/ceupp/t27708.htm.

29 Council of the European Union, *Cooperation between the European Parliament and the Council in the Field of Human Rights*, 8033/08, Brussels, 16 May 2008, p. 3.

rounds, which was not noticed by the EU's head of delegation. Although Commission and Council Secretariat possess desk officers, who tend to attend the dialogue process over several years, surely notice the occasions when the dialogue fails to advance from previously covered ground, they have little influence over how the discussion evolves between the heads of delegation during the dialogue session.

In the accompanying legal seminar, academics and, at times, NGO (non-governmental organisations) representatives meet to discuss various issues, with officials attending as observers. Funded by the Commission, the seminars are meant to underpin and feed into the political dialogue. However, over the past decade, no clear procedure had been established to ensure this link. Furthermore, there is no agreement on the desirability of this link among participating academics on the European side. While some view it as essential, others firmly reject it as an infringement of academic freedom and an instrumentalisation for political purposes. The latter group views the seminar as a purely academic gathering between researchers. This perception flatly ignores the parameters of human rights scholars in China. Clearly, an international meeting on human rights, attended not only by academics but also by government officials is not simply an academic conference. The Chinese academics are selected to represent China abroad. They have to walk a fine line between stating what they may personally hold to be right and not offending the government. At the same time, it is clear that those excluded from power in China, including not only dissidents and independent rights activists but also "non-establishment intellectuals" and even critical members of government organisations, are not only cut off from the political dialogue but also not invited to the seminars.[30] In addition, China has put the EU under pressure, demanding that it will not include specific organisations and individuals into its own delegation. In one case, a member of the European delegation was directly threatened when attending the academic seminar in Beijing. While this is unacceptable, China holds the right to deny visas when it deems necessary and the EU can do little if that happens to be the case. However, China has also made clear that it will not tolerate the participation of certain organisations and/or people during seminars on European soil. When the EU did not accept this request, China cancelled the academic seminars under the German and Portuguese presidencies in 2007.

On a positive note it should be mentioned that thanks to the human rights dialogue, the EU and China talk more about human rights than ever

[30] The author has been informed about instances where individual members of establishment organisations, such as the Chinese Youth League, did not receive the government's permit to participate.

before. On most issues, the two parties know their respective positions. However, the EU often does not believe what China says. This is best illustrated by looking at two examples.

Example 1

Under the British presidency, the dialogue took place on 24 October 2005 in Beijing. The Chinese delegation was headed by Director General Liu Jieyi, Department of International Organisations and Conferences, the MFA and the EU delegation was headed by Mr. Sebastian Wood, Director Asia Pacific, British Foreign and Commonwealth Office. In a discussion on the right to a fair trial, Director General Liu explained that the judiciary in China was independent and that the Politics and Law Commissions did not interfere in individual cases. After a number of follow-up questions on the role of the Politics and Law Commissions in China, the representative of the Supreme People's Court, Mr. Hu Yunteng, intervened and explained that China was a "democratic dictatorship" and that the courts had to "implement the decisions of the Party." He also stated that the Commissions interfered into individual cases. He suggested that the Commissions were comparable to the role of "friends of the court" in the United Kingdom (UK) or in the US, a comparison that was rejected by Mr. Wood. Director General Liu concluded that the EU's questions convinced him that the EU had either not listened to China's explanations or that China had not properly explained its system.

Example 2

Under the Finish Presidency in 2006, the dialogue took place on 19 October in Beijing. The Chinese delegation was headed by Director General Wu Hailong and the European delegation by Tom Grönberg, Ambassador of the Finnish MFA. Freedom of expression was one of the main topics of the session and the EU raised concerns about censorship on the internet. The Chinese delegation strictly rejected this view. The problems that foreigners had encountered when trying to access the internet in China were justified as being caused by technical problems. Restrictive measures were only taken regarding information on violence, pornography, ethnic issues or fake advertisements because they had a negative impact on the public. The Chinese delegation acknowledged that there was a small number of foreign websites blocked in China and stated that 90% of these blockages related to pornography. It did not provide an explanation for the remaining 10% but reassured the EU that there was no censorship and no screening of web pages for keywords like human rights, democracy or freedom. After the session, the EU decided to compile data on censorship by regularly accessing specific websites in

China, so as to take note of when they were blocked and when they were accessible. This list was presented to the Chinese delegation at the following dialogue session to demonstrate that flat-out denial did not serve as a convincing explanation.

The impact of such exchanges and of the overall dialogue is difficult to gauge. At the European level, human rights concerns are almost exclusively discussed in the dialogue and only during exceptional circumstances at a higher political level. When the Chinese side raises human rights concerns *vis-à-vis* the EU Troika, on issues related to racism and discrimination, there is hardly any follow up – not least because the Troika is of course not mandated to look into violations in a specific member state. In terms of China's human rights policy and practice, the key problem in assessing impact is the multiplicity of factors that cause such changes. Speaking strictly in terms of goal attainment, based on the EU benchmarks, and without discussing the complex question of attribution, progress can be noted only on a few points, such as the ratification of the International Covenant on Economic Social and Cultural Rights (ICESCRs), the visits of the *Rapporteur* on Education (2004), the Working Group on Arbitrary Detention (2005) and the *Rapporteur* on Torture (2006).

It is highly questionable whether the exchanges of the type reported above are pertinent to convincing decision-makers in China to change their position on political issues. In addition, assuming hypothetically that they were convinced by the EU's arguments, the dialogue counterparts would not be in a position to change policy as they lack the decision-making authority. Confidential interviews with EU officials and officials in EU member states point to a widely-held belief that the dialogue would, in the long run, contribute positively to human rights policies in China, for example, by exposing officials to difficult questions and by encouraging and supporting change-agents. However, the policy dialogue is not structured around a detailed conceptual framework that specifies just how the dialogue could lead to change in China, or to how it could provide support for change-agents in the country. Whilst analysing changes in China's human rights practice, indications that discernable improvements of human rights policy were only made when domestic pressure existed for reform (for example demanding the abolition of the administrative procedure "custody and repatriation" after the tragic death of Sun Zhigang in custody; or the recent return of the death penalty review to the Supreme People's Court triggered by a public debate on wrong verdicts). Given that the dialogue provides no direct support for these change-agents and does not induce the government to make public statements on normative matters, nor does it lead to changes in the EU's own human rights policy (for example a reassessment of the importance of economic, social and cultural rights), it is difficult to discern either a theoretical or a practical validation of the dialogue's impact.

Equally important to consider is the dialogue's failure to effectively resolve key differences on normative matters and to prevent these differences from triggering a crisis in the bilateral relationship, as it happened in the autumn of 2008. In an unprecedented move, China postponed the 11th EU-China Summit scheduled to take place on 1 December 2008 in Lyons, protesting against the visit of the Dalai Lama to several EU member states.[31] Just prior to this, on the very same day that the EU-China human rights dialogue took place in Beijing, businessman Wo Weihan was executed. Not only the EU and several of its member states, notably Austria, but also other Western governments, and NGOs had repeatedly intervened on this case. The EU used the dialogue meeting to reiterate its desire to annul Wo Weihan's execution. The MFA took note but did not provide any information on the execution. Later that day, after receiving information through its own channels, the EU issued a public statement, saying that both detention conditions and trial procedures had not met international standards – Wo Weihan allegedly confessed under torture. Furthermore, the EU stated: "this execution seriously undermines the spirit of trust and mutual respect required for this EU-China dialogue on human rights."[32] Chinese Foreign Ministry spokesman Qin Gang immediately retorted:

> The accusation made against the Chinese judicial authorities intervened brutally into Chinese judicial sovereignty, trampled the spirit of the rule of law, and undermine [sic] the basis of the healthy development of bilateral talks on human rights. [...] We were strongly dissatisfied with and opposed to (the accusation) and urged all concerned parties to immediately correct the mistake and stop the words and actions concerning interventions in another country's judicature.[33]

The human rights dialogue failed not only as a mechanism to resolve substantive differences – but also as the previous examples from the dialogues under the UK and the Finnish presidencies suggest – failed as a

---

31 Presidency-in-Office of the Council of the European Union, France, *EU-China Summit Postponed – European Union Statement*, Paris, 28 November 2008, retrieved on 15 July 2009, http://www.ue2008.fr/PFUE/lang/en/accueil/PFUE-11_2008/PFUE-26.11.2008/Declaration_UE_Report_Sommet.html.

32 Presidency-in-Office of the Council of the European Union, France, *Déclaration de la Présidence au Nom de l'Union Européenne sur l'Exécution de M. Wo Weihan (Chine)*, Paris, 28 November 2008, retrieved on 15 June 2009, http://www.ue2008.fr/PFUE/lang/de/accueil/PFUE-11_2008/PFUE-28.11.2008/PESC_Chine.html.

33 Xinhua News Agency, 'EU, Austria's Accusation on Spy Execution Rejected,' *Window of China*, 1 December 2008, retrieved on 19 February 2009, http://news.xinhuanet.com/english/2008-12/01/content_10436540.htm.

process to increase mutual understanding. What is more, it does not function as a trustworthy mechanism to exchange information on identified points of concern, which is perhaps less than what the EU would like to achieve through the medium of the dialogue, but which would at least ensure that unplanned clashes on normative matters between the EU and China could be avoided.

Concluding Remarks: Getting Real on the Normative Dimension of the EU-China Relationship

The PCA negotiations and particularly the negotiations on the essential elements clause provide a window of opportunity to reinforce the normative dimension of the EU-China relationship. Here, the process may be more important than the final adoption of the clause. Taking into consideration the EU's "past practices," during negotiations with its Chinese counterparts, it remains difficult to imagine that the EU would suspend, even partially, the PCA on the basis that the essential elements clause has been violated. The EU's approach to human rights violations in China is characterised by a strong reluctance to take public action. Even the violent response to the March 2008 uprising in Tibet, for example, or the intimidation and arrest of Charter 08 activists led only to standard reactions by the EU, such as public statements and demonstrations. The Union did not consider calling for a special session at the UN Human Rights Council.[34] In the UN Human Rights Council's Universal Periodic Review of China (published last February), most EU member states (with the exception of the Czech Republic) spoke in very general terms, avoiding reference to current developments and individual cases.[35]

With the ongoing PCA negotiations, the key opportunity in terms of process is to associate non-governmental actors, including the EP and human rights experts, in the negotiation on the implementation and monitoring of the essential elements clause. There is little hope for optimism in this regard. China would most likely firmly oppose the proposal, and the EU does not have a strong track-record of getting what it wants from the Chinese government either. As Agnoletto pointed out in

[34] According to confidential interviews with officials in EU member states, such a move is considered unconceivable given that the EU would most likely fail to get support from the necessary number of Council members.

[35] Human Rights Council Working Group on the Universal Periodic Review, *Report of the Working Group on the Universal Periodic Review: China*, A/HRC/11/25, Geneva, 3 March 2009.

a 2006 study for the EP: "the role of civil society is very weak in the whole procedure of the human rights clause."[36]

Nevertheless, it is a precondition for making the essential elements clause meaningful for the normative dimension of the EU-China relationship. Otherwise, the PCA clause would merely be business as usual: this implies the drafting of yet another rhetorical statement that is not underpinned by the willingness to take action, should the situation require so. The clause would, in that case, be void of any relevance for Chinese human rights defenders, but would act as a formal requirement adhered to primarily, to appease the European public. To avoid this, the negotiations on the essential elements clause in the EU-China PCA should lead to a genuine partnership on human rights with:

- The involvement of independent human rights experts in the negotiation, implementation and monitoring of the clause;
- A public reconfirmation of the universality and indivisibility of human rights standards;
- The identification of areas for technical cooperation based on a joint definition and publication of measurable goals and time-bound indicators;
- An agreement on regular, high-level political consultations regarding those issues where the EU and China continue to hold differing views, including on contentious individual human rights cases;
- The commitment to provide public information on the progress in the human rights dialogue;
- The identification of clear criteria and consultation procedures for invoking the non-execution clause.

If the PCA negotiators do not live up to the task of substantially redesigning the current EU-China relationship on normative matters, any agreement on an essential elements clause for the PCA would merely be a continuation of current practice, namely the encryption of normative conflict, the misrepresentation of an ongoing normative power struggle between equal partners that exhibit mutual respect, and the continuation of a human rights dialogue that is officially consensus-oriented, but in reality that represents antagonism in disguise.

---

36 European Parliament Committee on Foreign Affairs, *Report on the Human Rights and Democracy Clause in European Union Agreements (2005/2057(INI)). Rapporteur: Vittorio Agnoletto*, A6-0004/2006, Strasbourg, 23 January 2006, p. 14.

CHAPTER 9

The Significance of the PCA in Sino-European Relations

A Step Forward or a Stumbling Block?

Carmen AMADO MENDES

Sino-European relations, shaken by the events of Tiananmen Square (1989) and the subsequent European imposition of economic sanctions and the arms embargo, have evolved since the mid-1990s in a very constructive way. Since 1998, EU-China annual summits assemble European heads of government and Chinese leaders to discuss bilateral and global issues. Sino-European relations also gained a new meaning in 2003, with the adoption by the European Commission of a policy paper towards China and the subsequent signature of a Strategic Partnership with that country. Since then, the idea of negotiating a new comprehensive framework agreement evolved with the need of finding joint responses to global challenges. During the 9th EU-China Summit in Helsinki, the two sides agreed to open negotiations for a PCA. This agreement is expected to go beyond the commercial area, framed by the 1985 TECA, and cover both political and economic relations. The final joint statement of the 10th EU-China Summit, held in Beijing under the auspices of the Portuguese Presidency in November 2007, announced the formal opening of PCA negotiations.[1]

This chapter aims to contribute to the debate as to whether this agreement will merely constitute an institutional framework for the actual state of Sino-European relations or if it will be a step forward, opening doors to solve the main points of contention between both sides. After reviewing the evolution of Sino-European relations, this chapter will focus on the current PCA negotiations, from the EU's perspective. The chapter will take Portugal as a case study among EU member states, where the public opinion's protectionist desires became more noticeable after China's WTO accession. Finally, this chapter will analyse whether the PCA is perceived in the same way by the EU member states and

1 Commission of the European Communities, Joint Statement, *10th China-EU Summit*, Beijing, 28 November 2007.

Beijing, thus questioning the true meaning of "strategic partnership" for China.

The Evolution of Sino-European Relations

Until the beginning of the 1970s, countries from Western Europe played a very limited role in China's foreign policy. Chinese leaders considered those countries as satellites of the US and perceived the European Economic Community (EEC) as an instrument of the North Atlantic Treaty Organisation (NATO). After its rapprochement with Washington and its entrance in the UN in 1971, Beijing made informal contacts with the EEC and official relations were established in 1975.[2] The relationship eventually evolved and was supported by both mutual trade interests, and the 1985 TECA. However, this period of growing contacts between China and the Community was interrupted by the Tiananmen Square incident in June 1989.

Since the establishment of the Open-Door Policy by Deng Xiaoping in 1978, the perception in Europe was that political issues, such as human rights, should not be an obstacle for trade, as China was moving in "the right direction," as described in the next section. The Chinese authorities were therefore very surprised by the strong reactions provoked by the Tiananmen Square incident. In fact, Sino-European relations suffered a serious collapse after the events of June 1989: the EEC, along with other world powers, imposed a series of sanctions on China and embargoed the sale of military equipment. The European Council strongly condemned the crackdown by the Chinese authorities and expressed its dismay at the subsequent executions, despite the appeals of the international society. Besides, it formally asked Beijing to respect human rights and to take into account the hopes of freedom and democracy expressed by the population as an important aspect of the Chinese modernisation policy. The President of the European Commission, Jacques Delors, and the Vice-President, Frans Andriessen, refused to receive Minister Zheng Tuobin, expected to co-chair the EEC-China Joint Committee meeting on the day after the massacre; all high-level negotiations were cancelled and the Chinese delegation returned to Beijing.[3] The Madrid European

2 Carmen A. Mendes, 'Relações Económicas Europa – China,' in A. M. Amaro and C. Justino (eds.), *Estudos Sobre a China*, II, Lisbon, Instituto Superior de Ciências Sociais e Políticas (ISCSP), 2000, pp. 439-440.

3 Mendes, 'Relações Económicas Europa – China,' *op. cit.*, pp. 442-443.

Council of late June confirmed the previous national decisions and adopted a number of measures towards China.[4]

At the same time, the Group of Seven most industrialised countries (G7) unanimously condemned the massacre and confirmed the establishment of economic and political sanctions towards Beijing. This G7 decision had serious consequences for the Chinese leaders: the G7 decided to postpone the analysis of new World Bank loans[5] and blocked all its credits to China. It was followed by other international institutions such as the Asian Development Bank (ADB) that suspended a US$500 mn loan in progress. At the political level, the UN adopted, in September 1989, a resolution on the human rights situation in China, which clearly condemned the massacre.[6]

The restrictive measures adopted at the Madrid European Council in June 1989 affected EEC-China relations: high-level contacts between representatives of the Commission and the Chinese government and decisions on new cooperation projects were suspended.[7] However, in October 1990, the EEC member states agreed to gradually normalise relations with Beijing,[8] which evolved towards a new economic and political order. On the European side, the creation of the Single Market and the WTO changed the framework of trade and the Community aimed to become one of Asia's major political and economic partners. On the Chinese side, with the end of the Cold War, Beijing had growing international ambitions. In 1990-91, the PRC returned to the international political arena, using the Gulf War crisis[9] to settle the diplomatic consequences of the 1989 repression. In order to achieve normalisation with the West, China's officials used their position as permanent member of the Security Council to support or abstain during crucial resolutions.[10]

4 Commission of the European Communities, *Bulletin of the European Union*, point 1.1.24., Brussels, June 1989, p. 17 and *General Report on the Activities of the European Union*, No. 23, Brussels July 1989, p. 372.

5 Commission of the European Communities, General Report on the Activities of the European Union, *op. cit.*

6 François Joyaux, *La Tentation Impériale*, Imprimerie Nationale, Paris, 1994, pp. 79-82.

7 The programmes of scientific and technical cooperation agreed before 4 June 1989 were, however, maintained.

8 Commission of the European Communities, *General Report on the Activities of the European Union*, No. 24, Brussels 1990, p. 333.

9 The United Nations condemned Iraq for the invasion of Kuwait in August 1990 and authorised the employment of all necessary means to free this state.

10 Pierre Gentelle, 'Chine. La Cage et l'Oiseau,' *L'État du Monde*, 1992, pp. 77-78 and 'Un Ordre International Insaisissable,' *RAMSES*, 1992, p. 144.

Thus, although Sino-European relations cooled down, the consequences of the Tiananmen Square events were quickly forgotten, allowing for the resumption of the dialogue. China was becoming increasingly attractive for European businessmen and governments decided to adopt economic pragmatism, as Beijing benefited from a positive economic conjuncture. From 1994 onwards, trade, investments and bilateral cooperation were re-established and a new mechanism for political dialogue was created.[11] After having strongly condemned China, all Western countries followed the same line: the US and Europe, quickly forgot about the political quarantine, resumed negotiations, as trade remained the priority.

The idea that the Chinese political authoritarian regime would not change with sanctions but with the gradual evolution of society and its deeper integration into Western culture spread very conveniently among European decision-makers. Political and economic contacts would encourage the Chinese leaders to pursue the reforms (of the Open-Door Policy) and to respect human rights. Europe argued that China's accession to the WTO would encourage its reforms and would integrate it further into the multilateral trade system, pushing for the respect of international rules. In bilateral terms, it would abolish tariffs, opening the Chinese market to European business interests. By 1995, the Council of the European Union defined the EU's strategy towards the PRC, arguing that the relationship between both sides should reflect the Chinese weight and influence at the regional and international levels. The EU adopted, for the first time, a global approach to China, defined from a long-term perspective, covering different dimensions. This long-term strategy, based on several specific cooperation programs, aimed not only to encourage the development of Sino-European trade, but also to promote the emergence of civil society in the PRC, to eradicate poverty and protect the environment. According to the EU, these steps would contribute to implement trade liberalisation and democracy in China and to integrate it in the global system.[12]

By 2001, China considered the EU as a "strategic partner." China's entry into the WTO, after fifteen years of hard negotiations,[13] and the US involvement in the "War on Terror" after the events of 11 September 2001, may have contributed to changing the Chinese perception of Europe's significance. The US' unilateral invasion of Iraq in 2003 further contributed to this and also challenged the transatlantic relationship,

---

11 See Commission of the European Communities, *A Long Term Policy for China-Europe Relations*, COM(1995) 279, Brussels, 5 July 1995.

12 *Ibid.*

13 See 'China Abre La Muralla,' *El Exportador*, January, 2001, p. 7.

prompting new effects on EU-China relations. Soon after the release of a European Commission policy paper in September 2003 updating its China policy,[14] in October 2003, the PRC made public for the first time, its strategy. The *Policy Paper on the Relationship with the EU*[15] outlined an optimistic scenario for the economic exchanges between the two sides and the absence of conflicts.[16] These unilateral moves, inaugurated a "honeymoon" period in China-Europe relations,[17] culminating with the announcement of a "comprehensive strategic partnership."

The role of the US in the Sino-European relationship, known as the "silent actor," frames the bilateral dynamics into a triangular architecture. As aforementioned, both China and Europe seem to accommodate the American strategy into their bilateral reactions. The Chinese pragmatic vision of balancing its relationships with the US and the EU is noticeable in a report produced by the Chinese Academy of Social Sciences: *China's Modernisation 2008*, introducing the "Peace Dove Strategy."[18] This new concept represents the priorities of China's foreign policy in the body of a dove: the UN emerges as the top priority, at the head of the bird; Asia appears in the chest; Latin America, Africa and Oceania in the tail; Europe as a wing and the US as the other.[19] By stressing the importance of representing the US and the EU as each of the bird's wings, the study highlights China's interest in finding a balance in its relationship with these blocs. Although Washington is far more important to Beijing than Europe, the EU is perceived as a precious alternative during bilateral negotiations with the US, increasing Chinese bargaining power.

---

14 Commission of the European Communities, *A Maturing Partnership – Shared Interests and Challenges in EU-China Relations*, COM(2003) 533 final, Brussels, 10 September 2003 (updating the European Commission's Communications on EU-China relations of 1998 and 2001).

15 Susanne Weigelin-Schwiedrzik and Nele Noesselt, 'Striving for Symmetry in Partnership: An Analysis of Sino-EU Relations Based on the Two Recently Published Policy Papers,' in S. Weigelin-Schwiedrzik *et al.*, *As China Meets the World: China's Changing Position in the International Community*, Vienna, Austrian Academy of Sciences, 2006.

16 People's Republic of China, *China's EU Policy Paper*, Beijing, October 2003, pp. 7-8.

17 See David Shambaugh *et al.*, 'From Honeymoon to Marriage: Prospects for the China-Europe Relationship,' as cited in D. Shambaugh *et al.*, *China-Europe Relations: Perceptions, Policies and Prospects*, New York, Routledge, 2008, p. 314.

18 Chinese Academy of Social Sciences (CASS), 'China's Modernisation 2008,' Beijing, January 2008 and Xinhua News Agency, 'Chinese Think-Tank Initiates "Peace Dove Strategy,"' 29 January 2008, retrieved on 20 February 2009, http://news.net.com/english/2008-01/29/content_7515266.htm.

19 Carmen A. Mendes and Maria R. Freire, 'A Organização de Cooperação de Xangai como Instrumento Geopolítico Sino-Russo na Ásia Central,' *Geopolítica*, No. 2, Aveiro, June 2008, p. 211. See Xinhua News Agency, *loc. cit.*

The Partnership and Cooperation Agreement

From 1998 onwards, the EU-China political dialogue has been framed by annual summits, which assemble European Heads of State and Government and the Chinese leadership. One of the most important topics on the agenda has been, since its announcement at the 9th Summit in September 2006, the PCA, aiming at covering both political and economic bilateral relations. The 10th EU-China Annual Summit meeting, which took place in Beijing in January 2007 under the auspices of the EU's Portuguese Presidency, officially launched the beginning of the PCA negotiations.[20] Both sides were very optimistic at the time: the 17th Congress of the Chinese Communist Party, held in Beijing in the previous month, had been particularly successful, and the EU had just signed the Lisbon Treaty, after lengthy negotiations.[21] Thus, the Summit enjoyed a particularly favourable context, being conducted within a very cordial and "politically correct" tone, giving little relevance to the most sensitive issues in Sino-European relations, thus delaying any step forward to sort out the main points of contention between both sides.[22]

Instead, the meeting summarised the ten previous years of bilateral relations and emphasised common interests. The European leaders said they were willing to find solutions through cooperation, not protecttionism.[23] In commercial terms, China is the EU's second largest trade partner (after the US) and the EU is China's largest trade partner.[24] Therefore, along with the political meeting, the 4th China-EU Business Summit was held in Beijing, encouraging dialogue between companies on both sides, focusing on the role of the financial sector and of Small and Medium Enterprises (SMEs) in sustainable development and resolution

20 The summit assembled José Sócrates, President of the Council of the European Union, José Manuel Barroso, President of the European Commission, and Peter Mandelson, Former Commissioner for Trade. China was represented by its President, Hu Jintao, its Prime Minister, Wen Jiabao, and the Minister of Commerce, Bo Xilai.

21 'EU Ambassador to China: Summit to Enhance Cooperation,' *People's Daily Online*, 13 November 2007.

22 Xulio Rios, 'El Desencuentro entre la UE y China: que Acerca y que Separa a Bruselas y Beijing,' 12 December 2007, retrieved on 20 February 2009, http://spanish.safe-democracy.org/.

23 'EU Ambassador to China: Summit to Enhance Cooperation,' *People's Daily Online*, 13 November 2007. See The Federal Government, *Europe – Succeeding Together*, German EU Presidency Program, 2007, pp. 22-23.

24 Nicola Casarini, 'The Evolution of the EU-China Relationship: from Constructive Engagement to Strategic Partnership,' *Occasional Paper*, Institute for Security Studies, No. 64, October 2006, p. 7.

of environmental issues through usage of innovative technologies.[25] In the closing session, the EU announced a €500 mn loan from the European Investment Bank (EIB) to Chinese banks in the area of energy efficiency and environmental protection. In the education sector, €10 mn were invested in a programme to train managers in the *China-Europe International Business School* in Shanghai[26] and the creation of a *China-EU Law School* was announced. In fact, as part of the commercial and political pillars, cooperation represents an important dimension of Sino-European relations, as the EU is the most important Chinese partner in science and technology (S&T). For example, the agreements of the 6th EU-China Summit in 2003 enabled Beijing to participate in the Galileo Global Navigation Satellite System.

The political dimension of the 10th EU-China Summit focused on shared responsibility, leadership and joint response to international challenges, such as peace-keeping operations, security, stability and multilateral involvement. The EU asked for a more active role for the PRC in the establishment of the international agenda, reminding it of its interests and responsibilities. There was a clear strategy for pressing for cooperation and integration from China in the international system, requiring an active involvement in several areas. One of those areas concerned weapons proliferation, namely in the cases of North Korea, in which China has a crucial role in the six party talks, and Iran.[27] A second area was sustainable development and security in Africa, where Beijing has become a major player, given the dimension of its investment and interest in natural resources. A third area regarded energy issues, environment and climate change, where the EU identified common interests (security and sustainability of energy resources) and common responsebilities (environmental protection and alternative energy resources). Furthermore, the EU requested China's involvement in contentious regions, such as the Middle East and Burma/Myanmar, and with other global concerns, such as terrorism, organised crime and migration control.[28]

---

25 Carmen A. Mendes *et al.*, 'Председательство Португалии в Европейском союзе: шаг вперед или отражение тупика?,' *Европа*, Vol. 8, No. 1 (26), 2008, pp. 27-28.

26 'UE e China Encerram Cimeira com Promessas de Amizade,' *Diário Digital/Lusa*, 11 January 2008.

27 See Council of the European Union, *18 Month Program of the German, Portuguese, and Slovenian Presidencies*, 17079/06, POLGEN 125, Brussels, 21 December 2006, p. 65.

28 Portuguese Presidency of the EU, *Diálogo Estratégico UE-China Reúne em Lisboa*, Lisbon, 25 October 2007, retrieved on 20 February 2009, http://www.eu2007.pt/UE/vPT/Noticias_Documentos/20071026senec.htm.

As many analysts have noted, the Portuguese Presidency of the EU was rich in events but poor in results: some steps forward were taken in areas of increasing convergence, but the most controversial issues remained unsolved.[29] The annual Summit was a clear example of this, doing little to improve bilateral divergences. For the EU, these divergences mainly concerned issues such as the trade deficit, intellectual property rights (IPRs) and the devaluation of the RMB, in economic terms – and, from a political point of view, the issues covered human rights, relations with Taiwan and the international responsibility of the PRC, namely in Africa.[30] For the Chinese leaders, the EU should not force China to respect strict environmental regulations before it has reached a certain level of development, the EU should extend market economy status to China, and it should lift the embargo on arms sales.

The PCA, which is currently being negotiated, will probably summarise the ideas that were discussed in the previous summit instead of bringing new perspectives to those sensitive issues. From this viewpoint, it is difficult to understand why these two actors consider themselves "strategic partners." The Chinese approach to the "strategic partnership" is that cooperation should be long-term and stable, bearing on the larger picture of China-EU relations. It transcends the differences in ideology and social systems and is not subjected to the impacts of individual events that occur from time to time. By "partnership," it means that the cooperation should be equal-footed, mutually beneficial and win-win for all involved. The two sides should base this relationship on mutual respect and mutual trust, endeavour to expand converging interests and seek common ground on the major issues while shelving differences on the minor ones.[31] Does Europe share this approach? The EU considers that "partnerships with key actors" are the best way to pursue its objectives, especially in Asia. With China, the partnership would ideally allow better access to its market than what is enforced by WTO regulations and should include a clause on human rights. By "strategic," the EU does not mean "military" partnership, keeping a

---

29 Mendes *et al.*, 'Председательство Португалии в Европейском союзе: шаг вперед или отражение тупика?,' *op. cit.*, p. 34.

30 Commission of the European Communities, *EU Troika Meets with New Chinese Foreign Minister*, Brussels, 28 May 2007, retrieved on 20 February 2009, http://ec.europa.eu/external_relations/china/intro/index.htm.

31 Wen Jiabao, Speech, *Vigorously Promoting Comprehensive Strategic Partnership Between China and the European Union*, Speech by the Premier of the State Council of the PRC at the China-EU Investment and Trade Forum, Brussels, 6 May 2004, retrieved on 20 February 2009, http://www.fmprc.gov.cn/ce/cebe/eng/zt/t101949.htm.

cautious approach regarding the arms embargo.[32] In fact, rather than having a substantive meaning, the EU-China "strategic partnership" in fact reveals the absence of a "strategic competition" between the two.

We may take Portugal as case study among the five EU member states considered by China as strategic partners. The signature of a comprehensive strategic partnership with the PRC, during the visit of the Chinese Prime Minister to Lisbon in December 2005, did not translate into any significant steps. It was the consequence of the good relationship maintained by the two countries, in part because of the history related to Macao and the positive tone of the Sino-Portuguese negotiations on the handover. It also revealed Chinese interests in using Lisbon and Macao as a platform for cooperation with previous Portuguese colonies, namely in Africa, where Beijing has growing energy interests. The *Forum for Economic and Trade Cooperation between China and Portuguese-speaking Countries*, known as the "Macao Forum" – because its Permanent Secretariat is based in Macao – was created in 2003, as a mechanism:

> to reinforce the cooperation and the economic exchange between the People's Republic of China and the Countries of Portuguese Language; to give dynamism to Macao as a platform of connection to these countries; and to promote the development of the links between the People's Republic of China, Macao and the Countries of Portuguese Language.[33]

But the official discourse reveals a very different perception. In February 2009, during the 30th anniversary of the establishment of diplomatic ties between the two countries, the congratulatory messages of Chinese President Hu Jintao and his Portuguese counterpart Aníbal Cavaco Silva mentioned the strategic partnership as an important chapter in bilateral relations. Cavaco Silva said that "the building of the China-Portugal comprehensive strategic partnership in 2005 creates conditions for their mutually beneficial cooperation on a broader range." Hu pointed out that:

> China attaches importance to Portugal's role in the EU and international affairs and is willing to work together with the country in enhancing exchanges and cooperation, boosting trust and friendship, and constantly

---

32 See Sebastian Bersick, 'Europe in Asia,' in D. Shambaugh and M. Yahuda (eds.), *International Relations in Asia: The New Regional System*, Roam & Littlefield, 2008.

33 Forum for Economic and Trade Cooperation between China and Portuguese-Speaking Countries, 'Sobre o Fórum,' 2003, http://www.forumchinaplp.org.mo/pt/aboutus.asp. This Forum includes the PRC, Portugal, Brazil, East Timor, Mozambique, Angola, Cape Verde, Guinea-Bisau, and São Tomé & Príncipe as an observer (as it maintains diplomatic relations with Taiwan).

> enriching the content of bilateral relations in order to push their comprehensive strategic partnership to a new high.[34]

It should be noted that Hu's mention of the Portuguese intermediate role between China and the EU is recurrent in official speeches. For example, the Chinese Ambassador to Portugal Gao Kexiang said in a recent interview with the Xinhua News Agency that "China highly values its ties with Portugal and regards it as a reliable partner in the EU."[35] This idea, along with the Macao Forum, may count as one of strongest reasons why China signed the agreement with Portugal.

In this interview, Gao also said that the partnership "usher[ed] in a new era of friendly cooperation between the two countries [as they] have deepened political mutual trust through frequent exchanges of high-level visits."[36] The ambassador also highlighted that:

> [b]oth countries have further enhanced their bilateral cooperation in trade, culture, education, science and technology, health care and judicial affairs system. As a result, the goal of doubling bilateral trade volume within three years set by the two heads of government was fulfilled a year ahead of schedule.[37]

This increase of the volume of trade was only beneficial for China, and prompted a series of negative reactions against the proliferation of Chinese shops and restaurants in Portugal. Moreover, this trade volume was related to the impact of China's WTO accession (most noticeable in Portugal after 2005, as explained in the forthcoming section on trade), not to the signature of the partnership.

The ambassador referred to the fact that "two Confucius institutes have been opened in Portugal and more Chinese universities have started to offer Portuguese language courses," and concluded his interview by saying that "with joint efforts from both sides, comprehensive strategic partnership between the two countries will undoubtedly be able to advance further and bilateral cooperation will produce more fruits in the coming 30 years."[38] Those institutes are primarily designed to enhance China's culture and its image and status in the international community.

---

34 'Chinese, Portuguese Leaders Exchange Congratulatory Messages on 30th Anniversary of Diplomatic Ties,' *Xinhua News Agency*, 8 February 2009, retrieved on 20 February 2009, http://news.xinhuanet.com/english/2009-02/08/content_10781274.htm#.

35 Gao Kexiang, Interview with *Xinhua News Agency*, 'Ambassador: China-Portugal Strategic Partnership will be More Fruitful,' 7 February 2009, retrieved on 20 February 2009, http://news.xinhuanet.com/english/2009-02/08/content_10781914.htm.

36 *Ibid.*

37 *Ibid.*

38 Gao, *op. cit.*

Thus, they are used as an aspect of Chinese foreign policy to promote Chinese national interests in several EU countries. However, in Portugal this is not very noticeable. Besides, the creation of Confucius institutes in Braga and Lisbon resulted from personal efforts of professors from the respective University of Minho and the University of Lisbon and were not an outcome of the signature of the bilateral strategic partnership (although the inaugurating ceremony of the Minho institute took place during Wen Jiabao's visit to Portugal in December 2005).

Therefore, high level political contacts, growing bilateral trade or cultural and academic events can hardly be related to the existence of a Sino-Portuguese comprehensive strategic partnership. Will the EU-China PCA lack this kind of significance as well (i.e. will it make any difference in terms of the progress of the bilateral relationship)? In order to analyse the PCA negotiations, this chapter will now focus on the most important dimensions and problematic issues of Sino-European relations.

Different Human Rights Conceptions

Divergences over human rights have been constant in Sino-European relations. The concept of human rights and democracy, which originated from certain Western countries and that was further adopted by the US, is based on a "dynamic" interpretation of the UN Charter, which argues that an issue regulated by international law is not under national jurisdiction of a state.[39] On the contrary, the PRC, based on a narrow interpretation of the UN's competences, refuses all types of external regulations, considering them as "interference in China's internal affairs." Moreover, Beijing does not accept the notion of "universality of human rights," arguing that it should consider the historical, cultural and political constraints of each country. When the issue is approached by a foreign counterpart during an official meeting, Chinese leaders usually adopt an explicit posture of disapproval regarding their interlocutor.[40]

Formally, Chinese law has many similarities with European laws. In 1979, the PRC promulgated a regulation on "arrest," limiting the undetermined detention of suspects, and the 1982 Constitution regulates basic rights and freedoms. Indeed, judicial organisation, according to the Chinese Constitution, respects the principles adopted in most Western countries: the judiciary is independent of the executive and legislative powers, and the judges and prosecutors are elected by popular assemblies. However, there is no real independence of the judiciary, and

---

39 Elisabeth Fouquoire-Brillet, 'Chine: Droits de l'Homme et Démocratie,' *Défense Nationale*, October 1995, pp. 56-57.

40 Claudie Joussé, 'La Chine et l'Union Européenne,' *Politique Étrangère*, No. 4, 1996, p. 875.

individual rights and freedoms are not observed.[41] Although the introduction of the market economy in China prompted the emergence of new forms of social behaviour, it did not result in the adoption of a democratic political system based on Western characteristics.

European expectations regarding the reform of the Chinese legal system and its harmonisation with international standards, suffered a blow in June 1989 with the Tiananmen Square events.[42] Although being an unavoidable trading partner, China had lost much of its sympathy for Western public opinion and its international image deteriorated.[43] In October 1989, during the celebration of the 40th anniversary of the PRC, Deng Xiaoping declared that social order had been restored. The Western diplomats based in Beijing agreed among themselves to participate in the banquet hosted by the Chinese prime minister but to boycott the subsequent festivities.[44] The Nobel Peace Prize in that year was attributed to the Dalai Lama for opposing the use of violence in his fight for the liberation of Tibet,[45] causing an "extreme indignation" and a feeling of "deep regret" in Beijing.[46] In the period of implementation of its economic and social reforms, China believed Western pressure, for the respect of human rights and Western support for the Tibetan people and Taiwan, exacerbated the emerging political opposition movements within

41 In practice, the judges and prosecutors apply the directives from the Chinese Communist Party. The role of lawyers is to "help" their client to recognise the facts in order to mitigate the sentences handed; and they have no guarantee of achieving the (required) annual renewal of their licenses. Michel Brasier, 'Les Relations Franco-Chinoises,' *Conseil Économique et Social*, 6 June 1995, pp. 15-16.

42 Brasier, *op. cit.*, p. 17.

43 Patrice De Beer and Jean-Louis Rocca, *La Chine à la Fin de l'Ère Deng Xiaoping*, Brussels, Le Monde Éditions, 1995, p. 188.

44 Commission of the European Communities, *Bulletin of the European Union*, 2 October 1989.

45 Besides facing dissidents in the Tiananmen Square incident, the Chinese authorities were also confronted with Tibet's claims for independence. The more moderate reformist policy adopted by Deng Xiaoping from 1978 onwards, that ultimately inspired the demonstrations in Tiananmen Square, had also allowed for an increased expression of discontent in Tibet, often resulting in incidents witnessed by tourists and foreign journalists. In March 1989, while Tibetans called for the "independence of Tibet!" the rebellion was quickly silenced by the Chinese police and Beijing declared martial law in Lhasa. Valérie Niquet-Cabestan, 'Chine. Rééquilibrages,' *L'État du Monde*, 1988-1989, p. 76; Pierre-Antoine Donnet, *Tibet: Mort ou Vif*, Paris, Éditions Gallimard, 1990, pp. 126-127.

46 Commission of the European Communities, *Bulletin of the European Union*, 10 November 1989.

a weakening domestic situation that already had a fragile foundation.[47] The reactions of the European Community to the Tiananmen Square incidents[48] were condemned by the PRC as "interference in its internal affairs,"[49] referring to the Western trend of imposing sanctions, China's unequal treatment and the persistent attacks on its sovereignty.[50] An editorial in the *People's Daily*, commenting on the *communiqué* published by the G7, considered it unacceptable that those countries refused to understand what had happened in China.[51] The Chinese leaders regretted the Council of the European Union's declaration, arguing that, according to China's Constitution, the government had the sovereign right to put an end to the social unrest.[52]

The Chinese international position regarding human rights evolved from a less hostile attitude in the early 1980s to a defensive posture after 1989 and to a more assertive approach from 1990 onwards. China's Open-Door Policy adopted in 1978 by Deng Xiaoping resulted in the signature of international agreements and in the participation of Chinese officials, from 1985 onwards, in the UN Commission on Human Rights' meetings in Geneva. In 1988, they said to be willing to sign the Universal Declaration of Human Rights and the two 1966 Covenants (the International Covenant of Civil Rights and the International Covenant on Economic, Social and Cultural Rights). Given the reactions to the crackdown, the Chinese leaders opted for a defensive policy, mainly asking for non-interference in domestic affairs and arguing that their priority was economic development and poverty eradication.

From the early 1990s onwards, the Chinese strategy evolved to promote a broader international debate, defending specific views on human rights and democracy.[53] Linking the political and commercial issues and stressing the importance of economic rights for achieving

---

47 The Chinese leaders also feared that the human rights policy and democracy had become major instruments of American foreign policy. Fouquoire-Brillet, *op. cit.*, pp. 56-57.

48 European Parliament, Resolution, *Tibet/Droits de l'Homme*, Strasbourg, 16 March 1989, as cited in *Documents d'Actualité Internationale*, No. 9, 1 May 1989, p. 191.

49 National People's Congress of the People's Republic of China, 'Déclaration de la Commission des Affaires étrangères de l'Assemblée Populaire Nationale de la République Populaire de Chine (Pékin, 19 mars 1988),' *Documents d'Actualité Internationale*, No. 9, 1 May 1989.

50 Alain Boublil, *Le Siècle des Chinois*, Monaco, Éditions du Rocher, 1997, p. 176.

51 Commission of the European Communities, *Bulletin of the European Union*, 17 July 1989.

52 Commission of the European Communities, *Bulletin of the European Union*, 29 June 1989.

53 Fouquoire-Brillet, *op. cit.*, p. 58.

freedom, the official rhetoric was constantly repeated: "we could not isolate the political rights from other fundamental human rights as the level of awareness of individuals and nations, and thus its freedom, are directly related to their economic conditions."[54] Countries at different stages of economic development, as was the case of the PRC and European states, could not concentrate on the same type of rights – for the Chinese, sufficient nutrition and basic material needs were far more important than political and civil rights.[55]

During the first global debate on human rights,[56] Western countries were obliged to take into account the views of Asian countries, due to their demographic, economic and political weight, providing China with the opportunity to disclose its position on the subject: "the concept of human rights is very broad and includes individual and collective rights. No one should put their own rights and interests above those of the state and society."[57] The words of then Vice Foreign Minister Liu Huaqing highlight the conceptual difference between China and the West. In short, the Chinese defensive approach, post-Tiananmen, became more offensive from the mid-1990s onwards, reflecting the support of other Asian countries against the Western agenda on human rights and democratisation.[58]

Although China's economic development was followed by improvements at the level of social and political freedoms, as suggested by the adoption of the 2007 Labour Contract Law and the attempts towards creating a more equal society,[59] this development is still far from fulfilling Western conceptions of respect for human rights and democracy. Religious movements in China are also affected by the Chinese approach to human rights: despite the spread of various forms of Christianity throughout the whole society (including the Chinese Communist Party), it is not easy for Christians to survive the persecution

---

54 *Ibid.*, p. 59.

55 Jing Men, 'EU-China Relations Need More Mutual Understanding,' *EU-China Observer*, No. 1, 2009, retrieved www.coleurop.be/template.asp?pagename=EUCO, p. 6.

56 United Nations World Conference on Human Rights, Vienna, 14-25 June 1993.

57 Liu Huaqing, Speech as cited in S. Marks, 'Nightmare and Noble Dreams: The 1993 World Conference on Human Rights,' *The Cambridge Law Journal*, Vol. 53, No. 1, 1994, pp. 54-62.

58 Fouquoire-Brillet, *op. cit.*, p. 59.

59 Giuseppe Balducci, 'Prospects and Challenges for the European Promotion of Human Rights in China,' *EU-China Observer*, No. 1, 2009, retrieved on 20 February 2009, www.coleurop.be/template.asp?pagename=EUCO, p. 12.

of an atheistic regime, with such a restrictive approach to human rights.[60] The China-Africa Seminars on Human Rights held by the Forum on China Africa Cooperation (FOCAC) is a more recent example of Beijing's strategy to negotiate support for its own conceptions.[61]

Due to these differences, many argue that progress may rely more on dialogue than on the imposition of sanctions. The European Commission and governments, despite several initiatives undertaken regarding human rights in China, have the dilemma of choosing between economic interests and political censorship. Faced with the susceptible nature of Chinese leaders, Europe tends to avoid confrontation, opting for an economic and pragmatic approach.[62] In fact, the European response to Tiananmen did not establish a causal link between granting economic benefits to China and its human rights respect, as the US did, in its reaction to this incident. Instead, the Commission's line of conduct was inspired by principles of *realpolitik* – by not subordinating economic relations to any pre-conditions. European officials tried to avoid confrontation and pursued dialogue with their Chinese partners, by separating the human rights issue from economic negotiations.[63] This choice for political cooperation, in which criticism of human rights abuses was mostly made in private to Chinese leaders, was allegedly part of a comprehensive strategy for promoting the liberalisation and Open-Door Policy, eventually adopted by the Chinese government.[64] The difference of approaches between the EU and the US will be further developed in the next section.

In conclusion, due to dissensions in regards to human rights issues, the year 1989 was marked by a turning point in Sino-European relations. The months of international sanctions were quickly forgotten and the four years that followed the massacre were more positive than expected by the Chinese leaders: profiting from a favourable economic environment, they rapidly reduced China's isolation in the international system. Some argue that the normalisation of relations between Beijing and the West promoted "social peace" and support for capitalist change in China.[65] The

---

60 See David Aikman, *Jesus in Beijing: How Christianity Is Transforming China and Changing the Global Balance of Power*, Washington, Regnery Publishing, INC., 2003.

61 See Forum on China-Africa Cooperation, 'FOCAC to hold China-Africa Seminar on Human Rights,' 13 October 2004, retrieved on 20 February 2009, http://www.focac.org/eng/zt/zfrqyth/t164223.htm.

62 Joussé, *op. cit.*, p. 876.

63 Carmen A. Mendes, 'A Concepção Chinesa de Direitos Humanos,' *Via Latina*, No. 4, VI Series, March 2007, p. 120.

64 Joussé, *op. cit.*, p. 875.

65 *Le Monde Diplomatique*, July 1992.

fact is that Europe failed in conducting a coherent human rights policy towards China, mainly due to individual economic interests of its member states.[66] Only the arms embargo remained as a legacy of the Tiananmen Square incident.

EU Arms Embargo on China: Reasons for its Maintenance

Although the idea evolved in Europe that embargos are not the best way to change the Chinese leaders' perceptions on human rights, the embargo remains in force. Some argue that lifting the embargo should depend on progress for human rights in China. Others, based on strategic reasons, defend the view that the embargo guarantees the balance of power in East Asia, particularly in the Taiwan Strait. This is the US' official position, which has strongly encouraged the EU to maintain the arms ban.

The embargo, disrupting China's access to modern military technology, is perceived by Beijing as a shadow in its relations with Europe. In its 2003 EU policy paper, the Chinese government stated that:

> China and the EU will maintain high-level military-to-military exchanges, develop and improve, step by step, a strategic security consultation mechanism, exchange more missions of military experts, and expand exchanges in respect of military officers' training and defence studies.[67]

In line with the Chinese pressure on the EU for the lifting of the arms embargo, the paper argued that this would "remove barriers to greater bilateral cooperation on defence industry and technologies."[68]

The Chinese leaders have two main goals to accomplish with the lifting of the embargo. The first one is of political symbolism: the absolution by the international community regarding the Tiananmen Square incident,[69] which would allow China to recover its legitimacy as a great power in the international system, instead of just belonging to a list of embargoed states. Moreover, the lifting of the embargo by the EU and the strategic partnership with the EU would limit Washington's attempts to contain Beijing.[70] Having the EU as an ally would be highly beneficial in this strategy of counterbalancing the US, for example, during potential confrontational debates within multilateral institutions. Besides, the

---

66 Balducci, *op. cit.*, p. 10.

67 People's Republic of China, *op. cit.*, pp. 7-8.

68 *Ibid.*

69 Peter Brookes, 'The Lifting of the EU Arms Embargo on China: An American Perspective,' *The Heritage Foundation*, 2 March 2005.

70 Lora Saalman and Yuan Jing-Dong, 'The European Union and the Arms Ban on China,' Center for Nonproliferation Studies, July 2004, pp. 4-5.

European lifting of the arms ban would divide the transatlantic alliance, weakening the Western block on future anti-Chinese decisions. Regarding the Taiwan issue, the lifting of the embargo would be perceived in Europe as a defeat for Taipei, contributing to isolate the island from the international community, promoting Beijing's intentions for reunification.[71]

The second major objective is related to the Chinese military modernisation programs and the need to reduce dependence on Russian equipment, which is technologically inferior to that of NATO and of the EU. Beijing does not find in Russia the military technology it needs – systems of command and control, communications, computers, intelligence and surveillance.[72] The lifting of the embargo would give the People's Liberation Army (PLA) access to foreign technology of dual use (civil and military). Furthermore, Beijing would gain advantages in future negotiations of military purchases from Russia and the Middle East[73] and the US government would be pressured by its weapon producing industry to follow the EU, granting the PLA access to American weapons.[74]

As mentioned in the previous section, the US also imposed sanctions on China following the events of Tiananmen Square, including the arms embargo and the suspension of high-level meetings. The Public Law, adopted in February 1990, suspended:

> the issuance of licenses for the export to China of any military article on the US Munitions List. It exempted from this prohibition US Munitions List items that are designated specifically for use in civil products [and barred] the export of US-origin satellites for launch on Chinese launch vehicles. Because the US Munitions List includes nonlethal military equipment (for example, radios and radars) in addition to lethal equipment (such as missiles), the US prohibition on arms sales to China covers a broader range of items than the EU embargo.[75]

The US is the main opponent to a shift in EU policy regarding the arms ban. The American objections are of various kinds, but the main motive is related to China's refusal to renounce to the use of force against Taiwan –

---

71 Brookes, *op. cit.*

72 *Ibid.*

73 Saalman, *op. cit.*, p. 4.

74 Frank Ching, 'Changing Dynamics in EU-China Arms Relations,' *China Brief*, The Jamestown Foundation, Issue 5, March 2004, http://www.jamestown.org/single/?no_cache=1&tx_ttnews%5Btt_news%5D=3631.

75 Public Law 101-246, February 1990. 'Military Imports From the United States and the European Union Since the 1989 Embargoes,' *Report to the Chairman,* Joint Economic Committee, US Senate, General Accounting Office, GAO/NSIAD-98-176, 16 June 1998, p. 5.

this idea was reinforced by its adoption of the "Anti-Secession" Law.[76] In the event of a military incident in the Strait, the lifting of the embargo would allow the PLA to use European arms against American soldiers. Besides, it would endanger the balance of conventional military power across the Strait, giving Beijing the incentive of being able to resolve the conflict through the use of force.[77]

A second aspect that worries the US regarding the lifting of the embargo is that it would increase Chinese military power, threatening American predominance in the Pacific.[78] In case of the deterioration of relations between Japan and Korea, the transfer of weapons to Beijing could put Washington in strategic disadvantage. Another American argument relates to the issue of proliferation of technology and equipment to third states: the laws controlling Chinese exports may allow the transfer of European technology to countries like Pakistan, Iran, Myanmar and North Korea, among others, with severe consequences for the balance of power in Asia and in the Middle East.[79] Finally, the US government argues that, with the end of the embargo, the EU could lose its ability to influence China on human rights issues and would send a wrong signal to other "repressive regimes."[80]

Unlike the US Public Law adopted for the imposition of the embargo on arms sales to China, the EU issued a vague, although legally binding, policy statement, which did not specify the duration of the embargo or measures of verification for the observance of the embargo, leading to different member states' interpretations of this policy statement. While some nations embargoed all military items to China, others only banned lethal weapons.[81] The clause called for the suspension of military cooperation and embargoed the sale of military items, allowing the member states to decide what cannot be sold.[82] For this reason, the main instrument to regulate the European transfer of arms to Beijing is not the embargo, but the EU Code of Conduct for Arms Exports, which lists a

76 National People's Congress of the People's Republic of China, *Anti-Secession Law*, Adopted at the Third Session of the Tenth National People's Congress (NPC), on 14 March 2005.

77 Brookes, *op. cit.*

78 *Ibid.*

79 Saalman and Yuan, *op. cit.*, p. 4.

80 Brookes, *op. cit.*

81 US Senate General Accounting Office Joint Economic Committee, 'Military Imports From the United States and the European Union Since the 1989 Embargoes,' *Report to the Chairman*, GAO/NSIAD-98-176, 16 June 1998, p. 3.

82 Richard C. D'Amato and Roger W. Robinson Jr., 'US-Europe Paper Regarding China,' *US-China Economic and Security Review Commission*, Washington, D.C., 19 January 2005.

number of conditions to be fulfilled by a country before being allowed to import weapons from an EU member state – such as the country's political system and potential threats to regional stability. This Code of Conduct, an agreement issued by the Council of the European Union that has more political than legal weight, could be strengthened in case the EU decided to lift the embargo.

By 2003, there was the widespread view within the European Commission that the end of the arms ban would not necessarily lead to an increase on military sales to China, being rather a symbolic gesture.[83] Many EU member states, especially France and Germany, were in favour of lifting the embargo (probably to favour their own weapons sales). While France considered it an anachronism,[84] Germany and Spain argued that lifting it would increase Sino-European trade. The UK assumed a dubious position and Belgium demanded China's ratification of the UN's International Covenant on Civil and Political Rights. The Netherlands, Finland, Portugal and Sweden, traditionally opponents of removing the arms ban accepted to reconsider, and Denmark was willing to align with the position of the majority of the member states.[85] Fearing a shift in EU policy, some members of the European Parliament submitted a resolution criticising the Commission for not reacting to the public declarations made by certain members of the Commission, that were cited in the media "as being in favour of the lifting of the embargo" and calling "on the EU to maintain the arms embargo until the human rights situation in China improves drastically."[86] However, as the lifting of the embargo requires consensus at the Council of Ministers, the entry of ten new members in 2004 (many of them pro-American),[87] and another two in 2007, crushed any hope of reaching an agreement.

The official position of the European Commission and of the EP is that the arms ban should be maintained for human rights and strategic reasons: lifting it would reward the Chinese leaders for their controversial behaviour on human rights issues and cross Strait relations.[88] But is the embargo compatible with the emerging PCA? Lifting it would actually

83 D'Amato and Robinson Jr., *op. cit.*

84 Ching, *op. cit.*, p. 2.

85 Saalman and Yuan, *op. cit.*, pp. 1-2. As for the Portuguese position, see the Joint Communiqué between the People's Republic of China and the Portuguese Republic during the visit of the Portuguese President to China, Beijing, 12 January 2005: the lifting of the embargo would contribute to "the consolidation of bilateral political relations between the European Union and China."

86 European Parliament, Resolution, *On Lifting the EU Arms Embargo on China*, B5 0552/03, Strasbourg, 15 December 2003.

87 Ching, *op. cit.*, p. 2.

88 D'Amato and Robinson, *op. cit.*

have positive implications for EU-China relations. In economic terms, it would assure preferential treatment in bilateral trade and would open a new arms market for European companies, which face the reduction of European defence budgets. At the political level, it would help the EU to counterweight American hegemony and, from the point of view of individual member states, it would diminish their responsibility regarding the human rights situation in China.

But it would also bring some negative consequences for Europe, in its relationship with the US. The US lobbying against the lifting of the embargo is very strong,[89] as the sale of military or dual use technology to Beijing threatens American security interests in Asia. The fact that the US signed the *Taiwan Relations Act* represents a responsibility that Europe does not have to shoulder. Thus, security issues assume a different significance for Washington or Brussels in its relationship with China: the EU focuses on economic issues, while for the US the priority appear to be strategic issues.[90] Washington fears that European arms could be used against American soldiers in case of war in the Taiwan Strait and would blame the EU for changing the balance of power in East Asia, increasing the possibilities of a military conflict, without taking any responsibility for regional security. The US could react by penalising European companies involved in the arms sale to China and the gap in the transatlantic relationship would certainly grow wider.[91]

China's WTO Accession and EU Trade Policy

While Beijing tends to focus on the arms embargo as one of the main points of contention with Europe, the EU is much more worried about the deficit, due to its very negative performance in the balance of trade: China is its largest import supplier and Europe has become the main market for Chinese exports. The deficit drastically increased, especially after the PRC joined the WTO.

The Republic of China under Chiang Kai-shek was one of the 13 signatory countries of the General Agreement on Tariffs and Trade (GATT) in 1948. However, the Chinese nationalist government lost the civil war with the communists in 1949, moved to Taiwan and, soon after, decided to leave the GATT.[92] In 1971, the PRC became the legal representative of China at the UN and formally asked to join the GATT in

89 Ching, *op. cit.*, p. 2.

90 D'Amato and Robinson, *op. cit.*

91 Brookes, *op. cit.*

92 Secretaría General de Comercio Exterior, 'La Adhesión de China a la Organización Mundial de Comercio,' *Boletín Económico de ICE*, No. 2713, 17 December 2001, p. 3.

1986.[93] The process for joining the GATT, WTO since 1995, took fifteen years of hard negotiations. On the one hand, this was due to political issues, as China claimed that her statute of founding member should not be affected by the withdrawal of the Taiwanese government in 1950, and that the island should not join the GATT before the PRC. On the other hand, from an economic point of view, it was problematic to integrate a communist country in an institution created for market economies.[94] After making several bilateral concessions, especially to the US – as the EU supported its accession – the PRC gained membership in December 2001.[95] The EU and the US agreed that it was easier to control the impact of the Chinese economy if it was included within the system.

This brought some costs in the short-term: the multilateral system had not been conceived with China's soon-to-be vastly expansive rise in mind.[96] The textile and clothing industry, relying on intensive labour force, was the sector in which the impact for Europe of China's WTO accession was most noticeable. The world textile and clothing market had been regulated by international agreements that went against the principles of the multilateral system: the *Short-Term Arrangement Regarding Cotton Textiles*[97] and the *Long-Term Agreement Regarding International Trade in Cotton Textiles*, signed in 1962 within the GATT, imposed limits on cotton trade. Several times re-negotiated, this long-term agreement was replaced in 1974 by the *Arrangement Regarding International Trade in Textiles*, which extended the restrictions of trade to other textiles. This agreement opposed GATT principles as it infringed the most favoured nation (MFN) principle; established quantitative restrictions instead of tariff restrictions; discriminated against developing countries; and was not a transparent agreement. Renegotiated four times, it expired in 1994 and was replaced by the *Agreement on Textiles and Clothing* that came into force with the creation of the WTO in 1995, establishing a transitory regime to the full integration of textiles and

93 Jean-Pierre Cabestan and Leïla Choukroune, 'China's Accession to the WTO: A Historic Turning Point?,' Special Edition 'China – WTO,' *China Perspectives*, No. 40, March-April 2002, pp. 4-8.

94 Nicholas R. Lardy, *A China na Economia Mundial*, Gabinete de Estudos e Planeamento, Lisbon, Ministério da Economia, 1995, pp. 67-69.

95 Banning Garrett, 'China Faces Debates, The Contradictions of Globalization,' *Asian Survey*, Vol. XLI, No. 3, May-June 2001, p. 425.

96 Nicolas Occis, 'Les Enjeux de l'Adhésion à l'OMC,' *Politique Étrangère*, No. 2746, 30 January 2002, p. 4.

97 Yang Yongzheng, 'China's Textile and Clothing Exports: Changing International Comparative Advantage and its Policy Implications,' *Asia Pacific School of Economics and Management Working Papers*, Asia Pacific Press, Australian National University, 1999, p. 15.

clothing in the multilateral system.[98] The period of ten years foreseen by this agreement for the transition, meant that almost half of the products of this sector kept the restrictive quotas until 1 January 2005.[99] Therefore, the impact of China's WTO accession was most noticeable after this date.

China was the developing country gaining most advantage from this textile and clothing liberalisation as the majority of its exports are manufactured products, while others exports mainly concern raw-materials and primary products that are subject to higher tariffs.[100] The end of fourty years of protectionism opened the door to the structural decline of the textile and clothing industries in the US, Canada and Europe.[101] Portugal is a paradigmatic example of this, due to the traditional weight of the textile, clothing, ceramics and shoe sectors in the country's exports.[102] These industries cannot compete with Chinese goods, based on the price level, due to the huge gap in social rights and salaries between China and Europe.[103] Therefore, especially from 2005 onwards, daily news articles on factories closing down (leaving a few more hundred people unemployed) created a strong feeling of dismay, amongst the Portuguese, against the liberalisation of imports from China, and the Chinese immigrants' facility in opening new shops and restaurants.

Nevertheless, the EU trade policy towards China, besides being perceived as a threat to this important sector of the national economy, also opened a window of opportunity. As previously mentioned the Portuguese textile industry may not succeed in medium range or cheap goods but in high quality products, with perfect finish and design. Its advantage relies on the knowledge of the European market and taste, in marketing and innovation (technical textiles).[104] Therefore, there are two types of companies in the Portuguese textile industry: those that compete in low ranges without any added-value, which are highly exposed to this liberalisation; and modern, competitive companies that had been prepared for the opening-up to Chinese competition during the ten years

98 Hildegunn K. Nordås, 'The Global Textile and Clothing Industry Post the Agreement on Textiles and Clothing,' *World Trade Organization*, Geneva, 2004, p. 13.

99 Yang, *op. cit.*, p. 15.

100 Lardy, *op. cit.*, pp. 65-66.

101 Comtrade Database, as cited in Nordås, *op. cit.*

102 Luís Villalobos, 'Isto é que é Bom,' *Fortunas & Negócios*, September 2001, p. 43.

103 Paulo Nunes Almeida, Interview held with the President of the Portuguese Textile and Clothing Association, Lisbon, *Expresso*, 8 January 2005.

104 *Jornal Têxtil*, September 2004, pp. 3-4.

of transitory regime and are oriented towards industrial innovation.[105] These competitive companies even increased their exports with the opening of the Chinese market after its WTO accession.

From this perspective, China's entry into the WTO also brought some advantages to the EU, such as the removal of protectionist barriers to the Chinese market, through the reduction of tariffs and fulfillment of international trade regulations, such as the protection of IPRs. This facilitates European exports and acquisition of cheaper raw-materials and safeguards foreign companies that operate or de-localise production on the Chinese market.[106] Therefore, bringing China into the multilateral trade system, despite having a very negative short-term impact in the EU in general, and in Portugal in particular, also offers many opportunities. From the Chinese perspective, the suppression of custom-duties threatened many state companies[107] and exposed the old technology of the textile industry to competition with modern European factories, leading to unemployment in the sector,[108] but it also granted China access to European markets and to more FDI.

Conclusion

This chapter has analysed the most sensitive issues in Sino-European relations and the perspectives from both sides in terms of the need to resolve them. As a growing economic power, China is perceived as a major world market. The Chinese leaders use that power as an instrument of resistance to the adoption of universal human rights' values, which they consider as "Western" norms. A scheduled meeting between the Dalai Lama and the French President Nicolas Sarkozy, who held the presidency of the EU, was enough for Beijing to postpone the annual Summit in 2008.[109] Since the first EU-China Summit took place ten years ago, it was the first time that the annual meeting did not occur, highlighting the Chinese stance in its human rights conception and on the principle of non-interference in internal affairs.

---

105 Findings of the fieldwork of my Post-Doctorate research, funded by the Portuguese Foundation for Science and Technology, on 'The Impact for the Portuguese Economy of China's Entry into the World Trade Organization,' Institute for Political Studies, Catholic University of Portugal, 2005-2006.

106 Francisco Utrera Mora, 'La Entrada de China en la Organización Mundial de Comercio,' *Boletín Económico de ICE*, No. 2661, 31 July-3 September 2000, p. 4; Villalobos, *op. cit.*, p. 43; Jornal Têxtil, *op. cit.*, p. 4.

107 Odile Cornet, 'Nouvelle Etape de la Longue Marche Vers l'OMC,' *Moniteur du Commerce International*, No. 1423, 6 January 2000, p. 72.

108 Dorothy J. Solinger, 'Chinese Urban Jobs and the WTO,' *The China Journal*, Vol. 49, January 2003, pp. 78-79.

109 Jing Men, *op. cit.*, p. 4.

From the sanctions imposed by the West in the wake of the Tiananmen Square incident, only the embargo on arms sales and military cooperation prevails. Imposed for reasons linked to human rights, they are now maintained mainly for strategic interests. Due to the conflict across the Taiwan Strait, lifting the embargo could lead to an arms race and regional instability. However, certain officials in the European Commission argue that the military build-up across the Strait will always take place and that tension will rise, despite the maintenance of the embargo. But others refer to the symbolic aspect of the embargo and worry that, by lifting it, the EU would send the wrong message to Beijing and to non-European suppliers of military technology, encouraging Chinese military strategists.

The issue of the arms embargo is thus far from being solved and Europe is at a crossroads. On the one hand, the EU is pressured by the Chinese leaders and is strongly attracted by offering a new market to its military industry. On the other hand, the EU is pressed in the opposite direction by the US, concerned about the strategic implications resulting from the end of the embargo, particularly in East Asia. Apart from American objections, other factors explain the postponement of a European decision, such as divergences among EU member states, issues on human rights and concerns in regards to technological proliferation.[110] However, as argued above, this is an "intentionally permeable" embargo,[111] which has not prevented arms sales to China – and which has only limited the export of lethal weapons. Thus, the end of the arms embargo is inevitable: the issue is not whether it will be lifted but when and how will it be lifted.[112]

Following the economic dimension, the Sino-European relationship has been mainly driven by geopolitical dynamics and the EU will not put at risk its strategic interests in China. Some European leaders, such as the Germans and the French, see Beijing as a political partner in the project of achieving a multipolar world: a stronger China would help to create other centres of power, counterbalancing US hegemony. The Chinese leaders share this view of willing to contain the excesses of American power, mainly after the disintegration of the Soviet Union, and of looking forward to having China and Europe as two other poles of the

110 Saalman and Yuan, *op. cit.*, p. 6.

111 Alexandre Carriço, 'Um Jogo de Espelhos: Percepções em torno da Dimensão do Orçamento de Defensa da RP da China,' *Revista Militar*, No. 2465/2466, June/July 2007.

112 Alexandre Carriço, 'O Embargo de Armas à China: Motivações e Vulnerabilidades,' *Revista Militar*, No. 2443/2444, Lisbon, August/September, 2005.

international system.[113] The significant place occupied by the UN in the "Peace Dove Strategy," as explained in the first section of this chapter, reveals Beijing's commitment at the multilateral level, to achieving a multipolar world.[114]

Therefore, despite all the ideological differences between the two parties, and taking into account the economic challenges that China's WTO accession brought to Europe, namely a growing trade deficit, Brussels and Beijing perceive themselves as partners and are willing to improve cooperation. Whether we can add the word "strategic" to this partnership or whether the strategic partnership is still under construction is another question.[115] The PCA may be a reality, as it was reaffirmed by the two sides during Premier Wen Jiabao's visit to the European Commission in January 2009[116] and, last May, at the 11th EU-China Summit in Prague.

---

113 D'Amato and Robinson, *op. cit.*; Brookes, *op. cit.*; Ching, *op. cit.*, p. 2.

114 See Carmen A. Mendes, 'National Motives, Approaches and Goals of China's Foreign Policy,' in Luís Tomé (ed.), *East Asia Today*, Lisbon, Observatório de Relações Exteriores da UAL, 2008; Mendes and Freire, *op. cit.*, pp. 207-235.

115 See Jing Men, *op. cit.*, pp. 3-4.

116 See Commission of the European Communities, Joint Statement, *EU-China Joint Statement*, Brussels, 30 January 2009.

Bibliography

Abbott, K. W. and Snidal, D., "Hard and Soft Law in International Governance," *International Organization*, Vol. 54, No. 3, Summer 2000, pp. 421-456.

Abernathy, F. *et al.*, *Lean Retailing and the Transformation of Manufacturing – Lessons from the Textile and Apparel Industries*, Oxford, Oxford University Press, 1999.

Afilalo, A., "Constitutionalization through the Back Door: a European Perspective on NAFTA's Investment Chapter," *New York University Journal of International Law and Politics*, Vol. 34, No. 1, 2001, pp. 1-55.

Aguilera, R. V. and Williams, C. A., "Corporate Social Responsibility in a Comparative Perspective," in A. Crane, *et al.*, *Oxford Handbook of Corporate Social Responsibility*, Oxford, Oxford University Press, 2006, pp. 452-472.

Aikman, D., *Jesus in Beijing: How Christianity Is Transforming China and Changing the Global Balance of Power*, Washington, Regnery Publishing, 2003.

Algieri, F., "EU Economic Relations with China: An Institutionalist Perspective," *The China Quarterly*, Vol. 169, 2002, pp. 64-77.

Anca, R., "Foreign Investors in the EU – Which Best Treatment? Interactions between Bilateral Investment Treaties and EU Law," *European Law Journal*, Vol. 14, No. 2, 2008, pp. 237-260.

Andreosso-O'Callaghan, B. and Nicolas, F., "What Scope for an EU-ASEAN Free Trade Agreement?," *Journal of World Trade*, Vol. 42, No. 1, 2008, pp. 105-128.

Baker, P., "Human Rights, Europe and the People's Republic of China," *China Quarterly*, Vol. 169, 2002, pp. 45-63.

Barysch, K. *et al.*, *Embracing the Dragon: The EU's Partnership with China*, London, The Center for European Reform, May 2005.

Bersick, S., "Die Europäische Union und Ostasien," in A. Bendiek and H. Kramer (eds.), *Die Außenpolitik der Europäsichen Union*, Baden-Baden, Nomos, 2009, pp. 94-111.

Bersick, S., "Europe in Asia," in D. Shambaugh and M. Yahuda (eds.), *International Relations in Asia: The New Regional System*, Plymouth, Rowman & Littlefield, 2008.

Böhm, M., "Lieferantenauditierung und Runde Tische in China," in I. Schönheit, *et al.*, *Corporate Social Responsibility. Verantwortung für Nachhaltiges Wirtschaften in China*, Berlin, Beuth, 2006, pp. 70-74.

Boublil, A., *Le Siècle des Chinois*, Monaco, Éditions du Rocher, 1997.

Bradley, R. *et al.*, *Levelling the Carbon Playing Field: International Competition and U.S. Climate Policy Design*, Washington, Peterson Institute for International Economics, 2008.

Bradley, R., *Testimony to the U.S. House of Representatives Select Committee On Energy Independence And Global Warming*, Washington, World Resources Institute, February 2009, pp. 1-13.

Bridges, B., *Europe and the Challenge of the Asia Pacific*, Cheltenham, Edward Elgar, 1999, pp. 90-120.

British Petroleum, *Statistical Review of World Energy 2007*, London, BP, 2007.

Bu, Q., "Tighter Control on Foreign Acquisitions in China? – The XCMG Case," *European Business Law Review*, Vol. 19 (2), 2008, pp. 293-309.

Bubb, R. J. and Rose-Ackerman, S., "BITs and Bargains: Strategic Aspects of Bilateral and Multilateral Regulation of Foreign Investment," *International Review of Law and Economics*, Vol. 27, No. 3, 2007, pp. 291-312.

Buckley, P. J. *et al.*, "China's Inward Foreign Direct Investment Success: Southeast Asia in the Shadow of the Dragon," in *Multinational Business Review*, Vol. 13, No. 1, 2005, pp. 3-31.

Cabestan, J. P., "Learning from the EU?: China's Changing Outlook Towards Multilateralism," in G. Wang and Y. Zheng (eds.), *China and the New International Order*, New York, Routledge, 2008.

Cabestan, J. P. and Choukroune, L., "China's Accession to the WTO: A Historic Turning Point?," *China Perspectives*, No. 40, March-April 2002.

Casarini, N., "The Evolution of the EU-China Relationship: from Constructive Engagement to Strategic Partnership," *Occasional Paper*, Institute for Security Studies, No. 64, October 2006, pp. 1-50.

Ceyssens, J., "Towards a Common Foreign Investment Policy? – Foreign Investment in the European Constitution," *Legal Issues of Economic Integration*, Vol. 32, No. 3, 2005, pp. 259-291.

Chan, A., "A 'Race to the Bottom': Globalisation and China's Labour Standards," *China Perspectives*, No. 46, March-April 2000, pp. 41-49.

Chan, A., "China Says No To Developed Countries' Corporate Social Responsibility," *Asian Analysis*, February 2005, retrieved at http://www.aseanfocus.com/asiananalysis/article.cfm?articleID=816.

Chan, A., "Recent Trends in Chinese Labour Issues: Signs of Change," *China Perspectives*, No. 57, January-February 2005, pp. 1-22.

Chapple, W. and Moon, J., "Corporate Social Responsibility (CSR) in Asia. A Seven-Country Study of CSR Web Site Reporting," *Business and Society*, No. 44, 2005, pp. 415-441.

Chen, E. K. Y., "China-EC Economic Relations: Experience and Prospects," in G. Sciavoni (ed.), *Western Europe and Southeast Asia: Cooperation or Competition?*, London, Palgrave Macmilllan, 1989, pp. 174-196.

Chen, X., *From Political Alliance in China's Conception to Comprehensive Partnership in Building: the Relations between China and the European Community/European Union*, PhD Dissertation, Tübingen, Eberhard-Karls Universität, 2003.

Cheng, T. H., "Power, Authority and International Investment Law," in *American University International Law Review*, Vol. 20, No. 3, 2005, pp. 465-520.

Ching, F., "Changing Dynamics in EU-China Arms Relations," in *China Brief*, The Jamestown Foundation, Issue 5, March 2004 retrieved at http://www.jamestown.org/single/?no_cache=1&tx_ttnews%5Btt_news%5D=3631.

Choi, W. M., "The Present and Future of the Investor-State Dispute Settlement Paradigm," *Journal of International Economic Law*, Vol. 10, No. 3, 2007, pp. 725-747.

Comeaux, P. E. and Kinsella, N. S., *Protecting Foreign Investment under International Law: Legal Aspects of Political Risk*, New York, Oceana Publications, 1997.

Comino, A., "A Dragon in Cheap Clothing: What Lessons Can Be Learned from the EU-China Textile Dispute?," *European Law Journal*, Vol. 13, No. 6, November 2007, pp. 818-838.

Commission of the European Communities, *20 20 by 2020: Europe's Climate Change Opportunity*, Brussels, 2008.

Commission of the European Communities, *A Maturing Partnership – Shared Interests and Challenges in EU-China Relations*, COM(2003) 533 final, Brussels, 10 September 2003.

Commission of the European Communities, *Bilateral Trade Relations. EU-China Relations*, Brussels, May 2009.

Commission of the European Communities, *Building a Global Climate Change Alliance between the European Commission and Poor Developing Countries Most Vulnerable to Climate Change.* COM(2007) 540 final, Brussels, 2007.

Commission of the European Communities, *Commission Communication to the Council and Parliament: Human Rights, Democracy and Development Cooperation Policy*, SEC(1991) 61 final, Brussels, 25 March 1991.

Commission of the European Communities, *Commission Proposes an Integrated Energy and Climate Change Package to Cut Emissions for the 21st century*, Press Release – IP/07/29, Brussels, 2007.

Commission of the European Communities, *Communication from the Commission: Corporate Social Responsibility. A Business Contribution to Sustainable Development*, COM(2002) 347 final, Brussels, 2 July 2002.

Commission of the European Communities, *Communication from the Commission: Implementing the Partnership for Growth and Jobs: Making Europe a Pole of Excellence on Corporate Social Responsibility*, COM(2006) 136 final, Brussels, 22 March 2006.

Commission of the European Communities, *Communication from the Commission. Building a Comprehensive Partnership with China*, COM(1998) 181 final, Brussels, 25 March 1998.

Commission of the European Communities, *Communication from the Commission on the Inclusion of Respect for Democratic Principles and Human Rights in Agreements between the Community and Third Countries*, COM(1995) 216 final, Brussels, 23 May 1995.

Commission of the European Communities, *Communication from the Commission to the Council and the European Parliament. EU – China: Closer*

Partners, Growing Responsibilities, COM(2006) 631 final, Brussels, 24 October 2006.

Commission of the European Communities, *Communication from the Commission to the Council and the European Parliament: The European Union's Role in Promoting Human Rights and Democratisation in Third Countries*, COM(2001) 252 final, Brussels, 08 May 2001.

Commission of the European Communities, *Communication from the Commission to the European Parliament, the Council, the European Economic and Social Committee and the Committee of the Regions: The EU, Africa and China: Towards Trilateral Dialogue and Cooperation*, COM(2008) 654 final, Brussels, 17 October 2008.

Commission of the European Communities, *Communication from the Commission to the Council: Towards a New Asiatic Strategy*, COM(1994) 314 final, Brussels, 13 July 1994.

Commission of the European Communities, *Communication from the Commission to the Council and the European Parliament: Strategy of the EU vis-à-vis China: Implementation of the 1998 Communication and Measures to Take to Strengthen Community Policy*, COM(2001) 265 final, Brussels, 15 May 2001.

Commission of the European Communities, *Communication from the Commission: A Strategic Framework to Strengthen the Europe-Asia Partnership*, COM(2001) 469 final, Brussels, 4 November 2001.

Commission of the European Communities, *Communication from the Commission: A New Partnership with South-East Asia*, COM(2003) 399 final, Brussels, 9 July 2003.

Commission of the European Communities, *Communication from the Commission to the Council, to the European Parliament and to the European Economic and Social Committee: An EU-India Strategic Partnership*, COM(2004) 430 final, Brussels, 16 June 2004.

Commission of the European Communities, *Communication from the Commission to the Council, to the European Parliament, to the European Economic and Social Committee and to the Committee of Regions: A Competitive Europe in a Globalized Economy*, COM(2006) 567 final, Brussels, 4 October 2006.

Commission of the European Communities, *EU and China Partnership on Climate Change*, MEMO(2005) 298, Brussels, 2005.

Commission of the European Communities, *Europe's Climate Change Opportunity*, COM(2008) 30 final, Brussels, 2008.

Commission of the European Communities, *Limiting Global Climate Change to 2 Degrees Celsius: The Way Ahead for 2020 and Beyond*, COM(2007) 2 final, Brussels, 2007.

Commission of the European Communities, *Report of the Commission to the Council and to the European Parliament on the Implementation of the Communication: Towards a Global Partnership with China*, COM(2000) 552 final, Brussels, 8 September 2000.

Commission of the European Communities, *Strategic Document on EU-China Trade and Investments: Competition and Partnership*, COM(2006) 632 final, Brussels, 24 October 2006.

Commission of the European Communities, *The European Union's New Generalized System of Preferences (GSP) Scheme*, MEMO(1995) 1, Brussels, 19 January 1995.

Commission of the European Communities, *Towards a Comprehensive Climate Change Agreement in Copenhagen*, COM(2009) 39 final, Brussels, 2009.

Commission of the European Communities, *Trade Sustainability Impact Assessment of the Negotiations of a Partnership and Cooperation Agreement between the EU and China*, Final Report, Brussels, August 2008.

Commission of the European Communities, *Working with Developing Countries to Tackle Climate Change*, Report, Brussels, 2007.

Connolly, K., "Say What You Mean – Improved Drafting Resources as a Means for Increasing the Consistency of Interpretation of Bilateral Investment Treaties," *Vanderbilt Journal of Transnational Law*, Vol. 40, No. 5, 2007, pp. 1579-1610.

Cornet, O., "Nouvelle Étape de la Longue Marche vers l'OMC," *Moniteur du Commerce International*, No. 1423, 6 January 2000.

Council of the European Union, *A Secure Europe in a Better World*, 10881/03, Brussels, 25 June 2003.

Council of the European Union, *Council Conclusions on the Implementation of the EU Policy on Human Rights and Democratisation in Third Countries*, 16719/06, Brussels, 13 December 2006.

Council of the European Union, *EU Guidelines on Human Rights Dialogues with Third Countries: Update*, 16526/08, Brussels, 22 December 2008.

Council of the European Union, *Joint Press Communiqué, 11th EU-China Summit*, Prague, 20 May 2009.

Council of the European Union, *Joint Statement of the 10th EU-China Summit*, Beijing, 28 November 2007.

Council of the European Union, *Joint Statement of the 7th EU-China Summit*, La Haye, 8 December 2004.

Council of the European Union, *Joint Statement of the 8th EU-China Summit*, IP/05/478, Brussels, 5 September 2005.

Council of the European Union, *Report on the Implementation of the European Security Strategy: Providing Security in a Changing World*, 17104/08, Brussels, 10 December 2008.

Crawford, G., "Partnership or Power? Deconstructing the 'Partnership for Governance Reform' in Indonesia," *Third World Quarterly*, Vol. 24, No. 1, 2003, pp. 139-159.

Cremona, M., "Rhetoric and Reticence: EU External Commercial Policy in a Multilateral Context," *Common Market Law Review*, Vol. 38, 2001, pp. 359-396.

Cuesta González, M. and Valor Martinez, C., "Fostering Corporate Social Responsibility Through Public Initiative: From the EU to the Spanish Case," *Journal of Business Ethics*, No. 55, 2004, pp. 275-293.

Dai, Bingran, "Sino-European Political and Economic Relations in the Post Cold War Era," *Paper Presented to the 3rd ECSA-World Conference*, Brussels, September 1996.

Davis, G. and Hall, J., *Circular Economy Legislation. The International Experience*, Washington, World Bank, May 2006.

De Beer, P. and Rocca, J. L., *La Chine à la Fin de l'Ere Deng Xiaoping*, Brussels, Le Monde Éditions, 1995.

Dillon, M., *Contemporary China. An Introduction*, Oxon, Routledge, 2009.

Doh, J. P. and Guay, T. R., "Corporate Social Responsibility, Public Policy, and NGO Activism in Europe and the United States. An Institutional-Stakeholder Perspective," *Journal of Management Studies*, Vol. 43, No. 1, 2006, pp. 47-73.

Dolzer, R. and Schreuer, C., *Principles of International Investment Law*, Oxford, Oxford University Press, 2007.

Dolzer, R. and Stevens, M., *Bilateral Investment Treaties*, The Hague, Martinus Nijhoff Publishers, 1995.

Donaldson, T. and Preston, L. E., "The Stakeholder Theory of the Corporation: Concepts, Evidence, and Implications," *Academy of Management Review*, Vol. 20, No. 1, 1995, pp. 65-91.

Donnet, P. A., *Tibet: Mort ou Vif*, Paris, Éditions Gallimard, 1990.

Dunford, M., "The Changing Profile and Map of the EU Textile and Clothing Industry," in M. Faust *et al.*, *European Industrial Restructuring in a Global Economy: Fragmentation and Relocation of Value Chains*, Göttingen, SOFI, 2004, pp. 295-318.

Elkington, J., "Towards the Sustainable Corporation: Win-Win-Win Business Strategies for Sustainable Development," *California Management Review*, Vol. 36, No. 2, 1994, pp. 90-100.

European Community, *Association Agreement Between the EC and Its Member States and Chile*, OJ L 352, 30 December 2002.

European Community, *Euro-Mediterranean Agreement Establishing an Association Between the European Communities and Their Member States, of the One Part, and the Kingdom of Morocco, of the Other Part*, OJ L 70, 18 March 2000.

European Community, *Partnership and Cooperation Agreement Establishing a Partnership Between the European Communities and their Member States on one Hand and the Russian Federation on the Other*, OJ L 327, 1997.

European Court of Justice of the European Communities, Opinion 1/94, 1994, ECR I-5267.

European Court of Justice of the European Communities, Opinion 2/92, 1995, ECR I-521.

European Economic Community, *Agreement on Commercial and Economic Cooperation between the European Economic Community and the People's Republic of China*, OJ L 250, 1985.

European Parliament Committee on Foreign Affairs, *Report on the Communication from the Commission – Building a Comprehensive Partnership with China. Rapporteur: Mr Pierre Bernard-Reymond*, PE 228.395/fin, Strasbourg, 4 December 1998.

European Parliament Committee on Foreign Affairs, *Report on the Human Rights and Democracy Clause in European Union Agreements (2005/2057 (INI)). Rapporteur: Vittorio Agnoletto*, A6-0004/2006, Strasbourg, 23 January 2006.

European Parliament, "Tibet/Droits de l'Homme – Résolution du Parlement Européen sur les Droits de l'Homme au Tibet (Strasbourg, 16 mars 1989)," *Documents d'Actualité Internationale*, No. 9, 1 May 1989.

European Parliament, *European Parliament Resolution on Lifting the EU Arms Embargo on China*, B5 0552/03, Brussels, 15 December 2003.

European Union, "Consolidated Version of the Treaty on European Union: TEU," *Official Journal of the European Union*, No. C 325, 2002.

European Union, "Treaty of Lisbon Amending the Treaty on European Union and the Treaty Establishing the European Community: Lisbon Treaty," *Official Journal of the European Union*, No. C 306, 2007.

Evenett, S. J., "Trade Policy: Time for a Rethink?," in André Sapir (ed.), *Fragmented Power: Europe and the Global Economy*, Brussels, Bruegel, July 2007, pp. 61-94.

Fallows, J., *China's Way Forward*, Washington, The Atlantic, Asia, April 2009.

Faris, S., *Forecast: The Consequences of Climate Change, from the Amazon to the Arctic, from Darfur to the NAPA Valley*, New York, Henry Holt and Company, 2009.

Faya Rodriguez, A., "The Most-Favored-Nation Clause in International Investment Agreements – A Tool for Treaty Shopping?," *Journal of International Arbitration*, Vol. 25, No. 1, 2008, pp. 89-102.

Fei, T. *et al.*, *Mitigation Actions in China*, London, E3G, June 2008.

Ferdinand, P., "Economic and Diplomatic Interactions Between the EU and China," in R. Grant (ed.), *The European Union and China: A European Strategy for the 21st century*, London, The Royal Institute of International Affairs, 1995, pp. 26-41.

Foot, R., *Rights Beyond Borders: The Global Community and the Struggle over Human Rights in China*, Oxford, Oxford University Press, 2000.

Fowler, A., "Introduction – Beyond Partnership," *IDS Bulletin*, Vol. 31, No. 3, 2000, pp. 1-13.

Fox, J. and Godement, F., *A Power Audit of EU-China Relations*, London, European Council on Foreign Relations, 2009.

Friedman, S., *Expropriation in International Law*, London, Stevens, 1953.

Gentelle, P., "Géo-Histoire: de l'An Mil à l'An 2000, un Centre Bousculé Entre le Continent et la Mer," in M. Foucher (ed.), *Asies nouvelles*, Paris, Belin, 2002.

Gereffi, G., "International Trade and Industrial Upgrading in the Apparel Commodity Chain," *Journal of International Economics*, Vol. 48, No. 1, 1999, pp. 37-70.

Giuli, M., *The Competitiveness of the European Textile Industry*, Research Papers in International Business, No. 2, Centre for International Business Studies, London, South Bank University, 1997.

Grant, C. and Barysch, K., *Can Europe and China Shape a New World Order?*, London, The Centre for European Reform, May 2008.

Gupta, J., and Grubb, M., *Climate Change and European Leadership: A Sustainable Role for Europe?*, London, Kluwer Academic Publishers, 2000.

Haley, U. C. V. and Haley, G. T., *Subsidies and the China Price*, Cambridge, Harvard Business Review, June 2008.

He, Z., "Corporate Social Responsibility. Herausforderung und Ansporn für die Chinesische Wirtschaft," in I. Schönheit *et al.*, *Corporate Social Responsibility. Verantwortung für Nachhaltiges Wirtschaften in China*, Berlin, Beuth, 2006, pp. 24-31.

Heymann, M. C. E., "International Law and the Settlement of Investment Disputes Relating to China," *Journal of International Economic Law*, Vol. 11, No. 3, 2008, pp. 507-526.

Hickman, M. M. *et al.*, "Introduction: Foreign Investment in Post-WTO China," *International Financial Law Review*, Vol. 22, No. 7, 2003, pp. 31-37.

Hoekman, B. and Newfarmer, R., "Preferential Trade Agreements, Investment Disciplines and Investment Flows," *Journal of World Trade*, Vol. 39, No. 5, 2005, pp. 949-973.

Hofstede, G., *Cultures and Organizations. Software of the Mind*, New York, McGraw-Hill, 2004.

Horng, D. C., "The Human Rights Clause in the EU's External Trade and Development Agreements: Law and Practice," *EurAmerica*, Vol. 34, No. 1, 2004, pp. 143-202.

Howard, S. and Wu, C., *Climate Revolution*, Washington, Climate Group, 2008.

Human Rights Council Working Group on the Universal Periodic Review, *Report of the Working Group on the Universal Periodic Review: China*, A/HRC/11/25, Geneva, 3 March 2009.

Human Rights in China, *From Principle to Pragmatism: Can 'Dialogue' Improve China's Human Rights Situation?*, New York, 1998.

Human Rights Watch, *Chinese Diplomacy, Western Hypocrisy and the U.N. Human Rights Commission*, New York, 1997.

Intergovernmental Panel on Climate Change, *Climate Change 2007: The Fourth Assessment Reports*, Valencia, 2007.

International Energy Agency, *World Energy Outlook 2007*, Paris, IEA, 2007.

International Energy Agency, *World Energy Outlook 2007: China and India Insights*, Paris, IEA, 2007.

International Labour Organization, *Labour Practices in the Footwear, Leather, Textiles and Clothing Industries*, Geneva, 2000.

Jimenez Cortes, C., *GATT, WTO and the Regulation of International Trade in Textiles*, Vermont, Ashgate Publishing Company, 1997.

Joussé, C., "La Chine et l'Union Européenne," *Politique Étrangère*, No. 4, 1996, pp. 867-879.

Joyaux, F., *La Tentation Impériale*, Paris, Imprimerie Nationale, 1994.

Kahn, P. and Walde, T. (eds.), *Les Aspects Nouveaux du Droit des Investissements Internationaux*, The Hague, Académie de Droit International de Martinus Nijhoff Publishers, 2007.

Kaufmann-Kohler, G. and Stucki, B. (eds.), *Investment Treaties and Arbitration*, Zurich, Swiss Arbitration Association, 2002.

Kent, A., *China, the United Nations, and Human Rights: The Limits of Compliance*, Philadelphia, University of Pennsylvania Press, 1999.

Klein, J., "Creating Ethical Food Consumers? Promoting Organic Food in Urban Southwest China," *Social Anthropology*, No. 1, 2009, pp. 74-89.

Klein, N., *No Logo*New York, , Picador, 2002.

Krenzler, H. G. and Pitschas, C., "Progress or Stagnation?: The Common Commercial Policy After Nice," *European Foreign Affairs Review*, Vol. 6, 2001, pp. 291-313.

Kroeber, A., "Rising China and the Liberal West," *China Economic Quarterly*, No. 193, Beijing, March 2008, pp. 29-44.

Kurlantzick, J., "China's Charm: Implications of Chinese Soft Power," *Policy Brief*, Carnegie Endowment for International Peace, No. 47, June 2006, pp. 1-8.

Lan, X. and Forbes, N., "Will China Become a Science and Technology Superpower by 2020? An Assessment Based on a National Innovation System Framework," *Innovations*, Vol. 1, No. 4, 2006, pp. 111-126.

Landsmeer, A., "Capital Movements: On the Interpretation of Article 73b of the EC Treaty," *Legal Issues of Economic Integration*, Vol. 27, No. 2, 2000, pp. 195-200.

Landsmeer, A., "Movement of Capital and Other Freedoms," *Legal Issues of Economic Integration*, Vol. 28, No. 1, 2001, pp. 57-69.

Lardy, N. R., *A China na Economia Mundial* (*China in the World Economy*, translated to Portuguese), Lisbon, Gabinete de Estudos e Planeamento, Ministério da Economia, 1995.

Leeks, A., "The Relationship between Bilateral Investment Treaty Arbitration and the Wider Corpus of International Law: the ICSID Approach," *University of Toronto Faculty of Law*, Vol. 65, No. 2, 2007, pp. 1-40.

Lowenfeld, A. F., "Investment Agreements and International Law," *Columbia Journal of Transnational Law*, Vol. 42, No. 1, 2003, pp. 123-130.

Malaga, J. and Mohanty, S., "The Agreement on Textiles and Clothing: Is It a WTO Failure?," *Estey Centre Journal of International Law and Trade Policy*, Vol. 4, No. 1, 2003, pp. 75-85.

Maniruzzaman, A. F. M., "The International Law of Foreign Investment in the Age of Globalization: from Panic to Panacea," *International Environmental Agreements Politics Law and Economics*, Vol. 6, No. 4, 2006, pp. 365-370.

Marks, S., "Nightmare and Noble Dreams: The 1993 World Conference on Human Rights," *The Cambridge Law Journal*, Vol. 53, No. 1, 1994, pp. 54-62.

Maull, H. *et al.*, *Europe and the Asia Pacific*, London, Routledge, 1998, pp. 183-197.

Mayeda, G., "Playing Fair: the Meaning of Fair and Equitable Treatment in Bilateral Investment Treaties," *Journal of World Trade*, Vol. 41, No. 2, 2007, pp. 273-291.

Mayer, J., *Not Totally Naked: Textiles And Clothing Trade In A Quota Free Environment*, Geneva, United Nations Conference on Trade and Development, 2004.

McLachlan, C. *et al.*, *International Investment Arbitration: Substantive Principles*, Oxford, Oxford University Press, 2007.

Meadowcroft, J. *et al.*, "Developing a Framework for Sustainability Governance in the European Union," *International Journal of Sustainable Development*, Vol. 8, No. 1-2, 2005, pp. 3-11.

Men, J., "Building A Long-Term EU-China Partnership," Paper Presented to the 2nd Annual Research Conference, Dalhousie University, Canada, May 2008.

Men, J., "EU-China Relations Need More Mutual Understanding," *EU-China Observer*, No. 1, 2009, pp. 3-6.

Men, J., "EU-China Relations, from Engagement to Marriage," *EU Diplomacy Papers*, No. 7, College of Europe, June 2008, pp. 1-25.

Mendes, C. A., "A Concepção Chinesa de Direitos Humanos" (The Chinese Human Rights Conception, translated from Portuguese), *Via Latina*, University of Coimbra, No. 4, March 2007, pp. 118-121.

Mendes, C. A., "National Motives, Approaches and Goals of China's Foreign Policy," in L. Tomé (ed.), *East Asia Today*, EDIUAL, Lisbon, 2008, pp. 107-118.

Mendes, C. A., "O Impacto para Portugal da Adesão da China à Organização Mundial do Comércio" (The Impact in Portugal of China's Entry into the World Trade Organization, translated from Portuguese), *Zoom – Revista do Centro de Estudos do Curso de Relações Internacionais*, Ano XI, No. 14, 2006, pp. 45-49.

Mendes, C. A., "Relações Económicas Europa-China" (Europe-China Economic Relations, translated from Portuguese), in A. Amaro and C. Justino (eds.), *Estudos sobre a China*, II, Lisbon, I.S.C.S.P., 2000, pp. 438-464.

Mendes, C. A. and Freire, M. R., "A Organização de Cooperação de Xangai como Instrumento Geopolítico Sino-Russo na Ásia Central," *Geopolítica*, Aveiro, No. 2, June 2008, pp. 207-235.

Ministry of Foreign Affairs of the People's Republic of China, *China's EU Policy Paper*, Beijing, 13 October 2003.

Mora, F. U., "La Entrada de China en la Organización Mundial de Comercio" (China's Entry into the WTO, translated from Spanish), *Boletín Económico de ICE*, No. 2661, 31 July-3 September 2000.

Mouffe, C., *On the Political*, London, Routledge, 2006.

Muchlinski, P., "Caveat Investor? The Relevance of the Conduct of the Investor Under the Fair and Equitable Treatment Standard," *International and Comparative Law Quarterly*, Vol. 55, No. 3, 2006, pp. 527-559.

Muchlinski, P. *et al.*, *The Oxford Handbook of International Investment Law*, Oxford, Oxford University Press, 2008.

Narain, S., "Lectures Don't Make Lessons: What's the Rich World Doing on Energy Conservation besides Giving Lectures?," *Business Standard*, New Delhi, February 13, 2009.

National Bureau of Statistics of China, *Key Advancements of the First National Economic Census with New Changes of China's GDP Aggregates and its Structure*, Beijing, 2005.

National Development and Reform Commission, *China National Climate Change Programme*, People's Republic of China, Beijing, June 2007.

New Economics Foundation, *Up in Smoke: Asia and the Pacific – The Threat from Climate Change to Human Development and the Environment*, London, NEF, 2007.

Nordås, H. K., "The Global Textile and Clothing Industry post the Agreement on Textiles and Clothing," *World Trade Organization Discussion Paper No. 5*, Geneva, 2004, pp. 1-41.

Occis, N., "Les Enjeux de l'Adhésion de la Chine à l'OMC," *Politique Étrangère*, No. 2746, 30 January 2002, pp. 973-986.

Organization for Economic Cooperation and Development, *International Investment Law: A Changing Landscape*, Paris, 2005.

Organization for Economic Cooperation and Development, *Synthesis: Economic Study of China*, Paris, September 2005.

Pallemaerts, M. *et al.*, *Drowning in Process? The Implementation of the European Union's 6th Environmental Action Programme*, London, European Environment Bureau, 2006.

People's Republic of China, *11th Five-Year Guidelines (2006-2010)*, Beijing, 2006.

People's Republic of China, *China's EU Policy Paper*, Beijing, 13 October 2003.

People's Republic of China, *National Assessment Report on Climate Change*, Beijing, December, 2006.

People's Republic of China, *China's National Climate Change Programme*, prepared under the auspices of the National Development and Reform Commission, Beijing, 2007.

People's Republic of China, *White Paper: China's Policies and Actions on Climate Change*, Beijing, 2008.

Piepel, K., "CSR in China – Erfahrungen und Herausforderungen am Beispiel der Spielzeugindustrie," in I. Schönheit *et al.*, *Corporate Social Responsibility. Verantwortung für Nachhaltiges Wirtschaften in China*, Berlin, Beuth, 2006, pp. 81-94.

Presidency-in-Office of the Council of the European Union, *Déclaration de la Présidence au Nom de l'Union Européenne sur l'Exécution de M. Wo Weihan (Chine)*, Paris, 28 November 2008.

Presidency-in-Office of the Council of the European Union, *EU-China Summit Postponed – European Union Statement*, Paris, 28 November 2008.

Presidency-in-Office of the Council of the European Union, Portugal, *Diálogo Estratégico UE-China reúne em Lisboa* (Strategic Dialogue EU-China Meets in Lisbon, translated into Portuguese), Lisbon, 25 October 2007.

Remmers, B., "CSR – ein Mehrwert in China? Chancen und Risiken eines Mittelständischen Engagements auf dem Chinesischen Markt," in I. Schönheit *et al.*, *Corporate Social Responsibility. Verantwortung für Nachhaltiges Wirtschaften in China*, Berlin, Beuth, 2006, pp. 57-69.

Risse, T. and Ropp, S. C. (eds.), "International Human Rights Norms and Domestic Change: Conclusions," in T. Risse *et al.*, *The Power of Human Rights: International Norms and Domestic Change*, Cambridge, Cambridge University Press, 1999.

Rosen, D. H. and Houser T., *China Energy: A Guide for the Perplexed*, Washington, Center for Strategic and International Studies and the Peterson Institute for International Economics, May 2007.

Rosoff, R. J., "Beyond Codes of Conduct. Addressing Labor Rights Problems in China," *China Business Review*, March-April 2004, pp. 6-9.

Ryan, C. M., "Meeting Expectations: Assessing the Long-Term Legitimacy and Stability of International Investment Law," in *University of Pennsylvania Journal of International Economic Law*, Vol. 29, No. 3, 2008, pp. 725-761.

Salacuse, J. W. and Sullivan, N. P., "Do BITS Really Work? An Evaluation of Bilateral Investment Treaties and their Grand Bargain," *Harvard International Law Journal*, Vol. 46, No. 1, 2005, pp. 67-130.

Sally, R., "Looking East: The European Union's New FTA Negotiations in Asia," *Jan Tumlir Policy Essays*, ECIPE, No. 3, 2007, pp. 1-22.

Santarius, T. *et al.*, *Pit Stop Poznan: An Analysis of Negotiations on the Bali Action Plan at the Stopover to Copenhagen*, Wuppertal, Wuppertal Institute, 2009.

Sautenet, A., "Europe and China: a Cooperation with Complex Legal Dimensions," *Asie Visions*, Paris, Institut Français des Relations Internationales (IFRI), No. 3, March 2008, pp. 1-63.

Sautenet, A., "La Dynamique Juridique du Partenariat Stratégique," *Revue Économique et Sociale*, Vol. 67, No. 1, 2009, pp. 107-124.

Sautenet, A., "The Current Status and Prospect of the 'Strategic Partnership' between the European Union and China: towards the Conclusion of a Partnership and Cooperation Agreement," *European Law Journal*, Vol. 13, No. 6, 2007, pp. 699-731.

Sauvé, P. *et al.*, *Revealed Policy Preferences in Selected International Investment Agreements*, Investment Issues Series, Geneva, UNCTAD, 2006.

Schill, S. W., "Tearing down the Great Wall: The New Generation Investment Treaties of the People's Republic of China," *Cardozo Journal of International and Comparative Law*, Vol. 15, 2007, pp. 77-118.

Schönheit, I., "Corporate Social Responsibility – Deutsche und Internationale Perspektiven am Beispiel China," in I. Schönheit *et al.*, *Corporate Social Responsibility. Verantwortung für Nachhaltiges Wirtschaften in China*, Berlin, Beuth, 2006, pp. 9-23.

Schreuer, C., *The ICSID Convention: A Commentary*, Cambridge, Cambridge University Press, 2001.

Schwarzenberger, G., *Foreign Investments and International Law*, London, Stevens and Sons Publishing, 1969.

Seidl-Hohenveldern, I., *Collected Essays on International Investment and International Organizations*, The Hague, Kluwer Law, 1998.

Seligsohn, D., *China, the United States, and the Climate Change Challenge*, Washington, World Resources Institute, 2009.

Shambaugh, D., "China and Europe: The Emerging Axis," *Current History*, 2004, pp. 243-248.

Shambaugh, D., "China and the US: A Marriage of Convenience," *International Herald Tribune*, 6 January 2009.

Shambaugh, D. *et al.*, *China-Europe Relations: Perceptions, Policies and Prospects*, New York, Routledge, 2008.

Shan, W., "Towards a New Legal Framework for EU-China Investment Relations," *Journal of World Trade*, Vol. 34, No. 5, 2000, pp. 137-179.

Shan, W., *The Legal Framework of EU-China Investment Relations: A Critical Appraisal*, Oxford and Portland, Hart Publishing, 2005.

Shihata, I. F. I., *Legal Treatment of Foreign Investment: the World Bank Guidelines*, Dordrecht, Martinus Nijhoff, 1993.

Siebert, H., "China, Understanding a New Global Economic Player," *Kiel Institute for World Economics*, Kiel Working Paper, No. 1278, 2006.

Snyder, F. (ed.), *The European Union and China 1949-2008 Basic Documents and Commentary*, Hart Publishing, Oxford and Portland, 2009, pp. 197-227.

Snyder, F., "Soft Law and Institutional Practice in the European Community," in Stephen Martin (ed.), *The Construction of Europe – Essays in Honor of Emile Noël*, The Hague, Kluwer Academic Publishers, 1994.

Snyder, F., China, Regional Trade Agreements and WTO Law, *Journal of World Trade*, Kluwer Law International BV, Vol. 43, No. 1, 2009, pp. 1-57.

Solinger, D. J., "Chinese Urban Jobs and the WTO," *The China Journal*, No. 49, January 2003, pp. 61-87.

Sornarajah, M., *The International Law on Foreign Investment Second Edition*, Cambridge, Cambridge University Press, 2004.

Stengg, W., *The Textile and Clothing Industry in the EU – A Survey*, Brussels, DG Enterprises, European Commission, 2001.

Stern, N., *The Economics of Climate Change: The Stern Review*, London, Cambridge University Press, 2006.

Stiglitz, J. E., "Regulating Multinational Corporations: towards Principles of Cross-Border Legal Frameworks in a Globalized World – Balancing Rights with Responsibilities," *American University International Law Review*, Vol. 23, No. 3, 2008, pp. 451-558.

Strange, R., "EU Trade Policy towards China," in R. Strange *et al.*, *Trade and Investment in China: The European Experience*, London, Routledge, 1998, pp. 59-80.

Tamames, R., "China 2001: la Cuarta Revolución," (China 2001: the 4th Revolution, translated from Spanish), *Economía Exterior*, No. 17, Summer 2001, pp. 135-156.

Tong, Z., "The Development of China and World Trade," *Journal of World Trade*, Vol. 40, No. 1, 2006, pp. 129-136.

Tseng, Su-Ling, "The European Union's Commercial Policymaking towards China," in P. W. Preston and J. Gilson (eds.), *The European Union and East Asia: Interregional Linkages in a Changing Global System*, Cheltenham, Edward Elgar, 2001, pp. 171-197.

Tudor, I., *The Fair and Equitable Treatment Standard in International Foreign Investment Law*, Oxford, Oxford University Press, 2008.

Underhill, G. R. D., *Industrial Crisis and the Open Economy: Politics, Global Trade and the Textile Industry in the Advanced Economies*, London, Houndsmill Macmillan Press, 1998.

United Nations Development Program, *Fighting Climate Change: Human Solidarity in a Divided World*, New York, Human Development Report, 2007.

United Nations Development Programme, *World Report on Human Development 2005*, New York, Economica, 2005.

United Nations Foundation, *Global Leadership for Climate Action: Framework for a post-2012 agreement*, Washington, 2007.

United Nations Framework Convention on Climate Change, *Decision/CP.13 Bali Action Plan*, Bonn, 2007.

United Nations World Commission on Environment and Development, *Our Common Future*, New York, 1987.

United Nations, *Framework Convention on Climate Change*, Bonn, 1992.

Van Harten, G., "The Public-Private Distinction in the International Arbitration of Individual Claims against the State," *International and Comparative Law Quarterly*, Vol. 56, No. 2, 2007, pp. 371-394.

Van Harten, G., *Investment Treaty Arbitration and Public Law*, Oxford, Oxford University Press, 2007.

Van Harten, G. and Loughlin, M., "Investment Treaty Arbitration as a Species of Global Administrative Law," *European Journal of International Law*, Vol. 17, No. 1, 2006, pp. 121-150.

Wallace, D. Jr. and Shanks, R., *Model Foreign Investment Law: With Annotations*, Washington, International Law Institute, 1996.

Wan, M., *Human Rights in Chinese Foreign Relations: Defining and Defending National Interests*, Philadelphia, University of Pennsylvania Press, 2001.

Wassenbergh, H., "A Mandate to the European Commission to Negotiate Air Agreements with Non-EU States: International Law versus EU Law," *Air & Space Law*, Vol. 28, No. 3, 2003, pp. 126-139.

Weigelin-Schwiedrzik, S. and Noesselt, N., "Striving for Symmetry in Partnership: An Analysis of Sino-EU Relations Based on the Two Recently Published Policy Papers," in S. Weigelin-Schwiedrzik *et al.*, *As China Meets the World: China's Changing Position in the International Community*, Vienna, Austrian Academy of Sciences, 2006.

Weiler, T. J. (ed.), *International Investment Law and Arbitration: Leading Cases from the ICSID, NAFTA, Bilateral Treaties and Customary International Law*, London, Cameron, May 2005.

Welford, R., "Corporate Social Responsibility in Europe, North America and Asia," *Journal of Corporate Citizenship*, Vol. 17, 2004, pp. 33-52.

Wessel, R. A., "The Inside Looking Out: Consistency and Delimitation in EU External Relations," *Common Market Law Review*, Vol. 37, 2000, pp. 1135-1171.

Wiessala, G., "Beyond Distant Neighbours: The European Union and China," *The European Union and Asian Countries*, Sheffield Academic Press, 2002, pp. 89-105.

World Bank, *China Economic Indicators – Current*, Washington, 3 July 2008.

World Bank, *Mid-Term Evaluation of China's 11th Five Year Plan*, Washington, 2008.

World Health Organization, *Climate Change and Human Health: Risks and Responses*, Geneva, 2003.

World Health Organization, *Protecting Health from Climate Change: World Health Day 2008*, Geneva, 2008.

World Resources Institute, *Climate Analysis Indicators Tool (CAIT)*, Vol. 5, Washington, 2008.

World Resources Institute, *Earth Trends*, Washington, 2008.

World Trade Organization, *Dispute Settlement, Appellate Body and Panel Reports Adopted: China-Measures Affecting Imports of Automobile Parts*, WT/DS339/1, 3 April 2006.

World Trade Organization, *Protocol on the Accession of the People's Republic of China to the WTO*, Decision of 10 November 2001, WT/L/432, 11 December 2001.

World Trade Organization, *Report of the Secretariat, Trade Policy Review – People's Republic of China, Economic Environment, General Survey*, WT/TPR/S/161, 28 February 2006.

World Trade Organization, *Report of the Secretariat, Trade Policy Review – People's Republic of China*, WT/ TPRB/299, 16 April 2008.

World Trade Organization, *Transitional Review Mechanism of China, TRIPs Council, Contribution of the European Communities, Directorate-General for Trade*, 26 November 2004.

World Trade Organization, *Working Party Report on the Accession of China*, 2001.

World Wide Fund for Nature (WWF), *EU and China: Climate Policy Cut from the Same Cloth*, Brussels, 2005.

Wu, V., "Labor Relations in Focus: The PRC Government's Effort to Better Protect Worker's Rights Spring from Worries about China's Social Stability," *China Business Review*, November-December 2006.

Yahuda, M. B., "China and Europe: The Significance of a Secondary Relationship," in T. W. Robinson and D. L. Shambaugh (eds.), *Chinese Foreign Policy: Theory and Practice*, Oxford, Oxford University Press, 1994, pp. 266-82.

Yang, Y., *China's Textile and Clothing Exports: Changing International Comparative Advantage and its Policy Implications*, Working Paper Series, Asia Pacific School of Economics and Management, No. 3, 1999.

Young, N., "Three 'C's: Civil Society, Corporate Social Responsibility, and China," *China Business Review*, January-February 2002, pp. 21-25.

Zaborowski, M., "Facing China's Rise: Guidelines for an EU Strategy," *Chaillot Paper 94*, European Union, Institute for Security Studies, December 2006, pp. 71-81.

Zachary, D., "The Hybrid Foundations of Investment Treaty Arbitration," *British Yearbook of International Law*, Vol. 74, 2003, pp. 151-290.

Zachary, D., *The International Law of Investment Claims*, Cambridge, Cambridge University Press, 2009.

Zeng, L., "A Preliminary Perspective of Negotiations of EU-China PCA: A New Bottle Carrying Old Wine or New Wine or Both?," *European Law Journal*, Vol. 15, No. 1, January 2009, pp. 121-141.

About the Authors

Carmen AMADO MENDES is Associate Professor of International Relations at the School of Economics, University of Coimbra, and Board member of the European Association for Chinese Studies and of the Portuguese Political Science Association. She received her Ph.D. from the School of Oriental and African Studies, University of London, and her Master degree from the Institut des hautes études européennes, Université Robert Schuman, Strasbourg. Her fields of research focus on China's foreign policy, EU-China relations and Macau.

Frauke AUSTERMANN holds a position as Junior Lecturer in European Studies at Maastricht University (Faculty of Arts and Social Sciences; Department of Political Science). Here, she teaches a variety of courses in the BA and MA programmes, such as History and Theory of European Integration, Comparative Politics and Government, or European Social Policy. Her research interests include European social and employment policy, international/comparative employment relations, sustainable development, and corporate social responsibility. For her Ph.D. project, Frauke has taken a broader approach, by researching why and how the EU's changing perception of China has differed across EU institutions from 1975 until today.

Giuseppe BALDUCCI is Programme Officer for the Italian Development Cooperation Office in Afghanistan. He is a former Research Assistant of the InBev-Baillet Latour Chair of European Union-China Relations at the College of Europe. He is also a PhD candidate in the Department of Politics and International Studies at the University of Warwick, UK. His main research interests include EU-China relations and Asian politics. His publications include: "The Limits of Normative Power Europe in Asia: the case of human rights in China," *East Asia: an International Journal*, 2009, DOI 10.1007/ s12140-009-9090-3; "Prospects and Challenges for the European promotion of human rights in China," *EU-China Observer*, Bruges, College of Europe, Issue 1, 2009; "Inside Normative Power Europe: actors and processes in the European Promotion of Human Rights in China," *EU Diplomacy Paper Series*, No. 8, 2008; "The study of the EU Promotion of human rights: the importance of international and internal factors," *Garnet Working Paper*, No. 61, 2008; "Europe's Identity as a Democracy Promoter: where it comes from and what it does?," Book Chapter included in Jessica Bain and Martin Holland (eds.), *European Union Identity*, NESCA Series III, Baden-Baden, Nomos, 2007.

Edward CAMERON is a specialist on climate change, sustainable development, and governance reform. He is currently serving as a Consultant to the Social Dimensions of Climate Change Team in the World Bank's Social Development Department. He is a guest lecturer on climate change at four universities and has spent nine years working on EU policy in Brussels.

Andrew COTTEY is Senior Lecturer and Jean Monnet Chair in European Political Integration, Department of Government, University College Cork. A specialist in European and international security, he has been a Research Associate at the International Institute for Strategic Studies and a Visiting Researcher at the Stockholm International Peace Research Institute. His publications include Security in the New Europe (2007), *Reshaping Defence Diplomacy: New Roles for Military Cooperation and Assistance*, (with Anthony Forster, 2004) and East-Central Europe after the Cold War (1995).

Jappe ECKHARDT is Ph.D. candidate at the department of Political Science of the University of Antwerp (Belgium). He worked as a research and teaching assistant at the University of Amsterdam, as well as working for an international relations think-tank in Brussels. His current research, which is funded by the Research Foundation Flanders (FWO), concentrates on trade policy-making (especially in the EU context), EU-China (economic) relations and interest group politics.

Joern-Carsten GOTTWALD is Lecturer at the Irish Institute of Chinese Studies, University College Cork. He previously worked as assistant professor for Comparative Government, in the Department of Political Science, at the Trier University in Germany. Prior to that, he had worked as a researcher and lecturer on the politics of China and South East Asia, at the Free University of Berlin. He has extensively published in the area of EU-China relations, and specialises in the area of European Financial Services Regulation.

Katrin KINZELBACH is a researcher at the Ludwig Boltzmann Institute of Human Rights in Vienna and is a fellow of the European Foreign and Security Policy Study Programme jointly sponsored by the Swedish Riksbankens Jubileumsfond, the German Volkswagen Foundation and the Italian Compagnia di San Paolo. She holds a Magister/Laurea jointly awarded by the Universities of Florence and Bonn. She is currently a Ph.D. candidate in political science at the University of Vienna.

Hilary McMAHON is Senior Associate with the World Resources Institute (WRI). She leads WRI's work on international climate architecture and climate and development policy. She has previously worked for the World Business Council for Sustainable Development, the Institute of European Affairs, the Institute for International Integration Studies and for UNIFE in Brussels.

Jing MEN is the InBev-Baillet Latour Chair of European Union-China Relations at the College of Europe. She also works for the Vesalius College, Vrije Universiteit Brussel. She is specialised in EU-China relations and Chinese foreign policy. Her recent publications include: "East Asia: the acid test for Europe's common foreign policy," *Europe's World*, Summer 2009, pp. 12-15; "China's Rise and Its Relations with Other Major Powers: Competitors or Partners," in Sujian Guo and Jean-Marc F. Blanchard (eds.), *Harmonious World and China's New Foreign Policy* (Lanham: Rowman & Littlefield-Lexington, 2008), pp. 83-103; "Crisis across the Taiwan Strait," in Stanley Crossick and Etienne Reuter (eds.) *China-EU: A Common Future* (World Scientific Publishing Co Ltd of Singapore, 2007), pp. 81-92; "Changing Ideology in China and Its Impact on Chinese Foreign Policy," in Sujian Guo and Shiping Hua (eds.), *New Dimensions of Chinese Foreign Policy* (New York/Lexington: Rowman & Littlefield Publishers, 2007), pp. 7-39; *European Integration: Decision-Making and External Relations of the European Union* [Ouzhou yitihua jincheng: Oumeng de juece yu duiwai guanxi], (Beijing: China Renmin University Press, 2007, 237 pp. (written together with Youri Devuyst and published in Chinese); "The Construction of the China-ASEAN Free Trade Area: A Study of China's Active Involvement," *Global Society: Journal of Interdisciplinary International Relations*, Vol. 21, No. 2 (April 2007), pp. 249-268; and "Chinese Perception of the European Union: A Review of Leading Chinese Journals," *European Law Journal*, Vol. 12, No. 6 (November 2006), pp. 788-806.

Nayia PYRIDI is an attorney-at-law admitted at the Thessaloniki Bar Association, Greece. She provides her legal services to legal firms in several investment and commercial arbitration cases in Greece and abroad. She currently works also as a Teaching and Research Assistant of International Economic Law at the Department of International Studies in the Law Faculty of the Aristotle University in Thessaloniki, Greece. Moreover, she is a scientific and research associate of the Research Committee of the Aristotle University in Thessaloniki. Her Ph.D. thesis is on "the Legal Framework governing the External Economic Relations of the European Union with China." She holds a Bachelor of Law (LL.B.) from the Faculty of Law at the Aristotle University and a Masters of Law (LL.M.) on International Legal Studies, with a focus on WTO Law from Georgetown University Law Centre, in Washington, D.C.

Antoine SAUTENET is an associate research fellow at *Centre Asie, Institut Français des Relations Internationales* (IFRI), specialising in EU External Relations Law and in EU-Asia relations. He has published in peer review journals such as the European Law Journal and the *Annuaire de Droit Européen*. He is currently finishing his Ph.D. on the "Strategic partnerships between the EU and emerging countries of Asia – China, India, ASEAN" in the framework of the *Institut Ouest Droit Europe* (IODE), UMR CNRS 6262.

Kim VAN DER BORGHT is the Law Research Coordinator at the Brussels Institute for Contemporary China Studies (Vrije Universiteit Brussel) and Professor of International Economic Law at the Centre for Economic Law & Governance (Vrije Universiteit Brussel). He also holds positions at several high-ranking academic and non-academic institutes. He is an accredited arbitrator (CEPINA), a legal adviser on issues of international trade, investment and intellectual property rights, a member of the International Trade Law Committee and listed on the Roster of Panellists at the World Trade Organisation (WTO).

Lei ZHANG is a research fellow at Brussels Institute of Contemporary China Studies (BICCS) and the Centre for Economic Law and Governance of the Vrije Universiteit Brussel (VUB). She is doing her Ph.D. research on EU-China trade friction and dispute settlement in the legal context. Her research focuses on EU-China relations, Chinese law, European law and international economic law. She gives lectures on China's legal system, Chinese contractual law and Chinese investment regulation at BICCS. As a lawyer registered in China, she specialises in Chinese investment law, contractual law, commercial law and dispute resolution. She had practical experience as a legal consultant in AntwerpLaw law firm and CHAPS law firm. She worked as a journalist, director and editor at the China Central Television Station (CCTV) from 2000 to 2003.

College of Europe Studies

Europe is in a constant state of flux. European politics, economics, law and indeed European societies are changing rapidly. The European Union itself is in a continuous situation of adaptation. New challenges and new requirements arise continually, both internally and externally. The College of Europe Studies series exists to publish research on these issues done at the College of Europe, both at its Bruges and its Warsaw campus. Focused on the European Union and the European integration process, this research may be specialised in the areas of political science, law or economics, but much of it is of an interdisciplinary nature. The objective is to promote understanding of the issues concerned and to make a contribution to ongoing discussions.

Series Editors
Professors D. Hanf, D. Mahncke, I. Govaere,
J. Pelkmans, E. Lannon and J. Monar
for the College of Europe (Bruges and Warsaw)

Series Titles

N° 12 – Jing MEN & Giuseppe BALDUCCI (eds.), *Prospects and Challenges for EU-China Relations in the 21st Century. The Partnership and Cooperation Agreement*, 2010, 262 p., ISBN 978-90-5201-641-2

N° 11 – Jörg MONAR (ed.), *The Institutional Dimension of the European Union's Area of Freedom, Security and Justice*, 2010, p., ISBN 978-90-5201-615-3

N° 10 – Dominik HANF, Klaus MALACEK & Elise MUIR (dir.), *Langues et construction européenne*, 2010, 286 p., ISBN 978-90-5201-594-1

No. 9 – Jacques PELKMANS, Dominik HANF & Michele CHANG (eds.), *The EU Internal Market in Comparative Perspective. Economic, Political and Legal Analyses*, 2008, 314 p., ISBN 978-90-5201-424-1

No. 8 – Inge GOVAERE & Hanns ULLRICH (eds.), *Intellectual Property, Market Power and the Public Interest*, 2008, 315 p., ISBN 978-90-5201-422-7

No. 7 – András INOTAI, *The European Union and Southeastern Europe. Troubled Waters Ahead?*, 2007, 414 p., ISBN 978-90-5201-071-7

No. 6 – Inge GOVAERE & Hanns ULLRICH (eds.), *Intellectual Property, Public Policy, and International Trade*, 2007, 234 p., ISBN 978-90-5201-064-9

No. 5 – Dominik HANF & Rodolphe MUÑOZ (dir.), *La libre circulation des personnes. États des lieux et perspectives*, 2007, 329 p., ISBN 978-90-5201-061-8

2503135861

No. 4 – Dieter MAHNCKE & Sieglinde GSTÖHL (eds.), *Europe's Near Abroad. Promises and Prospects of the EU's Neighbourhood Policy*, 2008, 318 p., ISBN 978-90-5201-047-2

No. 3 – Dieter MAHNCKE & Jörg MONAR (eds.), *International Terrorism. A European Response to a Global Threat?*, 2006, 191 p., ISBN 978-90-5201-046-5

No. 2 – Paul DEMARET, Inge GOVAERE & Dominik HANF (eds.), *European Legal Dynamics – Revised and updated edition of* 30 Years of European Legal Studies at the College of Europe / *Dynamiques juridiques européennes – Édition revue et mise à jour de* 30 ans d'études juridiques européennes au Collège d'Europe, 2007, 571 p., ISBN 978-90-5201-067-0

No. 1 – Dieter MAHNCKE, Alicia AMBOS & Christopher REYNOLDS (eds.), *European Foreign Policy. From Rhetoric to Reality?*, 2004, 2nd printing/2e tirage 2006, 381 p., ISBN 978-90-5201-247-6

P.I.E. Peter Lang – The website

Discover the general website of the Peter Lang publishing group

www.peterlang.com